British Law and Govern
in Treaty Port China 184

British Law and Governance in Treaty Port China 1842-1927

Consuls, Courts and Colonial Subjects

Alex Thompson

Routledge
Taylor & Francis Group
LONDON AND NEW YORK

First published in 2024 by Amsterdam University Press Ltd.

Published 2025 by Routledge
4 Park Square, Milton Park, Abingdon, Oxon OX14 4RN
605 Third Avenue, New York, NY 10158

Routledge is an imprint of the Taylor & Francis Group, an informa business

ISBN: 9789463720397 (hbk)
ISBN: 9781041176442 (pbk)
ISBN: 9781003691938 (ebk)
NUR 691

Cover photo: Sir Sidney Barton, British Consul-General, inspects a detachment from the Sikh Branch of the Shanghai Municipal Police at the empire day parade held at the British Consulate General, Shanghai, in 1926. Photograph by Eugene Kobza (Kobza Jenõ). Special Collections, University of Bristol Library (www.hpcbristol.net).

Cover design: Coördesign, Leiden

DOI: 10.5117/9789463720397

Table of Contents

List of Tables

Abbreviations

BaFSP	British and Foreign State Papers
BPP, HC	British Parliamentary Papers, House of Commons
FO	Foreign Office
HChT	Hertslet's China Treaties
HCoT	Hertslet's Commercial Treaties
NCH	*The North-China Herald*
OIC	Order in Council
SCC	Her Britannic Majesty's Supreme Court for China (and Japan)
SMC	Shanghai Municipal Council
SMP	Shanghai Municipal Police
TNA	The National Archives, Kew, UK

Glossary

Concession an area of land leased from the Chinese government to a single foreign government, which adopted measures for the administration of the area. The foreign government sublet plots of land to its own nationals (and in addition, in some cases, to nationals of other countries). In the British case, concessions were governed by a municipal council of which the Chair was usually the local British consul. Important examples were the British concessions at Tianjin and Hankou.

Settlement an area of land allocated by the Chinese government for foreign residence at an open port. In some cases, municipal councils were created by foreigners to administer settlements. The land in a settlement was not leased and then sublet by a foreign government (as it was in the case of concessions). Land was leased directly from Chinese landholders. The most prominent example was the International Settlement at Shanghai.

Treaty port a place open to foreign trade according to treaty. Five ports were opened as a result of the 1842 Treaty of Nanjing (Fuzhou, Guangzhou, Ningbo, Shanghai and Xiamen) but dozens more were created in the following decades. The most important treaty ports were host to foreign concessions or settlements, but some treaty ports had no such area.

Preface

The nature of the European presence in China during the treaty port era (1843-1943) remains problematic and continues to warrant detailed examination: problematic, because scholars find it difficult to agree how best to define that presence, recognising that the short-hand term, 'informal empire', fails properly to explain its nature; warranting examination, because the inquiry itself requires us to focus on the way in which colonial practices were slowly and subtly insinuated into the country's sovereign territory. As Alex Thompson shows in this penetrating study, the process by which the British state and other European-controlled institutions, principally the Shanghai Municipal Council (SMC), achieved this was both novel and complex, frequently leading to tensions between the various agencies and to outcomes which were certainly not pre-determined and would no doubt have much surprised the architects of the Treaty of Nanjing (1842) which ended the First Opium War.

Underpinning the British and wider foreign presence were extraterritorial provisions in the portfolio of Sino-foreign treaties that would eventually come into force. Although this degradation of China's sovereignty has attracted a great deal of political and scholarly attention, it has not yet been adequately studied or understood. Exploring how it actually worked in practice for British subjects living and working in China and how it impacted on the Chinese, Thompson emphasises that extraterritoriality was introduced not only to prevent British nationals being subjected to what were portrayed as barbarous judicial practices but also to ensure that their conduct would be properly subject to British control. By the late 1850s, it was becoming clear that this aim was far from being achieved with 'rowdy' seamen, whom Consul Alcock described as drawn from "the lowest class of London and Liverpool seafaring men", being particularly troublesome, and the first British Minister, Bruce urging the government to introduce a more effective system of control.[1]

With the opening of the British legation in Peking and of a British Supreme Court in Shanghai five years later, a more effective system was certainly introduced but it was one which also made greater inroads into Chinese sovereignty. If the problem of rowdy seamen righted itself, there were other nationals who were brought before the court system, Indian traders, seamen or security personnel being one particular example. All British subjects were

1 Coates, *The China Consuls*, pp. 47-8.

not alike or equal in practice in the eyes of this British legal apparatus and colonial practices and prejudices, including racial differentiation, pervaded the judicial process. By focussing on these elements, Thompson shows that, however rowdy they may have been, these 'in-between peoples', formed a crucial element in the making of this 'hybrid colonial state'.[2] And although the Chinese fell outside the remit of extraterritorial jurisdiction, with over one million residing in the International Settlement by the early 1930s, they inevitably formed a key part of that process.

An additional value of Thompson's study is that it can, as he says, lead to further lines of inquiry; for example, exploring other ways in which these institutions furthered Britain's colonial presence, particularly in relation to its commercial aspects. It can also provide a basis for examining what T.G. Otte has called the 'Foreign Office mind' and its impact in this colonial context. Although officials in London necessarily played an important role, it was the British state institutions in China which took the lead. And whilst particular personalities stand out in this process, most obviously Ministers Bruce and Alcock and Chief Justice Edmund Hornby in the early days, it is the British consular officials who were the men on the spot responsible for implementing these practices, whose 'mind' also needs to be examined. Generally little- considered, save by P.D. Coates in his monumental study, they had a wide discretion, subject to overall control from the legation, when dealing with the SMC in Shanghai or with less formal bodies in other treaty ports, such as Chambers of Commerce, as well as with Chinese officials, and thus played a key part in shaping the British presence. As we see in the following chapters, these men faced considerable challenges in their day to day tasks – many mundane in themselves but which, taken cumulatively, would often have far-reaching consequences.

Andrew Hillier
University of Bristol

2 Cf. England, *Fortune's Bazaar*, pp. 12, 15, *passim*.

Chinese geographical names and note on romanisation

Chinese words in this book have been rendered using the *pinyin* system of writing Chinese with the roman alphabet, which is the standard used in the People's Republic of China (PRC) and most new academic writing. This has been done to assist readers using other sources, especially sources published in the People's Republic of China. The only exceptions are Hong Kong and Macao (which are rarely encountered written using the *pinyin* forms Xianggang and Aomen respectively, even in PRC English-language texts).

Alternative romanisations of place names and geographical features mentioned in the text are given below in the Wade-Giles format, used in many older academic texts, as are common forms used in contemporary texts such as newspapers, where the latter usage differs (as it often does) from the Wade-Giles. Common transliterations of Chinese place names given are often those formerly in use by the Chinese Post Office.

Pinyin/Chinese	Wade-Giles	Common form
Beijing 北京	Peiching	Peking
Fuzhou 福州	Fuchou	Foochow
Guangzhou 广州	Kwangchou	Canton
Hankou 汉口[1]	Hank'ou	Hankow
Hongkou 虹口	Hungk'ou	Hongkew
Huangpu 黄埔	Huangp'u	Whangpoo / Hwangpu
Humenzhai 虎门寨	Humenchai	Hoomun-Chae
Jinan 济南	Chinan	Tsinan
Nanjing 南京	Nanching	Nanking
Ningbo 宁波	Ningpo	
Niuzhuang 牛庄	Niuchuang	Newchwang
Qingdao 青岛	Tsingtao	
Shanghai 上海	Shanghai	Shanghae

1 Hankou is now part of the city of Wuhan.

Pinyin/Chinese	Wade-Giles	Common form
Shantou 汕头	Shant'ou	Swatow
Tianjin 天津	T'ienchin	Tientsin
Xiamen 厦门	Hsiamen	Amoy
Yangzi 扬子[1]	Yangtzu	Yangtze / Yangtse
Yantai 烟台	Yant'ai	Chefoo[2]
Zhenjiang 镇江	Chênchiang	Chinkiang
Zhoushan 舟山	Choushan	Chusan

1 Yangzi (扬子)/Yangtzu refers only to the lower part (from Nanjing to Shanghai) of the river known in Chinese as *Changjiang*. The name Yangzi (扬子)/Yangtzu is obsolete in China.

2 Chefoo was the name widely used for Yantai by foreigners in the treaty era is a rendering of Zhifu (芝罘), the name of the harbour at Yantai.

1 Britain and colonialism in China

Abstract
This chapter introduces the key argument that the role of the British state in the development of the treaty ports has not been well understood and places it in its historiographical context: existing historical work on the British empire, on colonialism in China and on imperial networks. It traces the lack of clarity over the role of the British state in treaty era China to problems with the deployment of the term informal empire. It then describes the sources used and the structure of the book.

Keywords: colonialism in China, imperial expansion, informal empire

> I am not the first who has been compelled to remark that it is more difficult to deal with our own countrymen at Canton, than with the Chinese government.[1]
>
> John Francis Davis, 1846

John Francis Davis was Britain's leading official in China — the plenipotentiary and superintendent of trade — when he wrote these lines of complaint to Lord Palmerston, only a few years after the end of the First Opium War. His complaint was prompted by feelings of extreme frustration while in the midst of a dispute surrounding violent behaviour towards Chinese people in Guangzhou by British merchants.[2] Later superintendents and subordinate British officials would also expend significant amounts of time and energy on dealing with challenges that they saw as arising out of their commitment to control British subjects in China. Their attitudes and practices, and the policies and legal measures they adopted in dealing with these issues, influenced the shape of the British state's presence in

1 Quoted in Morse, *The International Relations of the Chinese Empire: Vol. 1*, p. 384.
2 The city of Guangzhou was referred to as Canton by foreigners at the time. See pages 15-16 for more information on the rendering of Chinese place names in western languages.

Thompson, Alex: *British Law and Governance in Treaty Port China 1842-1927. Consuls, Courts and Colonial Subjects.* Taylor & Francis Group, 2024
DOI: 10.5117/9789463720397_CH01

China, and moreover had profound effects on the wider development of the Chinese treaty ports.

Some aspects and effects of Britain's intrusion into China in the nineteenth century are well known. There was of course the transfer of sovereignty over land and people that took place at Hong Kong and Weihaiwei, which became British 'possessions'. We also know much about the limitations placed on the Chinese government's sovereignty within its own borders through both legal treaties and the accretion of established practices. We know that Chinese state control over parts of its territory was taken away, so that cities or portions of cities in China became effectively micro-colonies governed by foreigners. We know that China's state finances were taken to a large extent out of Chinese hands, and especially we know that under the principle of extraterritoriality, foreigners in China were removed from Chinese jurisdiction, in a clear degradation of Chinese sovereignty, as understood (both then and now) in western international law. We might characterise this process as one of the relentless erosion of the power of the Chinese state, of the removal of mechanisms for order and control which are hallmarks of state power. This is an accurate picture, which has been painted in many ways by many different writers.[3] But it gives an incomplete picture of foreign expansion in China, at least in the British case, if we fail to give serious consideration to the steps which were taken by the British state to put in place an apparatus for order and control — consular jurisdiction — over its subjects in China. This is a step which we must take if we are to understand the way that the treaty ports operated. The research presented in this book interrogates for the first time the British state's project of governance in China and connects it with the institutions, practices and culture which grew up in the Chinese treaty port world.[4] As others have noted, this was a colonial world dominated by Britain, but the roles played by British officials, through regulations,

3 See especially Bickers, *The Scramble for China*; Feuerwerker, *The Foreign Establishment in China*; Hevia, *English Lessons* and Jürgen Osterhammel, 'Semi-Colonialism and Informal Empire in China: Towards a Framework of Analysis'.

4 Others have described aspects of the British state's involvement in China, including certain institutions, but there is no existing work which aims to analyse the British state's project of governance in China. See Cassel, *Grounds of Judgment*; Whewell, 'British Extraterritoriality in China; Coates, *The China Consuls*; Fairbank, *Trade and Diplomacy on the China Coast*; Feuerwerker, *The Foreign Establishment in China.* Cassel and Whewell examine extraterritoriality and the courts, Coates and Fairbank both give a good deal of information about consuls, and Feuerwerker provides a valuable overview of the working of the Shanghai International Settlement within which Britain was dominant. However, none of these works provides a survey or detailed analysis of the British state's project of governance as effected through the range of institutions and practices, and over the time period, encompassed by this book.

institutions and everyday practices, in creating, shaping and perpetuating this world have remained largely unexplored.[5]

This book examines a key aspect of the expansion of the British state in China, which was undertaken to implement consular jurisdiction following the conclusion of the Treaty of Nanjing in 1842, and it shows how this project of governance unfolded in subsequent years, up to 1927. This period covers the decades when the British machinery of governance was being established and also the years in the early twentieth century which can be considered to have been the 'apogee' of the foreign presence in China, before the treaty system began to be dismantled beginning in the late 1920s.[6] I show that the British state engaged in a substantial project of governance in China, and, to achieve this, deployed resources towards a settled, institutional presence which has hitherto been only weakly acknowledged in the historical writing on Britain in China. The lack of prominence given to this process has meant that the nature of imperial expansion in China has been misunderstood or misrepresented.

A key focus of the book is the structures and institutions developed to manage and control British subjects, especially two marginal groups: white Britons who committed violent crime, and 'martial' British Indian colonial subjects. It uncovers and evaluates the factors which lay behind official British attitudes and practices towards them. The attention of state actors was intensely focussed on these groups in the course of the implementation of the British state's project of governance in treaty port China. Examining attitudes and practices towards these marginal British subjects brings to the surface processes and everyday practices which were sometimes incoherent, or even illegal, and reveals connections and collaborations with other organisations both within and beyond China which developed without fanfare and could otherwise be easily overlooked. An analysis of the actions of the state, and the effects of those actions, explains aspects of the development of the treaty ports and reveals their nature as distinctively colonial settings in new ways.

Analysing empire and colonialism in China

Foreign expansion into China in the treaty century (1842–1943) was complicated, and historians continue to grapple with the best way to understand

5 Osterhammel, for example, makes the case for British domination of this colonial setting succinctly and convincingly, but, like others, does not direct significant attention towards the actions of the state. Osterhammel, 'Britain and China', pp. 146–69.

6 Feuerwerker, p. ix. Although the system was dismantled from the 1920s, and British influence waned, Britons retained extraterritorial treatment until the 1940s.

various aspects of it. It was an extensive, influential, destructive, creative, exploitative and profitable set of processes, which has cast a long shadow in Chinese minds, especially in the Communist Party official view of China's modern history as written in China, particularly from the 1980s onwards, in which the 'unequal treaties' forced on China by foreign powers are very prominent.[7] But despite its clear and obvious importance, it is hard to pin down the nature of foreign and British expansion in China conceptually, since on the one hand the situation in China does not fit in many ways alongside patterns seen in most examples of nineteenth-century European colonial expansion elsewhere in the world, yet on the other hand many features of the foreign presence, when examined carefully, look colonial from a historian's perspective, and have been shown clearly to have been experienced as colonial from the perspective of both foreign and Chinese contemporaries.[8] In this book I will show that, when the range of the British state's actions in China are properly examined, we can see that it behaved as a colonial power in many ways which stretch the meaning of the word 'informal' to its limits, and that these actions had serious consequences for the development of the treaty ports, places which were in turn hugely influential in the development of modern China in the late nineteenth and early twentieth centuries.

Given that most of China remained under Chinese sovereignty, it is unsurprising that many writers have turned to the concept of 'informal empire' to help to explain the case of treaty era China, but this has perhaps encouraged misconceptions. 'Informal empire' is generally used within a conceptual framework which posits two broad types of imperial expansion, drawing on the work of John Gallagher and Ronald Robinson, who suggested that the British state's approach to empire could be summarised as 'trade with informal control if possible; trade with rule when necessary'.[9] This theory has played a useful role in drawing the attention of imperial historians towards places which fell under varying degrees of external control without becoming formally politically subsumed within or attached to the imperial polity, including China.[10] Although Robinson and Gallagher

7 Bickers, *The Scramble for China*, pp. 4–6; Feuerwerker, pp. 110–11.

8 Jurgen Osterhammel provides a useful (and extensive) list of foreign phenomena in China which could be classed as imperial in his 'Semi-Colonialism and Informal Empire in China', pp. 290–91.

9 Gallagher and Robinson, 'The Imperialism of Free Trade', p. 13.

10 Historians who have made use the theory of informal empire effectively to incorporate studies of China into the British empire world include especially Robert Bickers and Jurgen Osterhammel. See for example, Bickers, *Britain in China*; Osterhammel, 'Semi-Colonialism'.

themselves argued that 'the difference between formal and informal empire has not been one of fundamental nature but of degree,' an awareness of this latter insight has not however always been evident in some subsequent work, so that 'informal' and 'formal' empire can appear as two clear and bounded categories, alternative modes of expansion with clear lines of distinction between them.[11] In this kind of framework, informal empire is all too easily cast as necessarily a diminished or secondary variety of empire. Formal empire is then seen as 'full' empire, whereas informal empire — and sometimes the alternative term 'semicolonialism' — is a lightweight, perhaps even 'light touch' alternative. For example, John Darwin sets out the contrast between formal and informal empire by describing the latter as 'nearly invisible', and stresses the importance of 'influence' in the exercise of control.[12] Darwin applies the label of informal empire to China and yet the expansion of Britain — including the British state — into China in the treaty era can only have appeared to be somewhat invisible when viewed from selected points, such as perhaps at times from within the walls of the Colonial Office in London; it was by no means invisible to the foreigners and Chinese living in or passing through the treaty ports.

This misleading dualism has also appeared in more specialist work focussing specifically on China. For example, in their discussion of colonialism in China, David and Bryna Goodman describe places such as Hong Kong, Qingdao and Weihaiwei, as 'clearly colonized pieces of China, each of which was governed by a single colonial power', and contrast them with the treaty ports, which they call 'a more restricted type of colonial formation.'[13] Clearly, differences in modes of governance should be recognised between kinds of colonised space, but the implication of the use of the term 'restricted' seems to be that the treaty ports, including even Shanghai, represented a type of more limited or less active colonialism, a position which is not supported by the evidence.[14] To take the most stark example, why should Weihaiwei, in which under British rule traditional village hierarchies and legal procedures were maintained more or less intact, and in which Britain invested very little administrative labour or capital, be a less 'restricted' example of colonialism than the International Settlement of Shanghai, in which officials of foreign governments, especially Britain, together with the

11 A point made recently by Isabella Jackson in relation to China: see her *Shaping Modern Shanghai*, p. 17.

12 Darwin, *Unfinished Empire*, pp. 391–92.

13 Goodman and Goodman, *Twentieth Century Colonialism and China*, p. 2.

14 Isabella Jackson argues forcefully for a recognition of Shanghai's International Settlement as a fully-fledged site of colonial governance. Jackson, *Shaping Modern Shanghai*.

Shanghai Municipal Council (SMC), a large foreign administrative body, instituted procedures of governance which clearly replicated asymmetrical colonial relations in a wide range of areas and in ways which bore a close resemblance to sites of colonialism elsewhere in the world? If the crucial point of difference is that the Chinese residents of Weihaiwei, numbering around 160,000 in 1918, were placed under Britain's sole authority, whereas the Shanghai International Settlement's approximately 630,000 Chinese residents in 1916 were still nominally under the control of the Chinese government, this fixation on tracing sovereignty can severely distort our understanding of specific conditions, arrangements and their effects.[15] When we consider that in the early part of the twentieth century the Shanghai Municipal Council oversaw what was thought to be the world's largest prison (Ward Road Gaol), its thousands of inmates being almost all Chinese citizens, the seriousness of this sort of distortion becomes obvious.[16]

When we study the British state in China, we must examine multiple institutions across a wide geographical area which engaged in both a colonial project and a diplomatic one. This multiplicity and blending of purposes is one of the most challenging features for writers seeking to explain British state actions and their effects in nineteenth- and early twentieth-century China. In the existing literature on the foreign presence in China, the role of the British state has often been examined in limited ways as most historians have focussed on its role in terms of actions, especially diplomatic and military, towards the governments of China and the other treaty powers, from the aggressions of the forcible opening of the Qing empire to trade in the nineteenth century, via the various crises of the last decades of the Qing dynasty, through to the turbulent years of republican China.[17] The existence of extraterritoriality and consular jurisdiction in China is generally noted in such writing, but the workings of the system and the administrative role played by the British state through its consuls and courts have not been explored in great detail.[18] Published works which have looked in more detail

15 For a study of British governance in Weihaiwei see Tan, *British Rule in China*. See also Atwell, *British Mandarins and Chinese Reformers*.

16 Dikötter, *Crime, Punishment and the Prison in Modern China*, p. 311.

17 A fairly comprehensive survey of such work up to 1990 can be found in Wang, *Anglo-Chinese Encounters*. For more recent literature, see Bickers, *Out of China*.

18 Whewell's 2015 thesis is a recent exception, although by making criminal law under extraterritoriality (rather than governance more broadly) the focus of her attention, she gives only a partial picture of the project of governance which was effected by the British state through a range of institutions and collaborations with other bodies in China. Whewell, 'British Extraterritoriality in China'.

at extraterritoriality in China have tended to focus on the international relations aspect of this issue. So, for example, both Pär Cassel and R. Randle Edwards focus much of their attention on the process of negotiating the contours of extraterritoriality which took place between Chinese and foreign officials.[19] However, relatively little research has been conducted which examines British consular jurisdiction as it was in fact practised following the Opium War, and the implications of this practice for the treaty ports and China more broadly. This book addresses this omission by examining how, on the basis of extraterritoriality, the British state engaged in a project of governance in China through its involvement in the day-to-day ordering of British activities in China, in ways which strongly influenced treaty port life, principally through the British consuls and the courts which administered justice to British subjects and corporate bodies. It was not only British subjects whose lives were shaped by the attitudes and practices of agents of the British state in China. Chinese in the Shanghai International Settlement lived for many practical purposes as though they were colonial subjects under foreign government, and I argue that the British state played a substantial role in the ambitious and elaborate project of governance exercised over them there, albeit in concert with other foreign governments and the SMC.[20]

Ann Laura Stoler has made a powerful critique of terms like 'informal empire' which she calls 'unhelpful euphemisms', and argues that instead we should think in terms of 'scaled genres of rule that produce and count on different degrees of sovereignty and gradations of rights'.[21] She prefers the expression 'imperial formations' to encapsulate all forms of empire, and thus advocates a more flexible framework which could help avoid the problems discussed above. Other scholars, some working in the field of Chinese history, have also advocated moving away from the use of multiple terms to particularise forms of empire. James Hevia, for example, proposes that we think of 'all the entities produced in the age of empire as forms of semicolonialism', a formulation which may at first appear perplexing, but which would in fact allow us to acknowledge that colonialism, however initiated or described in legal and political or administrative terms, was never a completed project, and was always a complex set of relations which need to be analysed as they unfolded in everyday life as much as in the lives

19 Cassel, *Grounds of Judgment*; Edwards, 'Ch'ing Legal Jurisdiction Over Foreigners'. See also Kayaoglu, *Legal Imperialism* and Ruskola, *Legal Orientalism*.

20 Feuerwerker, p. 5.

21 Ann Laura Stoler, 'On Degrees of Imperial Sovereignty', pp. 136, 128.

of imperial and local leaders.[22] Isabella Jackson argues for the uniqueness of Shanghai, and advocates using the description 'transnational colonialism' to fit the specific case of the Shanghai International Settlement, emphasising the variety of nations and nationalities involved in governance of the Settlement — but, as I argue in this book, the overwhelming importance of British influences (and especially the British state), at least in the period covered by this book, must be understood.[23] The adoption of a framework which emphasises the transnational aspect of Shanghai's governance could easily lead us too far from this fact.

The obvious counter-criticism to such moves is that without analytical tools to classify broader categories of empire or colonialism, attempts to make comparisons and draw conclusions on a larger scale are made very difficult. But if the tools used to distinguish lead to distortions such as those outlined above, we may be better off seeing the situation as too nuanced and complex to allow for the development of straightforward categories or shorthands.[24] Informal empire may be useful in metropole-oriented studies seeking to understand the various modes of expansion of a particular empire, and in drawing attention to expansion not definable in terms of the transfer of specifically demarcated territory, but it is of limited use for, and may in fact be unhelpful to, scholars whose primary aim is to explain, in Alan Lester's words, 'the nature of colonial relations in any one or more places, and how those relations shape those places'.[25] Instead of making sovereignty over territory the starting point and key to the defining framework of histories of empire, a focus on colonial relations, and the colonial practices which established and perpetuated them, can avoid the blind spots created by the older models discussed above.

The Foreign Office archive and other sources

In the course of their engagement in the processes described above, British officials in China, at other posts in Asia, and of course in London, produced a rich archive of documentary material, much of which was well looked after, and a good deal of which has been gathered together and preserved at the

22 Hevia, *English Lessons*, p. 26.

23 Jackson, *Shaping Modern Shanghai*, p. 6.

24 John Comaroff has made a similar argument against distorting generalisations of the colonial state: 'Reflections on the Colonial State', p. 336.

25 Lester, 'Imperial Circuits and Networks', p. 131.

National Archives, Kew, London. Despite the relative completeness of these records and the ease with which they can be accessed, this resource has been under-exploited by historians of British colonialism. These materials, together with (to a more limited extent) the India Office records at the British Library in London, have made up the key primary sources deployed in the research for this book. The research has entailed an examination of a wide range of records, reflecting the extensive range of state actors at different locations who played a role in British governance in China, and the aim to present a history of the British state in China which integrates the full range of official agents who played significant roles in the British project of governance. These archival sources have been read in two ways: first, as documents which can help us to determine what actions were taken by the British state in China; and second, as documents which contain evidence of the attitudes, often not explicitly articulated, of British officials dealing with processes connected with British expansion in China, and especially the management of marginal British subjects. The most important file series consulted were those containing records of key institutions engaged in the state's project of governance in China: the superintendent of trade/minister (FO 228), the FO in London (FO 17, FO 97 and FO 371), the law officers of the Crown (FO 83 and FO 96), the Shanghai Consulate (FO 671) and the British Supreme Court for China (FO 656). A complete list is given in the bibliography.

A further source of official documents which has been used extensively is published collections of British state papers, including laws, treaty texts, orders in council (OICs), and regulations. The key collections are *Hertslet's China Treaties* (two volumes), *Hertslet's Commercial Treaties* (31 volumes) and *British and Foreign State Papers* (170 volumes). British Parliamentary Papers have also been used, especially those which collect correspondence relating to China at moments when British actions were under scrutiny by the legislature.

Newspaper articles and editorials, mostly from the Shanghai-based English language press, have been used extensively for their reports of court cases, to supplement the details of cases contained in official papers held in the archives referred to above. As much as possible I have based analysis of court cases on both reports of proceedings published in the press and documents circulating between officials, which often reveal the ways in which practices deviated from legal procedures and are therefore highly revealing of official attitudes. However, although press reports sometimes reveal information lacking in official documents (and vice versa), it must be acknowledged that this will always be an incomplete picture, particularly where performative aspects of legal practices are concerned — there can only be a very partial reconstruction of what went on in the courtroom, in particular in areas such as bodily practices and ways of speaking.

Book structure

In this book the British state in China emerges as an important force of governance at the treaty ports, not always coherent but highly influential, driven to expand and collaborate by the impulse to control British subjects, especially marginal British subjects who were, to British officials, problem populations. The first of the following chapters examines the framework, in terms of laws and organisational structures, which was developed by the Foreign Office (FO) from the early 1840s following the end of the Opium War. This is an overview of British governance in China which is not to my knowledge available in any other recent published work. Having presented this overview, the remaining chapters delve into the primary causes of changes to British governance which were made over the course of the second half of the nineteenth and early part of the twentieth century: the response to British problem populations, namely 'rowdy' Europeans and 'martial' Indians.[26] Each chapter examines the wider effects on China of British state governance, especially the consequences at Shanghai, where British state support for the Shanghai Municipal Council, which governed the International Settlement, is shown to have been crucial.

Together the chapters that follow demonstrate that, in implementing British jurisdiction in China, the British state created structures and institutions, deployed personnel, and created or enabled practices in ways that combined to have profound consequences for the development of the treaty ports, especially Shanghai, as key sites of colonialism in China. Any analysis of the treaty ports which fails to incorporate an understanding of this influence is in danger of providing a distorted account, by failing to explain an essential feature of the treaty port world and furthermore an

26 A further important group of marginal British subjects who attracted a not insignificant amount of British official scrutiny and intervention were Chinese British subjects, often people who had obtained British nationality as a consequence of birth or naturalisation in the colonies of Hong Kong or the Straits Settlements. The story of British official engagement with members of that group who returned to China is not included in this book, because although they were a significant British problem population, there is no evidence that the development of the British state's structures and institutions in China were influenced to a great extent by the existence or actions of this group.

important factor affecting developments in China more widely up to at least the 1920s.[27]

Bibliography

Atwell, Pamela, *British Mandarins and Chinese Reformers: The British Administration of Weihaiwei (1898–1930) and the Territory's Return to Chinese Rule* (Oxford: Oxford University Press, 1985).

Bickers, Robert, *The Scramble for China: Foreign Devils in the Qing Empire, 1832–1914* (London: Allen Lane, 2011).

Bickers, Robert, *Out of China: How the Chinese Ended the Era of Western Domination* (London: Penguin, 2017).

Cassel, Pär Kristoffer, *Grounds of Judgment: Extraterritoriality and Imperial Power in Nineteenth-Century China and Japan* (Oxford: Oxford University Press, 2012).

Coates, P. D., *The China Consuls: British Consular Officers, 1843–1943* (Hong Kong: Oxford University Press, 1988).

Comaroff, John L., 'Reflections on the Colonial State, in South Africa and Elsewhere: Factions, Fragments, Facts and Fictions', *Social Identities*, 4, 3 (1998), 321–61.

Darwin, John, *Unfinished Empire: The Global Expansion of Britain* (London: Allen Lane, 2012).

Dikötter, Frank, *Crime, Punishment and the Prison in Modern China* (C. Hurst & Co., 2002).

Edwards, R. Randle, 'Ch'ing Legal Jurisdiction Over Foreigners', in Jerome Alan Cohen, Fu-mei Chang, and R. Randle Edwards (eds.), *Essays on China's Legal Tradition* (Princeton, NJ: Princeton University Press, 1980), 222–69.

Fairbank, John King, *Trade and Diplomacy on the China Coast: The Opening of the Treaty Ports, 1842–1854* (Stanford, CA: Stanford University Press, 1953).

Feuerwerker, Albert, *The Foreign Establishment in China in the Early Twentieth Century* (Ann Arbor: Center for Chinese Studies, University of Michigan, 1976).

Gallagher, John and Ronald Robinson, 'The Imperialism of Free Trade', *The Economic History Review*, New Series, 6, 1 (1953), 1–15.

Goodman, Bryna, and David S. G. Goodman, *Twentieth Century Colonialism and China: Localities, the Everyday, and the World* (Abingdon: Routledge, 2012).

27 It is widely acknowledged that Shanghai, which had developed into China's most important urban centre in many respects by the early twentieth century, has had an enormous influence on China's twentieth-century development in a vast range of areas. See Yeh's *Shanghai Splendor* for a description of the way that Chinese lived experiences within and beyond Shanghai were affected by the social formations which grew up in the city.

Hevia, James L., *English Lessons: The Pedagogy of Imperialism in Nineteenth-Century China* (Durham, NC: Duke University Press, 2003).

Jackson, Isabella, *Shaping Modern Shanghai: Colonialism in China's Global City* (Cambridge: Cambridge University Press, 2017).

Kayaoglu, Turan, *Legal Imperialism: Sovereignty and Extraterritoriality in Japan, the Ottoman Empire, and China* (Cambridge: Cambridge University Press, 2010).

Lester, Alan, 'Imperial Circuits and Networks: Geographies of the British Empire', *History Compass*, 4, 1 (2006), 124–41.

Morse, Hosea Ballou, *The International Relations of the Chinese Empire: Vol. 1, The Period of Conflict, 1834–1860* (London: Longmans, Green, 1910).

Osterhammel, Jürgen, 'Semi-Colonialism and Informal Empire in China: Towards a Framework of Analysis', in W. Mommsen and J. Osterhammel (eds.), *Imperialism and After: Continuities and Discontinuities* (London: German Historical Institute, 1986), 290–314.

Osterhammel, Jürgen, 'Britain and China, 1842–1914', in Andrew Porter and William Roger Louis (eds.), *The Oxford History of the British Empire: Volume 3, The Nineteenth Century* (Oxford: Oxford University Press, 1999), 146–69.

Ruskola, Teemu, *Legal Orientalism: China, the United States, and Modern Law* (Cambridge, MA: Harvard University Press, 2013).

Stoler, Ann Laura, 'On Degrees of Imperial Sovereignty', *Public Culture*, 18, 1 (2006), 125–46.

Tan, Carol G. S., *British Rule in China: Law and Justice in Weihaiwei 1898–1930* (London: Wildy, Simmonds and Hill, 2008).

Wang, Gungwu, *Anglo-Chinese Encounters since 1800: War, Trade, Science, and Governance* (Cambridge: Cambridge University Press, 2003).

Whewell, Emily, 'British Extraterritoriality in China: The Legal System, Functions of Criminal Jurisdiction, and its Challenges, 1833–1943', University of Leicester PhD thesis (2015).

Yeh, Wen-hsin, *Shanghai Splendor: Economic Sentiments and the Making of Modern China, 1843–1949* (Berkeley, CA: University of California Press, 2007).

2 British institutions of governance in China

Abstract
This chapter sketches British state involvement in China before 1842 as background to the expansion which began in the subsequent treaty era. It also gives an overview of the non-British foreign presence in treaty era China. It describes and analyses the chief structures established to implement extraterritoriality through consular jurisdiction: laws and regulations created in London, Hong Kong and Beijing; personnel tasked with putting these legal instruments into practice, the British consuls and the judges of the Supreme Court for China. It highlights the connections and networks engendered by the British state presence and practices in China and explains how the governance of Shanghai was influenced by, and dependent on, British state institutions and actors.

Keywords: Extraterritoriality, consular jurisdiction, the Shanghai Mixed Court, the Supreme Court for China, Rutherford Alcock, Edmund Hornby

Soon after the signing of the 1842 Treaty of Nanjing officials at the Foreign Office set to work on a Bill that they were anxious to get through Parliament without delay.[1] This was entitled 'An Act for the better Government of Her Majesty's Subjects resorting to China', and its aim was to create a system of jurisdiction exercised by British officials which would make the extraterritorial rights Britain had obtained through the treaty workable. Contemporary Foreign Office (FO) documents make it plain that this task was viewed as a highly important one:

> this admission on the part of the Chinese Government imposes upon Her Majesty's Government the obligation of providing in the most effectual

1 TNA FO 17/76B: Addington to Bethune [draft], 8 July 1843.

Thompson, Alex: *British Law and Governance in Treaty Port China 1842-1927. Consuls, Courts and Colonial Subjects.* Taylor & Francis Group, 2024
DOI: 10.5117/9789463720397_CH02

> manner against any prejudice resulting to China from the consent of its Government to renounce its right to control British Subjects within the Emperor's dominions.[2]

This chapter provides a survey of the formal outlines of the British state presence as it developed in China, made up of legal instruments, institutions and personnel. The settled, institutional aspect of the British state's expansion into China, and the connections which were formed through such institutions, had important effects. But these formations are easily overlooked when the role of the state is thought of as a largely indirect force, or as episodic and inconstant in the application of its power, as has been the case in some analyses of informal empire. This chapter will describe elements of Britain's presence in China which were not in any sense informal and which were furthermore fairly stable and long-lasting — the British state institutions and structures, made up of policymakers (principally the Foreign Office and the British minister in China), legislation, courts, consuls, constables and gaols — which together furthered the state's project of governance over British subjects and British interests in China, which underpinned the operations of British-dominated non-state institutions and British commerce, and which also curtailed the sovereignty of the Chinese state in important ways.

In order to gain a deep understanding of the actions of official and unofficial Britons, without doubt the most influential foreign community in China, with the aim of better evaluating their place in Chinese history, we must understand the legal and regulatory regime under which they lived, and which offered them certain rights but also constrained their actions in various ways. Simply noting that they were under British jurisdiction is not enough, for as this chapter will show, the British state created a system of governance in China which was adapted specially for its purposes there. It was based on English domestic law, and on British colonial practices elsewhere, but with important modifications, often prompted by the challenges created by marginal British subjects, as later chapters will demonstrate in some detail.

Britain in China before the treaties

This book focusses on the period from 1843 when British commercial and institutional expansion increased enormously following the end of the

2 TNA FO 17/76B: 'Memorandum: China Bill of 1843', 22 July 1843.

Opium War, the signing of the first treaties, and the opening of five ports to foreign commerce — the first treaty ports. There was a prehistory of interaction prior to this expansion, however, going back around two hundred years, including experiences and encounters which led to provisions for extraterritoriality being incorporated in the treaties made after the First Opium War. The commercial aspects of the early trade between Britain and China, which began in the seventeenth century, including the development of the opium trade and eventual war fought over its conduct, have been well covered elsewhere.[3] Here I will give a brief account of this period which focusses instead on British institutional developments and approaches to governance over British subjects.

Until 1834, British trade with China took place under the monopoly held by the East India Company (EIC), but involved both Company-owned and private ships, which operated under licence from the Company.[4] At first, such ships called speculatively at a variety of South China ports and attempted to trade profitably, hoping to interest Chinese buyers in foreign goods such as British woollens and Indian cottons, and purchasing Chinese goods such as tea, silk and porcelain. In 1699 the EIC appointed an officer with the title of president to supervise the trade. The first president, Allen Catchpoole, was also given the title of consul for China by the king, a common practice in connection with EIC presidents in other parts of Asia.[5] He sailed to Zhoushan and Ningbo to attempt to oversee trade there, thus technically becoming the first British official to visit China. While at Zhoushan, he experienced difficulties in exercising control over captains of private British ships, and in dealing with them the office of consul seems not to have had much practical use. Catchpoole was criticised by some captains for being unable to offer any protection to British subjects in China. It seems that the main aim in granting him the titles of president and consul was to assist him in making contact with Chinese officials, for the benefit of easing trading restrictions, at the highest level possible, preferably at Nanjing, a goal which was not successfully attained.[6]

The EIC failed to open satisfactory channels for trade at Ningbo, Zhoushan or Xiamen (where attempts were also made), but at Guangzhou they had more success, and trade there increased. From 1757, following further attempts

3 A concise summary is given in Bickers, *The Scramble for China*, pp. 80–86. A more detailed recent treatment can be found in Lovell, *The Opium War*.

4 Greenberg, *British Trade and the Opening of China*, p. 11.

5 Bruce, *Annals of the Honorable East-India Company*, vol. 3, p. 332.

6 Morse, *The Chronicles of the East India Company, Trading to China 1635–1834*, vol. 1, p. 109.

by the EIC to initiate trade at ports further north, the Chinese government stipulated that all foreign trade must thenceforth be done at Guangzhou.[7] At the latter port foreigners were subject to many restrictions, including the rule that trade was only to be done through Chinese merchants there accredited by the local authorities, who were known collectively by English speakers as the 'cohong' (in Chinese *gonghang* 公行).[8] The Chinese official attitude towards foreigners can be summarised as a desire to keep foreigners at arm's length, and minimise points of contact between foreigners and Chinese people and places. Foreigners in China were thus in an uncomfortable and precarious situation — only the security of the Portuguese territory at Macao, where most British figures engaged in trade lived for part of the year, made it possible to operate within the Chinese restrictions. Although the British were frequently frustrated by the limitations on their activities, a very valuable trade took place, especially in tea, increasingly in demand in Great Britain, and eventually, from the middle of the eighteenth century, also in opium, which although illegal found a ready market in China. Opium was brought from India by the private traders, many based in India, a number of whom were Parsis.[9]

The functioning of a basic system of control over British subjects in China was possible at this time because the EIC had both the incentive and the powers to oversee it. From the late eighteenth century, the EIC appointed a group of supercargoes (commercial agents responsible for trade), known as the Select Committee of Supercargoes, to lead their activities in China. They naturally wished to eliminate behaviour in China which might cause interruptions to trade resulting from disputes with the Chinese. The EIC was able to maintain some control over British subjects in China, because since it held a British government-sanctioned monopoly, all those engaged in the trade were either its employees or were licenced by it. Employees could be disciplined or dismissed, and private traders could be excluded from the trade by the EIC if they did not cooperate.[10] There were a number of outbreaks of violence committed by British subjects, especially seamen, in or near Guangzhou as the trade increased, and it fell to the Select Committee to decide how to respond. Other than in cases of homicide against Chinese, the

7 Morse, *International Relations*, vol. 1, p. 67.

8 Morse, *International Relations*, vol. 1, pp. 63–71. Most English-language texts use the contemporary rendering of this word, cohong or co-hong, which was presumably based on an interpretation of the pronunciation in the local Guangzhou dialect. Individual merchants were called Hong merchants by English-speaking foreigners.

9 Morse, *International Relations*, vol. 1, p. 228.

10 Morse, *International Relations*, vol. 1, pp. 109–19.

Chinese authorities did not generally try to assert Chinese jurisdiction with regard to legal process and punishment of crimes committed by foreigners, so that in the case of British subjects, the EIC Select Committee was left to handle matters.[11] In 1784 a Chinese man was killed by a salute fired from the guns of a British ship, *Lady Hughes*, and the Chinese authorities demanded that the person responsible be handed over to them for trial and punishment. A British gunner was eventually handed over to the Chinese authorities and was executed; following this punishment, seen by the British as unjust, the British refused from that point on to hand over European British subjects accused of homicide to the Chinese authorities.[12] The case cast a long shadow and was frequently used in later debates to demonstrate alleged Chinese barbarity and to justify foreign extraterritoriality in China.[13]

In 1834 the British government ended the EIC's monopoly on trade in China, and vested control over British activities there in a new institution created to oversee the trade with China — the Superintendency of Trade. This was the first true institution of the British state to be established on Chinese soil, and was headed by three men, one of whom was given the title of chief superintendent of trade. An act of parliament and two orders in council were made in 1833 to endow the superintendents with authority to exercise control over British subjects and to enable the creation of a British court of justice at Guangzhou, over which the chief superintendent would preside.[14] The first chief superintendent was Lord William Napier, formerly an officer of the Royal Navy. The other two superintendents were former EIC supercargoes: John Francis Davis (who later became chief superintendent and governor of Hong Kong) and George Robinson.[15] The court provided for by means of the legislation of 1833 was not established immediately, under

11 Edwards, 'Ch'ing Legal Jurisdiction Over Foreigners', 222–69; Morse, *International Relations*, vol. 1, p. 101.

12 Cassel, *Grounds of Judgment*, p. 43. According to Koo, a 'lascar' (a South Asian seaman) was handed over to the Chinese authorities in 1833 following the killing of a Chinese near Guangzhou. Koo, *The Status of Aliens in China*, p. 79.

13 Cassel, *Grounds of Judgment*, p. 43. For a detailed exploration of the *Lady Hughes* case, see Chen, 'Law, Empire, and Historiography of Modern Sino-Western Relations'.

14 Great Britain. 'An Act to Regulate the Trade to China and India: 3 & 4 Will. 4. c. 93'; Great Britain. 'Order in Council, Appointment of a Court of Justice at Canton, for the Trial of Offences Committed by British Subjects in China,' 9 December 1833; Great Britain. 'Order in Council, Relative to the Government and Trade of British Subjects, at Canton, in China', 9 December 1833. All printed in Great Britain. Foreign Office, *British and Foreign State Papers* (hereafter *BaFSP*), *1832–1833*, vol. 20, (London, 1836), pp. 256–59; 260–61; 262–63.

15 Initially, William Plowden, former president of the EIC Select Committee was appointed one of the superintendents, but he left China before Napier's arrival and Robinson was appointed to fill the resulting vacancy. Morse, *International Relations*, vol. 1, p. 119.

instructions from Lord Palmerston to postpone taking any steps to bring it into service, and indeed no permanent British court, with a regular schedule of operation or fixed premises, was opened in China before the Opium War.[16] When a man called Lin Weixi was killed in an incident involving British seamen in 1839, at a time when the dispute between Britain and China over the opium trade was growing in intensity, Chief Superintendent Charles Elliot held court proceedings under the 1833 Order in Council (OIC) in a temporary courtroom set up on a British ship, in response to Chinese demands that those responsible be punished.[17] He sentenced five men to imprisonment for engaging in a riot, but the sentence was not carried into effect and the men were released in Great Britain since the courts there decided that Elliot lacked the required authority over British subjects.[18]

Other aspects of the post-EIC establishment were also defective. Superintendent Elliot had between 1836 and 1838 attempted to stop armed British smuggling boats landing near the custom house at Guangzhou and created 'police regulations' as a step to prevent this activity. When he reported his actions to the FO, he was told that he had no power to create such regulations under the British legislation.[19] The removal of the monopoly of the EIC may have inserted professional British state officials into China for the first time, but it seems that owing to the faulty legislation created to endow them with authority, they were less able to effect order and control over British subjects than had been possible under the EIC's Select Committee prior to 1834. Reporting his inability to prevent a British subject absconding from China, having defrauded British and Chinese subjects of goods worth large sums of money, Elliot made the case to Palmerston in 1837 that greater powers were needed:

> This may be a convenient occasion respectfully to press the necessity for the early establishment of some formal and efficacious means of maintaining a state of good order amongst His Majesty's subjects in this country, and for the adjustment of disputes involving claim of money which may arise on the spot.[20]

16 Morse, *International Relations*, vol. 1, pp. 120–21. Koo, *The Status of Aliens*, pp. 109–10.

17 Morse, *International Relations*, vol. 1 pp. 237–38. The man's name is rendered in some texts as Lin Wei-hi or Lin Weihe. The killing of Lin Weixi played a significant role in escalating tensions between Britain and China which would lead to the outbreak of the Opium War. See Lovell, *The Opium War*, pp. 72–74.

18 Morse, *International Relations*, p. 238, fn. 114; Lovell, *The Opium War*, p. 74.

19 Koo, *The Status of Aliens in China*, p. 110.

20 Elliot to Palmerston, 2 June 1837. British Parliamentary Papers, House of Commons, Papers relative to the Establishment of a Court of Judicature in China, for the Purpose of Enabling the

In both 1837 and 1838, attempts were made to pass legislation in Parliament to remedy the problem, but they were blocked by opposition in the House of Lords.[21]

In 1842, the Opium War ended with the signing of the Treaty of Nanjing. The most significant provisions of the treaty were that five ports (the first 'treaty ports') would be opened to British subjects for residence and trade, Hong Kong island would be ceded to Britain and British consuls would be posted at each port and would have jurisdiction over British subjects in China.[22] One lesson clearly learned by British officials locally and in London, from their experiences prior to the Opium War, was that a more effective means of control would be needed as the British presence grew with the opening of the treaty ports and the expansion of trade which was subsequently expected to take place.

The wider foreign presence and the treaty ports in China 1843–1927

Although the focus in this book is on British institutions, officials and subjects, it is important to remember that the British were not the only foreign actors in China. Other foreign states and their nationals also entered into trading and other relations in China, on similar terms to the British. Prior to the Opium War other countries whose nationals engaged in trade in a substantial way included Portugal (especially important owing to its control over the territory of Macao near Guangzhou), the Netherlands and the United States.[23] Following the Opium War, the United States and France also made treaties with China, giving them the same privileges as the British. The treaties included 'most favoured nation' clauses, so that when one foreign state gained increased rights through a treaty, the other treaty powers also benefitted in the same way.[24] In this way the foreign expansion into China which Britain had spearheaded through its actions in the Opium

British Superintendents of Trade to Exercise Control over the Proceedings of British Subjects, in their Intercourse with each other and with the Chinese, vol. 41, [c.128], (1838), p. 7.

21 British Parliamentary Papers, House of Commons, A Bill to Authorize the Establishing a Court Or Courts with Criminal and Admiralty and Civil Jurisdiction in China, vol. 1, [c.431], (1837); TNA FO 17/76B: 'Memorandum: China Bill of 1843', 22 July 1843.

22 Bickers, *Scramble for China*, p. 84. The five ports were (from south to north) Guangzhou, Xiamen, Fuzhou, Ningbo and Shanghai. Foreign trade and residence was still kept at some distance from Beijing.

23 Morse, *International Relations*, vol. 1, p. 82.

24 Osterhammel, 'Semi-Colonialism and Informal Empire in China', p. 300.

War became a multinational phenomenon. Foreign countries which made treaties with China all gained extraterritorial rights for their nationals and were thus responsible for the administration of justice in relation to them. Two latecomers to foreign expansion into China, Germany and then Japan, made up for lost time towards the end of the nineteenth century, and became important treaty powers. Several foreign states founded institutional presences on the China coast, but none were as extensive as the British, until the rise of Japanese power beginning in the late nineteenth century.[25]

The first treaty ports grew and developed in an extremely uneven way, and most were a disappointment to the British and other foreigners. Shanghai was the exception and soon became an important centre for shipping, being strategically located near to the mouth of the Yangzi, and eventually it was also an important location for foreign investment in land, manufacturing, and services. None of the other four ports became important as large centres of foreign residence or investment. Fuzhou was dominated by the tea trade and when this declined from the late nineteenth century, it lost its importance as a treaty port. Xiamen was most important for its connections with southeast Asia, and much of the trade conducted through the port involved ethnic Chinese from southeast Asia, some of whom were British subjects through birth or naturalisation in the Straits Settlements. It was an important centre for the 'coolie' trade, from which British and other firms profited, transporting large numbers of Chinese labourers, not all of whom had been recruited voluntarily, to plantations and mines in southeast Asia, South America and the Caribbean where they worked under harsh conditions. Ningbo was never an important port for foreign trade, but attracted foreign 'convoyers', little different from pirates, who engaged in dubious maritime activities in the 1850s and 1860s.[26] Guangzhou was a busy port, with important trade connected with its relatively prosperous hinterland, but lost out to Shanghai as the main centre for foreign trade, residence and investment from the mid-nineteenth century onwards.

The physical space occupied by foreign residents and businesses at the treaty ports was established on terms which varied, often according to the way the first foreign officials negotiated the institutional and physical environments which they encountered at the different places where they were posted. The actions of the first British and other foreign consuls

25 For a comparison of foreign establishments in China in the early twentieth century, see Bickers, 'British Concessions and Chinese Cities, 1910s–1930s'.

26 Morse, *International Relations*, vol. 1, pp. 406–08. For more on convoying, see Chapter 3.

therefore influenced the subsequent development of some of the ports.[27] Chinese officials were in general hostile to foreigners taking up residence within the existing Chinese towns or cities at the treaty ports. At Fuzhou and Guangzhou, confrontations over this issue led to violence, and in the case of Guangzhou, British access to that city was a major contributing factor to the outbreak of the Second Opium War (or Arrow War, as it is sometimes called) in 1856.

At Shanghai, the British consul made an agreement with the leading local official — the *daotai*, usually translated as 'circuit intendant' — to establish a special area for British residence, north of the existing Chinese city, alongside the Huangpu River.[28] Land was apportioned for this purpose, lots were acquired by foreign merchants (not all British subjects) and their titles were registered at the British Consulate. This area was usually called the English Settlement by contemporaries, although sometimes the word concession was confusingly used in place of settlement. In Chinese only one term was used: *zujie* (租界) meaning 'leased area'.[29] In the following years the United States and French consuls also made agreements for the setting aside of areas, neighbouring the English Settlement, for the residence of their nationals. In 1845 the British consul agreed with the daotai on a set of regulations, known as the Land Regulations, which provided for residents of the English Settlement to set up an institution to manage basic functions of local government, called the Committee of Roads and Jetties. This was made up of three land renters (the land acquired in the settlement was technically leased, though it was effectively owned as the leases were perpetual, and the leaseholders were called land renters). The committee was held to account at an annual meeting of ratepayers chaired by the British consul.[30] This body eventually developed into the Shanghai Municipal Council (SMC) in the mid-1850s, following the making of new Land Regulations, prompted by the influx of Chinese into the foreign settlements who came seeking refuge from the upheaval of the great rebellions taking place at the time in eastern China. This rapid population growth posed greater administrative challenges, particularly in the area of policing. In 1863, the American Settlement merged with the English Settlement to form the International Settlement, which was governed by the SMC. The French settlement, known as the French Concession, remained a separate entity with different forms

27 Morse, *International Relations*, vol. 1, pp. 346–66.
28 On the office of daotai, see Leung, *The Shanghai Taotai*.
29 Bickers, 'British Concessions', p. 159.
30 Morse, *International Relations*, vol. 1, p. 351.

of governance.[31] Once it became the International Settlement, the SMC annual meeting of ratepayers was usually chaired by the senior consul (the most long-serving among the foreign consuls at the city), and the Shanghai consular body had a supervisory role over the Council while also serving as an intermediary between the SMC and the local Chinese authorities.[32]

Following the end of the Second Opium War in 1860, Qing officials agreed to the establishment of a further twelve treaty ports, and areas were acquired in some of these by treaty powers for their residents under different terms than the earlier settlements at Shanghai and elsewhere. Parcels of land described as concessions were rented on long leases from the Chinese government by individual treaty power governments, who then sublet plots of land to foreigners. Some of the foreign concessions established at this time grew to become fairly substantial, for example those at Hankou and Tianjin. Municipal Councils were formed at the concessions, usually headed in the British case by the British consul at each port where a concession was established.[33]

Although the treaties with China provided for favourable tariffs, rights of residence, extraterritoriality and other advantages for foreigners in China, trade never matched the extravagant hopes of British and other foreigners in the mid-nineteenth century. British business dominated foreign trade and investment in China in the nineteenth and early twentieth centuries, but exports of goods other than opium were disappointing.[34] Britain also dominated the shipping industry in China, and British businesses moreover saw healthy growth in other service industries such as insurance and banking. Some of the biggest foreign fortunes in China were made from the development of land at the treaty ports, especially Shanghai, where the Chinese population grew considerably as a direct result of its status as a foreign-controlled (and foreign-protected) enclave.

British and other foreign expansion in China was not limited to the cession of small areas of territory such as at Hong Kong and Macao, expansion of

31 Morse, *International Relations*, vol. 2, pp. 119–20.

32 In Shanghai and in Beijing, representatives of the foreign powers at each city formed in the 1860s a 'consular body' and a 'diplomatic body' respectively, in order to coordinate their position in a number of matters relating to foreign relations, trade, and administration in China. These bodies were especially important in dealing with the oversight of the constitution and administrative powers of the International Settlement at Shanghai. See Kotenev, *Shanghai: Its Mixed Court and Council*, p. 15.

See reports of annual meetings in the *North China Herald* (*NCH*). For the consular body as intermediary, see for example Morse, *International Relations*, vol. 2, pp. 113–14.

33 Bickers, 'British Concessions and Chinese Cities', pp. 167–68.

34 Osterhammel, 'British Business in China, 1860s–1950s', p. 192.

business under favourable conditions forced out of China and written into the treaties, and the establishment of the treaty ports as micro-colonies. Foreign power was embedded in China in various other ways which taken together combined to make the Chinese experience of imperial expansion a peculiar case. The Chinese customs service is the most obvious example, a body which was led by foreigners — usually a British subject, and most notably Ulsterman Robert Hart — and which meant that the Chinese central government's largest and most consistent source of revenue was administered by foreign staff under Qing control.[35] In the late nineteenth century new encroachments multiplied, both in number and form and there was also an increase in the number of foreign states which joined the rush to wring concessions from the ailing Qing Chinese state.[36] So, for example, in 1898 new leaseholds over pieces of territory were granted to Germany at Qingdao, Britain at Weihaiwei and the New Territories, France at Guangzhouwan and Russia at Dalian (Port Arthur).[37] The major foreign powers also established and agreed on spheres of influence, so that China was divided into areas in which each foreign power was, at least nominally, to be pre-eminent. In the area of commerce foreign powers pushed for businesses controlled by their nationals to be the providers of loans to the government (often partly needed to pay for indemnities incurred after China lost wars against foreign governments) and the developers of railway building schemes and mining concessions. The rise of Japanese power in the late 1890s had a profound effect: when China lost the Sino-Japanese war in 1895, not only did Japan obtain further concessions and indemnities, but Taiwan was also ceded, becoming by far China's most important loss of territory to a foreign power in the nineteenth century. After the fall of the Qing in 1911, China became fragmented and was under the rule of a variety of regional factions dominated by warlords. Only once the Guomindang rose to power from the end of the 1920s did the situation begin to change with regard to western powers, although Japanese expansion into China grew and had a huge impact until the defeat of Japan in the Second World War. From the late 1920s, Britain began to give up its concessions, beginning with Hankou in 1927, as part of a gradual process of official retreat which continued over the subsequent two decades, although extraterritoriality,

35 A range of work has been published on the Customs in recent years. See especially Bickers, 'Purloined Letters: History and the Chinese Maritime Customs Service'; Van de Ven, *Breaking with the Past* and Ladds, *Empire Careers*.

36 The best-known example illustrating the large number of foreign states involved is Tianjin, where there were foreign concessions belonging to nine different countries.

37 Feuerwerker, pp. 9–10.

and Britain's principal institution through which it was implemented, the Supreme Court for China at Shanghai, endured considerably beyond this policy change, not being abolished until the 1940s.[38]

Centres of British executive power in the treaty era: London, Hong Kong and Beijing

After the conclusion in 1842 of the First Opium War, with treaties providing for greater freedoms for British subjects to trade in China, a new act of parliament and orders in council were passed in London, which provided for the transfer of the British court (nominally based at Guangzhou) to the newly ceded colony of Hong Kong. The chief superintendent of trade, who was also made Hong Kong governor, was to be responsible for the overall governance of British subjects in all of the treaty ports to be opened under the new regime. The process involved in creating this system of control, which was an integral part of the system for free trade envisaged by the treaties, involved a negotiation between British officials on the spot and those in London, both within the FO and outside it, in particular the law officers of the Crown, who were frequently asked for their opinion on proposals to govern British subjects in China.[39] It is clear that the FO desired at the outset to put in place a system which would actually enable the superintendent to exercise authority over British subjects. Therefore, at precisely the same time as the FO instructed Superintendent and Plenipotentiary Henry Pottinger to secure recognition of the principle of extraterritoriality 'in the most formal manner' from the Chinese plenipotentiaries (who had, according to an FO memo, 'voluntarily recognized' it), moves were made in London to create a system which could provide a satisfactory means of managing the behaviour of British subjects in China.[40]

The FO and law officers drew on the precedent of consular jurisdiction in the Ottoman Empire when creating the new system of jurisdiction.[41] Experience there would also serve as an important model for policy in China

38 Chow, *Britain's Imperial Retreat from China.*

39 See Parry (ed.), *Law Officers' Opinions to the Foreign Office.*

40 TNA FO 17/76B: 'Memorandum: China Bill of 1843', 22 July 1843. We may justifiably be sceptical as to the true Chinese position notwithstanding the FO assertion that the Chinese had 'voluntarily' accepted extraterritorial rights for British subjects in China. Li Chen has exposed a number of inconsistencies in British claims in official documents surrounding earlier interactions with Chinese officials over who had the right to try British subjects accused of crimes in China. See Chen, 'Law, Empire, and Historiography of Modern Sino-Western Relations', p. 13.

41 TNA FO 17/76B: 'Memorandum: China Bill of 1843', 22 July 1843.

at various later times, especially in 1865 when the system was overhauled (the 1865 reforms are dealt with later in this chapter). The FO were also able to draw on the experience and advice of Undersecretary James Stephen at the Colonial Office, who commented on the draft Bill and argued forcefully for various amendments towards ensuring that British officials in China were given wide discretion in a range of areas. For example, he argued against proposed restrictions on the superintendent of trade's freedom to decree what punishment (including the death penalty) should be inflicted for breaking the superintendent's ordinances, stating that such powers were delegated in 'half our colonies', and that 'qualifications and restrictions' would lead to 'legal quibbles without end'.[42]

It is clear that foremost in official minds when creating the new regime was dissatisfaction with the powers of the superintendents under the 1833 Act; the FO was determined that the new superintendent should be better equipped to maintain the peace in China by exercising greater control over British subjects. He was therefore given the new and important power to create, with the advice of the Hong Kong Legislative Council, laws and ordinances 'for the peace, order, and good government of Her Majesty's subjects being within the dominions of the Emperor of China'.[43] This was chiefly justified first by the inability to anticipate precisely what powers would be needed, and second by the distance between Great Britain and China, which made it impractical for the superintendent to consult London before enacting new regulations.[44] The power meant that the superintendent could issue ordinances laying down specific rules to be observed by British subjects, often based on the treaties with China, or giving special powers to consuls in certain areas. This was an unusual but not unprecedented step — when the legislation was debated in the House of Lords it was pointed out, in response to accusations that it was a 'despotic power', that similar powers existed in relation to British subjects in independent chiefdoms or states neighbouring the colonies of the Cape of Good Hope and India.[45]

42 TNA FO 17/76B: Stephen to Bethune, 18 July 1843.

43 Great Britain. 'Act of the British Parliament, for the better Government of Her Majesty's Subjects resorting to China: 6 & 7 Vict. C. 80', printed in Great Britain. Foreign Office. *British and Foreign State Papers (hereafter BaFSP)*, vol. 31 (London, 1843) p. 1230–33; 'Order in Council of 4 January 1843, transferring the court from Canton to Hong-Kong, for the trial of offences committed by British subjects in China', in Tuson, *The British Consul's Manual*, pp. 189–90; 'Order in Council of 2 October 1843, relative to the laws and ordinances enacted by the superintendent of British trade in China', *BaFSP*, vol. 31 (London, 1843) pp. 1237–38.

44 TNA FO 17/76B: 'Memorandum: China Bill of 1843', 22 July 1843.

45 HL Deb. (3rd series), 7 August 1843, vol. 71, c. 316–17.

A few examples of early ordinances will give a flavour of the kinds of administrative actions taken at the time. Superintendent Henry Pottinger's Ordinance No. 4 of 1844, prohibiting trade north of 32 degrees latitude, set out very severe penalties for infringement — a fine of up to $10,000 or up to two years' imprisonment.[46] Samuel Bonham's Ordinance No. 2 of 1854 gave consuls jurisdiction over 'lunatics and persons of unsound mind' together with their property.[47] John Bowring's Ordinance No. 1 of 1855 enforced neutrality of British subjects in the 'civil war' in China (that is, the Taiping Rebellion), again with heavy penalties for infringement.[48] When from 1859 the position of superintendent was separated from the role of governor of Hong Kong and given to the minister in China, the superintendent-minister's edicts were called notifications or regulations and later, King's regulations, rather than ordinances, but were effectively the same in terms of their use and means of enforcement. In addition to regulations framed to meet particular issues, there were general regulations, later known as consular district regulations, which imposed various rules on British subjects in the treaty ports. These covered such areas as formalities for British ships entering and leaving port, prohibitions regarding the firing of guns in harbour, formalities for reporting deaths or crimes occurring on board ships, requirements for ships not to leave behind seamen at port without the agreement of the consul, licensing requirements for British subjects establishing certain concerns, such as boarding-houses, and definition of the distance from the port which British subjects were allowed to travel into the interior.[49]

In the normal course of events the superintendent consulted London when creating ordinances or regulations. When the FO received a draft of a new ordinance, this was generally referred to the law officers of the Crown, or later the FO's internal legal department, for comments on its legality.[50] Regulations were often amended and sometimes rejected altogether by the FO or the law officers. In case of urgency, the superintendent could issue

46 *Hertslet's Commercial Treaties* (*HcoT*), vol. 7 (London, 1850), pp. 175–78.

47 *HCoT*, vol. 10 (London, 1859), pp. 56–57.

48 *HCoT*, vol. 10 (London, 1859), pp. 61–62.

49 See for example 'General Regulations for British Trade, in the Five Ports of China, 18 May 1854', in *BaFSP*, 1856–57, vol. 47, (London, 1866), pp. 594–98; and also 'British Port Regulations', in *NCH*, 20 December 1913, p. 875.

50 Although from 1876 the FO created the role of Legal Assistant Under Secretary, which was initially filled by Pauncefote, who advised on legal questions, with the result that the law officers were consulted far less frequently. See Ward and Gooch (eds.), *The Cambridge History of British Foreign Policy*, vol. 3, pp. 608–09.

his ordinance or regulation to have immediate effect without referring to London, but it still needed to be approved retrospectively by the FO to remain in force. An example of this situation occurred in 1867 when Minister Rutherford Alcock issued an urgent notification authorising consuls to punish by fine or imprisonment certain unspecified acts which represented a breach of the treaties. The FO told Alcock, following the recommendation of the law officers, that the notification was disapproved (its stipulations and the penalties it set out were held to be insufficiently clear) and so it was necessary to publish its withdrawal in the *Supreme Court and Consular Gazette* in 1868.[51]

While there was, unsurprisingly, an abiding concern with order and stability evident in the kind of ordinances and regulations issued by successive superintendents, their purposes can be seen to have changed in important ways over the course of the treaty century. In the first decades, concerns with enforcing treaties, creating stable trading conditions, and keeping order among sailors were particularly evident.[52] Later on, with the development of ever more substantial municipal authorities in many treaty ports, regulations were created to support and control those institutions and also to assist multinational bodies such as the Shanghai Municipal Council and even foreign authorities like the Russian Municipality at Harbin — regulations were issued in 1914 for the enforcement of its municipal bye-laws on British subjects.[53] After its creation in the 1850s, a number of regulations were created to assist the work of the Chinese Maritime Customs Service, a Chinese government agency dominated by Britain, the work of which clearly served British interests and objectives in creating orderly structures to ensure the smooth running of trade.[54] Examples included the General Pilotage Regulations of 3 November 1868, 'for the better ordering of pilotage matters at the ports', the Shanghai Harbour regulations of 1900, the Customs Kongmoon Regulations of 1904 and the Quarantine Newchwang Regulations

51 TNA FO 233/67: 'Memorandum: general notifications and regulations issued from HM Legation Peking for the treaty ports, under Sec 85 of the Order in Council, 1865'.

52 In addition to those mentioned above, see also for example: Ordinance no. 5 of 10 April 1844, which made treaty provisions enforceable in the same way as ordinances, in *HCoT*, vol. 7, pp. 178–83; and Ordinance no. 3 of 19 July 1849, 'for the safe and better custody of offenders sentenced to imprisonment by the consular courts in China', in *HCoT*, vol. 8, pp. 129–30.

53 For example, 'Regulations respecting veto by His Majesty's consuls on action of British municipal councils in China', 2 January 1907, printed in *Hertslets China Treaties* (*HChT*), vol. 2, p. 1095; for Shanghai, see for example 'Regulation for the Shanghai Municipal Police', 12 October 1906, printed in *HChT*, vol. 2, pp. 1080–81; for Harbin, see Eric Teichman, *Vade-Mecum* (Tientsin, 1920), p. 68.

54 For a comprehensive survey of this body, see Van de Ven.

of 1906, all of which made Customs-originated rules legally enforceable on British subjects.[55] From the twentieth century, the emergence of new threats was reflected in the regulations created. The growing challenge presented by Indian revolutionaries based in China provoked a strong regulatory response — the issues their presence raised were considered important enough to be addressed through the creation of new OICs, as well as regulations, in some cases giving the minister special powers for dealing specifically with them, and also providing for close working with the SMC.[56]

As already noted, the superintendent held concurrently (after 1842) the position of governor of Hong Kong. This combination of roles sprang naturally from the fact that Hong Kong's purpose as a colony was as Britain's bridgehead in China, rather than as a valuable possession of itself. However, although Hong Kong when founded as a colony was clearly envisaged as serving the former role, its creation was quickly followed by the emergence of interests there which were the cause of difficulties for the British state in China and its chief official, the superintendent and governor. The existence of a Crown colony in such close proximity to, and sharing apparatus of governance with, a domain where the British state exercised extraterritorial jurisdiction created serious complications not experienced in the Ottoman Empire, where the FO had the most extensive prior experience of managing extraterritorial jurisdiction.[57] The key source of difficulty was the Hong Kong Supreme Court. From 1844 Hong Kong had its own court modelled on those in England, headed by an independent judge, and a jury system which drew on the non-official élite of the colony for its constituents. The court was created, like the colony, with the intention of serving the needs of British trade under the new treaty system, and its jurisdiction therefore extended not only over the colony of Hong Kong, but also over cases arising on the Chinese mainland where a British subject was defendant. It became clear however from an early stage that the kind of administration of justice which the FO and superintendent wanted to deliver to British subjects in the

55 *HChT*, vol 2, p. 658; *HChT*, vol 2, p. 1162; *HChT*, vol 2, p. 1182; *HChT*, vol 2, p. 1081.

56 For example, new rules to prevent 'seditious conduct' and providing for additional powers to control British subjects employed in municipal police forces were brought into force by the 'China and Corea (amendment) Order in Council, 1909' of 18 October 1909, printed in *HCoT*, vol. 25, pp. 203–05. See Chapter 4 for more on this subject.

57 The complications arising from the existence of the colony of Hong Kong alongside the treaty ports is discussed in the context of piracy suppression by Jonathan Chappell: Chappell, 'Maritime Raiding, International Law and the Suppression of Piracy on the South China Coast, 1842–1869'.

treaty ports, often in support of the aim of stable relations with the Chinese government under the treaties, was frequently of a different character from that which was on offer from the Hong Kong Supreme Court's juries, made up of the colony's non-official élites, and its judges, schooled in English legal traditions and generally uninterested in relations with the Chinese government or people.[58] This is a theme which will be further developed in Chapter 3, since the need to deal with criminal behaviour in China, especially when it was perceived as likely to cause disruption in relations with the Chinese authorities, was a major factor which affected officials' handling of this dilemma.

British officials in China, especially successive superintendent-governors, were infuriated on a number of occasions by the Hong Kong court's reversal of judicial decisions made by consuls, who heard less serious cases at first instance. This was a particularly serious problem in cases where the Chinese authorities were pushing for the British state to act against British subjects accused of wrongdoing, whether criminal acts or breaches of the treaties. Although Superintendent Davis had intended when establishing the system of consular jurisdiction that only cases of murder should be sent to Hong Kong for trial, in practice cases of various kinds arising out of the actions of British defendants in mainland China, including civil cases, were frequently moved to the Hong Kong Supreme Court, either by appeal, or through a process of judicial review (the legal term used was *writ of certiorari*).[59] Hearings in Hong Kong had clear potential disadvantages for Chinese complainants in particular: a combination of the court's fairly strict adherence to English legal forms (at least compared with the consular courts in China), the distance which complainants and witnesses might need to travel, the fact that juries were composed largely of British merchants, and the costs incurred in hiring counsel, all made the Hong Kong court an unsatisfactory forum.[60]

Ordinances were passed by the superintendent-governor which modified the rights of appeal to the Hong Kong court, but the problem of interference by the latter institution was not fully resolved, and it was this recurring difficulty which provided the initial impetus for the creation of a new order in council at the beginning of the 1850s. Superintendent and Governor

58 For a detailed survey of the contemporary Hong Kong legal system, see Munn, *Anglo-China*, pp. 107–254. Munn shows that legal principles were, however, readily discarded by Hong Kong's magistrates when dealing with lower status Chinese accused of crime in the colony.

59 John Francis Davis, 'Circular respecting consular jurisdiction', 22 November 1844, reprinted in Tuson, pp. 229–32; TNA FO 97/98: Alcock to Bonham, 10 January 1852.

60 Coates, *The China Consuls*, p. 53.

Bonham began the process by asking Shanghai Consul Rutherford Alcock to draft new ordinances to address the problem raised by the 1851 *Lady Mary Wood* case, in which the Hong Kong court had reversed Alcock's consular decision which found that a British defendant had committed a breach of the treaty.[61] Bonham described the main purpose of the draft ordinances as being to prevent the Hong Kong court interfering firstly with matters arising out of treaty rights and obligations, and secondly in all cases where Chinese subjects were plaintiffs or defendants.[62] The extent of the rift and difference of viewpoint already opened up between some Hong Kong officials and those involved in governance of the treaty ports, including the superintendent-governor, was made starkly apparent when Bonham forwarded Alcock's drafts to London and made a point while doing so of explaining that he had not consulted the Hong Kong Attorney General or the Legislative Council on the proposals, presumably because he feared that they might object to them:

> I think it right to comment that these ordinances were drawn up without the assistance of any legal advice — the Attorney General of Hong Kong — and have not been submitted for the consideration of the Legislative Council, my desire being to ascertain how far Her Majesty's Government may concur with me in the opinion, and in that of every Consul in China, of the inexpediency of allowing a Colonial Court of Justice to interfere in matters arising out of Treaty Rights to the great inconvenience of Her Majesty's plenipotentiary in China.[63]

The aim of the proposed ordinances was above all to avoid damaging relations with China and ensure that trade was conducted in conformity with the treaties, as Alcock emphasised in his letter accompanying his drafts.[64]

It may be noted here that the novelty of British policies towards the Chinese government of the 'cooperative era' of the 1860s can sometimes be exaggerated, and the conciliatory actions of leading China-based British officials in earlier periods may be overlooked. In fact in the 1850s many British officials wished to deal with Chinese officials in ways which supported rather than undermined what they judged to be the appropriate

61 Full details of this case can be found in Fairbank, *Trade and Diplomacy*, pp. 363–65.

62 TNA FO 97/98: Bonham to Addington, 3 July 1852.

63 TNA FO 97/98: Bonham to Addington, 3 July 1852.

64 TNA FO 97/98: Alcock to Bonham No. 5, 10 January 1852, enclosure in Bonham to Addington, 3 July 1852.

exercise of Chinese authority, and there was a strong desire on the part of the superintendents and many consuls to ensure that British subjects acted in accordance with the treaties.[65] John King Fairbank depicts Consul Alcock in the 1850s, promoting 'the aggressive designs of commercial imperialism' and contrasts the younger consul with his later self, the Minister Alcock of the 1860s who was 'determined to hold the treaty port extremists in check and give the Ch'ing [Qing] administration, with its new foreign-staffed Customs Service, a fair chance to govern China'.[66] However, as shown above, Alcock was clear in the early 1850s that British activities in China should be bound by the rules set down in the treaties, and assisted Bonham in trying to create the legal framework to ensure this.

Bonham forwarded Alcock's drafts to the Foreign Office while the former was on leave in London, and it was decided in London that a new OIC was needed, rather than the ordinances proposed by Bonham. In the course of its preparation, several drafts were passed to the law officers for their opinions. There was an internal debate over the relative desirability of measures offering the practical expediency of greater authority in the hands of the superintendent and consuls, unhampered by judicial interference from the Hong Kong court, which was desired by the FO, superintendent, and consuls on the one hand, and advocates of a system more firmly grounded in established English legal practices and principles on the other, which was the general position of the law officers.

The new OIC, made in 1853, did remedy the particular problem highlighted by the *Lady Mary Wood* case — appeals in treaty cases, and also for breaches of the superintendent's ordinances or regulations, were thenceforth to be decided by the superintendent, not the Hong Kong court. However, Hong Kong remained the court of appeal in civil cases between British subjects where the sum in dispute exceeded $1000 and, more importantly, retained, concurrently with consuls, civil and criminal jurisdiction, with the effect that in criminal cases where greater sentencing powers were required than were available to the consuls (i.e. imprisonment for twelve months),

65 The cooperative policy can be summed up briefly as an agreed aim on the part of the main treaty powers following the Second Opium War to deal with China broadly within a diplomatic framework, in a way that was intended to support the Qing government at a time when Chinese official reformers were in the ascendant and instituting reforms at the Qing court. See Bickers, *The Scramble for China*, p. 207; Wright, *The Last Stand*, pp. 21–42. See also Day, *Qing Travelers to the Far West*, for an account which covers Chinese attitudes and diplomatic actions at the time of this policy.
66 Fairbank, *Trade and Diplomacy on the China Coast*.

defendants had to be sent to Hong Kong for trial.[67] Although it began as a collection of draft ordinances intended to remedy the specific problem of the relationship of the Hong Kong court to consular jurisdiction, the 1853 OIC had by the time of its promulgation become a kind of code for consular jurisdiction, which consolidated the confusingly large number of earlier ordinances made by successive superintendents of trade for the governance of British subjects in China — more than twenty ordinances dealing with British governance in the treaty ports had been passed by the end of 1852. From this point onwards, British governance in China would always be based primarily on such a code, referred to from 1904 as the principal OIC, which was revised and reissued in 1865, 1904 and 1925. When amendments or new provisions were required in the interim, supplementary orders in council were passed. The principal OIC always contained certain core sections providing for the key ingredients of British consular jurisdiction in China: the operation generally of all English laws in China; and the operation of a body of law applicable only in China, contained in the treaties made between Britain and China, created by OIC, or made by the superintendent of trade (his ordinances, notifications or regulations, later called King's regulations), which had the effect of limiting, modifying or adding to the body of English law applicable in China.[68]

In 1857 the role of minister was given to Lord Elgin, but Hong Kong Governor Bowring remained superintendent until 1859, when the British China and Hong Kong administrations (though not the judicial systems) were finally fully separated, with the minister (by then Frederick Bruce) becoming concurrently superintendent.[69] British state governance in China would thenceforth be led by the minister resident at the Legation in Beijing. Hong Kong's position as bridgehead was, in its administrative aspect, much diminished by the move of Britain's key official in China away from the colony, but the Hong Kong court retained, for a time, an important position in the judicial apparatus involved in governance of British subjects

67 'Order in Council for the Government of British subjects resorting to China, etc., and for the repeal of certain ordinances relating thereto, enacted in Hong Kong between 1844 and 1852', *BaFSP*, vol. 42, pp. 254–76.

68 It should be noted here that all British subjects were theoretically subject to *English* law in China rather than the colonial law or national law effective in their place of origin. Only criminal offences which were offences in England (and any offences added by treaty or ordinances/regulations) were crimes in China. So a British Indian subject might in theory commit an act in China which was unlawful under the Indian Penal Code but not be prosecuted if the act was not illegal in England or had not been made illegal by treaty, ordinance or regulation.

69 Keeton, *The Development of Extraterritoriality in China*, vol. 1, p. 235.

in China. The British Hong Kong and China judicial systems were only comprehensively separated with the creation in 1865 of the Supreme Court for China (SCC), based at Shanghai.[70] From 1865 the courts at Shanghai and Hong Kong held separate, parallel positions in the British judicial hierarchy.[71] The most important consequences of this reform are discussed later in this chapter and also, in respect of criminal cases, in Chapter 3. But for now it may be noted that this attempted solution of the difficulties surrounding the Hong Kong court and consular jurisdiction immediately led to new problems, since the Hong Kong and treaty port commercial worlds were so closely intertwined. For example, the SCC and the Hong Kong Supreme Court gave contradictory rulings on the same point of law relating to the bankruptcy of a British firm with operations in both Hong Kong and Shanghai, separate proceedings in respect of which were simultaneously brought in both places.[72] Before turning to examine the SCC at Shanghai, in order to understand the post-Nanjing treaty institutional landscape more fully, it is necessary first to look more closely at those officials who represented both the executive and, with the exception only of Shanghai after 1865, the judicial branches of British governance at the treaty ports throughout the treaty century — the consular officers.

The consuls and British governance at the treaty ports

The consuls and their staff based at the treaty ports carried out a broad range of tasks, far more varied and complex than their counterparts in most other countries, largely because of the existence of extraterritoriality in China. Consuls were responsible for implementing policies and enforcing rules for British governance created by the FO and the superintendent-minister, as well as administering English law and ensuring adherence to the treaties with the Chinese government. In addition, consuls and their staff performed many administrative duties, including land (and later also company) registration, formalities related to shipping, providing commercial and other reports

70 See article 95 of the Order in Council (OIC) of 9 March 1865, in *BaFSP*, vol. 55, pp. 136–75.

71 With a few minor exceptions. For example, in 1877 the Hong Kong court was given by OIC jurisdiction over crimes or civil matters occurring within ten miles of the colony, presumably for reasons of economy. See Sir Richard Rennie, *Instructions to Her Majesty's Consular Officers in China and Japan* (Shanghai, 1885), p. 19. Also, a small link between the courts was established in 1912 when the Hong Kong Full Court was established. A panel of appeal judges was created for the colony, one of whom was the judge of the SCC (then Havilland de Sausmarez).

72 Norton-Kyshe, *History of the Laws and Courts of Hong Kong*, vol. 2, p. 132.

to the FO and the registration of births, deaths and marriages.[73] They also officiated at marriages held at the consulates.

Consuls exercised both criminal and civil jurisdiction in their respective ports. As law enforcers, consuls could be proactive or reactive, according to circumstances. In many cases, a hearing before a consul would begin with a complaint being made to him by the party aggrieved. This could be another British subject, another foreigner, a Chinese person or indeed, as was frequently the case where the treaties were alleged to have been breached, a local Chinese official, usually the daotai (circuit intendant). In the larger ports, such as Shanghai and Tianjin, which eventually had substantial municipal police forces, proceedings were often triggered by the arrest and handing over of the detainee to the consulate (or in Shanghai from 1865 the police court). Consuls might take the initiative and intervene where they saw British subjects engaging in troublesome behaviour, for example when British subjects in China exploited opportunities to make money which did not align with the British state's own view of British interests. An example which gives a sense of the problems presented by the mercenary approach to commerce often taken on the China coast dates from 1858, while Britain was at war with China. Shanghai Consul D. B. Robertson issued a circular to the British community at Shanghai noting that Chinese soldiers had been transported to Shantou in British ships and warning that British subjects were liable to prosecution for doing so while Britain and China were engaged in hostilities.[74]

Consuls faced practical problems when trying to maintain order, since in most consular districts there was just one poorly paid European constable to arrest suspects and supervise the consular gaol, and consuls therefore sometimes had to rely on the Chinese authorities and, more often, the police forces of the foreign municipalities which developed with the growth of foreign settlements and concessions to help keep order.[75] At British concessions, although the wages of these police forces were paid by the municipalities out of their taxation revenues, the authority to perform police duties was granted by the consul, sometimes by appointing municipal police as special constables.[76] Consular approval appears even to have been considered necessary at Shanghai in the early years of the existence of the Shanghai

73 The important consular role in relation to shipping, and in particular, sailors, is dealt with in Chapter 3.

74 TNA FO 233/4: Circular No. 1, Shanghai, 4 January 1858.

75 Details of the staff of each consulate in 1868 is listed in British Parliamentary Papers, House of Commons, Reports on Consular Establishments in China, 1869, vol. 69, [c.44], (1870).

76 See for example section 16 of the Tianjin Land Regulations of 1866, *HChT*, vol. 2, p. 642.

Municipal Council (SMC), showing how the British state's agents in China played an essential role in the expansion of the powers of the latter body.[77]

Police discipline was maintained in both the concessions and settlements, including the Shanghai International Settlement, with the direct assistance of the British state. In 1906 urgent regulations were issued by Minister J. N. Jordan, in response to a strike by Indians employed in the Shanghai Municipal Police (SMP), making it a breach of regulations, punishable under the 1904 principal OIC, for a British subject to disobey orders, to desert the force or to persuade others to do so.[78] Further regulations were issued in 1907 for discipline in British concession police forces which contained almost identical provisions.[79] By OIC in 1909 control over police in concessions and settlements was tightened further by providing powers for the superintendents of municipal police forces in concessions and settlements to act in a magisterial capacity and deliver judgment summarily over their men if they breached discipline or failed to follow orders.[80] Again we see the very close relationship between British state institutions and the municipal councils, including the SMC, despite the latter's formal status as an international body. This closeness was evident to other foreigners at the time and could be the cause of tensions — the 1909 OIC caused a diplomatic row with the German and American consuls, who interpreted the regulations as a proclamation of British control over the SMP.[81] The interests of the councils, especially the SMC, and the British state were very closely aligned in the case of the control of Indians in China, many of whom formed a key part of concession or settlement police forces.[82]

While the municipal councils generally employed a mixture of European, Chinese and Indian men as police, it was considered necessary to fill the

77 In the case of Shanghai, just as with many other institutional arrangements relating to the SMC, the legal basis for this procedure is not clear, nor is it clear what legal force it actually had. Nevertheless in 1855, the SMC obtained 'countersignature of the British Consul to instructions for Police under which instructions and power the men in the employment of the Municipal Council are to act'. Zhang (ed.), *The Minutes of Shanghai Municipal Council*, vol. 17, p. 230, 24 March 1909. *Minutes of SMC 1854–63*, vol. 4, 28 March 1855, p. 53.

78 'Regulation for the Shanghai Municipal Police', 12 October 1906, in *HChT*, vol. 2, p. 1080. See Jackson, 'The Raj on Nanjing Road', for more on the strike and Indians in the SMP generally. See also Chapter 4 of this book.

79 *HChT*, vol. 2, p. 1105.

80 'British Order in Council amending the China and Corea Order in Council, 1904', 18 October 1909, section 3(3) in *HCoT* vol. 25 (London, 1909), p. 204.

81 TNA FO 228/3413: 'New China Order in Council', unsigned notes. The treaty port wrongly referred to as Newchwang (Niuzhuang in pinyin) was actually located at the town of Yingkou.

82 See Chapter 4.

role of consular constable in the ports with a European British subject. However, it was not easy to find suitable recruits on the low wages offered. From Niuzhuang (Yingkou) in 1869 Consul W. E. King reported that 'three constables in the course of four years were dismissed for incompetency or drunkenness'.[83] Although the problem of British subjects engaged in theft and violent crime had apparently subsided by the early twentieth century, the problem of scant consular policing resources persisted.[84] Consul Tours asked the Legation for advice on how, in the absence of either gaol or constable, he was to exercise control over 'ruffians' at Jinan in 1923 and was advised by the Legation that he had three options: appoint locally based British subjects as special constables who would then have power of arrest; seek assistance from the Chinese authorities until arrangements could be made to transfer the prisoner to Shanghai; or, since seeking Chinese assistance might 'weaken the foundations of extraterritoriality', ask the Japanese consul for help.[85] This last suggestion was subsequently criticised by superior officials at the Legation, who saw serious objections to enlisting aid from the Japanese.[86]

Japanese consular policing in the treaty ports offers a stark contrast to the British approach. British consular constables were engaged locally by each consulate and in no way constituted a centrally coordinated 'force'. From the 1880s, the Japanese Foreign Ministry created a centrally organised and well-staffed police force which operated in China and Korea to maintain order among Japanese subjects, and also played a particularly important rolc in the fight against anti-Japanese Korean nationalists based in the Chinese treaty ports.[87] Britain instead relied heavily on the assistance of the municipal police forces in the settlements and concessions, particularly the SMP, a state of affairs which drew British officials into a close relationship of inter-dependence with such bodies.

There was often an improvisatory nature to judicial proceedings overseen by the consuls, especially in the first few decades, since consuls generally lacked legal training; most early consular officers were recruited on the strength of their China experience, often gained in the military, or on the basis of personal connections with officials at the FO.[88] Furthermore, consuls were often required to adjudicate in complicated cases, sometimes based

83 British Parliamentary Papers, House of Commons, *Reports on Consular Establishments in China*, p. 74.

84 Coates, *The China Consuls*, p. 160.

85 TNA FO 228/3168: A. D. P. Gascoigne to B. G. Tours, 30 July 1923.

86 TNA FO 228/3168: Minute of E. Teichman on Tours to Gascoigne, 2 August 1923.

87 Esselstrom, *Crossing Empire's Edge*.

88 Coates, *The China Consuls*, Chapter 1.

on somewhat imprecisely worded treaties or regulations, which often posed novel and unusual legal and practical problems and also frequently involved Chinese or other foreign parties as complainants and witnesses. Even Harry Parkes, instigator of the *Arrow* incident which led to the Second Opium War, and usually portrayed as endowed with abundant self-confidence, complained of the difficulty of satisfactorily fulfilling the consul's judicial role: when he was consul at Shanghai he referred to the trials he presided over in his capacity as judge as the 'worry of his life'.[89]

Whether out of legal ignorance or in the name of expediency, consuls sometimes viewed their ambit in maintaining peace and good order quite broadly and did not necessarily always base their actions on firm legal grounds. The lack of sufficient or effective staff, especially constables, also forced a flexible approach. For example, at Ningbo, due to the lack of a constable, Consul Thom admitted to deciding sentences in criminal cases based on his judgment of how likely a prisoner was to comply, so that more troublesome characters were less severely punished, if at all.[90] About a decade later at Shanghai British officials can be found to have sometimes leaned in the opposite direction in terms of their strictness towards British subjects there. Baker and confectioner H. E. F. Evans was fined ten dollars in 1856 merely for 'using disrespectful language' to the vice consul. The precise law or ordinance he had allegedly broken in so doing, if indeed there was any legal basis at all for the charge, is not clear from the records. No other charge against the man is recorded, so it would not appear to have been a case of contempt of court.[91] Later, with the advent of the SCC in 1865, staffed by professional judges, consuls at last had a source of guidance to which they could turn for advice on difficult questions, and they were also from that time onwards periodically issued with fairly detailed instructions explaining various aspects of their legal and other duties. Judges Hornby (1867), Rennie (1885) and de Sausmarez (1915) all issued lengthy documents to consuls which contained instructions to guide them in their judicial duties.[92]

89 Lane-Poole, *Sir Harry Parkes in China*, p. 293. For a description of Parkes' character and role, see Bickers, *Scramble for China*, pp. 138–42.

90 Coates, *The China Consuls*, p. 22.

91 TNA FO 97/106: Shanghai police sheets 1856–57.

92 Sir Edmund Hornby, 'Instructions to Her Majesty's Consular Officers in China and Japan, on the Mode of Conducting Judicial Business, with Comments on the China and Japan Order in Council, 1865, and the Rules of Procedure Framed under It' (Shanghai, 1867); Sir Edmund Hornby and Sir Richard Rennie, 'Instructions to Her Majesty's Consular Officers in China and Japan, on the Mode of Conducting Judicial Business, with Comments on the China and Japan Order in Council, 1865, and the Rules of Procedure Framed under It' (Shanghai, 1885).

Consuls could deal with lesser criminal and civil cases summarily under their magisterial powers, but for cases where a greater punishment was appropriate or cases where money or property of value higher than a certain limit were involved, they were required to hear cases with assessors drawn from British subjects resident in their districts. When the system was first introduced by Superintendent John Francis Davis in 1844, he made it clear that the use of assessors was intended to draw the 'respectable' members of the British community into voluntary participation in the administration of justice. There was no compulsion to serve as an assessor, 'because perfect reliance is placed upon the good feeling of the respectable portion of the British community in China.'[93] The assessors had no decision-making power in a case, but if they dissented their views were recorded in the record of proceedings (and the superintendent was notified of the fact of their dissent).[94] Consuls were expected only to refer the most serious cases to the Supreme Courts of Hong Kong, or from 1865, Shanghai, where juries were employed and greater sentencing powers were available. Unsurprisingly, given the lack of legal training and experience of most consuls and the complexity of the cases brought before them, some consular judgments were overturned on appeal, which was initially usually to the Hong Kong Supreme Court and from 1865 the SCC at Shanghai.[95]

Punishment was also somewhat extemporised, in large part owing to the lack of facilities and staff for the incarceration of convicts. Consuls had the power to fine or imprison those convicted of offences. Under the principal OICs, consuls could hand down sentences of up to twelve months in prison when sitting with assessors.[96] In the early years British subjects were sometimes held in the local Chinese gaol when there were no cells available at the consulate.[97] Consul Temple Layton at Xiamen in 1847 reported that

The instructions issued by de Sausmarez in 1915 are referred to in TNA FO 228/3413: circular to consuls of 12 March 1925.

93 Davis, 'Circular respecting consular jurisdiction', 22 November 1844, reprinted in Tuson, *The British Consul's Manual*, pp. 229–32, p. 231.

94 See section 3 of Ordinance no. 7 of 1844, in *HCoT*, vol. 7, p. 188; section 6 of the 1853 OIC, in *BaFSP*, vol. 42, p. 260; sections 33–34 of the 1865 OIC, in *BaFSP*, vol. 55, p. 145; section 33 of the 1904 OIC, in *HChT*, vol. 2, (1908), p. 849; and section 36(3) of the 1925 OIC, in *BaFSP*, vol. 121, p. 121.

95 Examples of consular decisions overturned on appeal include 'Keen-Show and others v T. L. Larken', *NCH*, 1 December 1860, (supplement — no page numbers); 'Hatch, Forbes & Co. v Forbes, Graham & Co.', *NCH*, 25 November 1885, p. 608; 'Yu Hi v D. O'Rourke', *NCH*, 19 May 1893, p. 731.

96 Section 71 of the 1865 OIC, *BaFSP*, vol. 55, p. 152. Section 59(2) of the 1904 OIC; section 63(2) of the 1925 OIC, *BaFSP*, vol. 121, p. 130.

97 Coates, *The China Consuls*, p. 22 (Thom at Ningbo), p. 50 (Sullivan at Xiamen); they were instructed to do so where necessary by Davis, see his circular in Tuson, *The British Consul's*

he had no gaoler or constable; instead he visited the prison room himself once or twice a day. He also had one prisoner flogged, a punishment not sanctioned by the OICs or ordinances.[98] In 1869 Consul J. Mongan at Tianjin complained that he was sometimes forced to punish offenders with fines when imprisonment with hard labour would be more appropriate. He found this particularly regrettable in the case of assaults on Chinese, when it was 'highly desirable that the complainant should have ocular demonstration that the guilty parties have been actually punished.'[99] At Yantai (Chefoo) the consul reported that more than one prisoner had escaped the gaol because the constable was too busy to oversee it properly.[100] Although probably not strictly justifiable under any treaty, Chinese were also arrested and detained in consular gaols, pending transfer to Chinese authorities for trial.[101] The British consuls at Shanghai in the 1850s and early 1860s went even further by dealing summarily with large numbers of Chinese accused of petty crimes, who were punished by hard labour under the supervision of the SMC.[102] In this way Britain's displacement of China's legal sovereignty at times went far further than provided for under the principle of extraterritoriality as outlined in the treaties.

British prisoners sometimes served long prison sentences at Shanghai, where a substantial consular gaol was built between 1869 and 1871, or more often at Hong Kong, but this entailed the additional costs and difficulties of transporting prisoners to the colony, so was used sparingly.[103] Consuls were advised by Judge Hornby in 1867 that imprisonment in China for any lengthy period should be considered as equal to punishment of three times the same length in England, because 'the effect of prompt punishment following on crime to be carried into effect as near to the scene of the commission of the crime as possible is far greater as a deterrent than conviction at a distant place'.[104] Another, and probably greater justification was also given: longer

Manual, p. 232.

98 TNA FO 228/70: Layton to Davis No. 4, 9 January 1847. Coates, *The China Consuls*, p. 56 has other examples of consular flogging, which he says ceased in 1852.

99 British Parliamentary Papers, House of Commons, *Reports on Consular Establishments in China, 1869*, p. 41.

100 BPP, HC, *Reports on Consular Establishments in China, 1869*, p. 99.

101 For example, at Xiamen: British Parliamentary Papers, House of Commons, *Reports on Consular Establishments in China, 1869*, p. 49.

102 Kotenev, *Shanghai: Its Mixed Court and Council*, p. 45.

103 TNA FO 671/444: memo enclosed in Office of Works to Fraser, 1 June 1920.

104 Hornby, *Instructions to Her Majesty's Consular Officers in China and Japan*, p. 17; and revised and reissued in 1881 by Judge Rennie: Hornby and Rennie, *Instructions to Her Majesty's Consular Officers in China and Japan*, p. 16.

sentences could only be inflicted by judges at Shanghai, so involved the greater cost of sending the accused away for trial or of bringing a judge to the district where the offence was committed. Even after the reforms of 1865, consular sentencing policy thus continued in some respects along the lines first introduced by Davis in 1844.

One of the most important powers available to consuls, first given to them in 1844, was the ability to order that a British subject be deported from China.[105] Deportation was initially viewed by Superintendent Davis as an 'extreme measure', aimed at removing from China persistent offenders when 'the character of the offender is such as to render his continuance in China incompatible with the peace and good order of society'.[106] But from 1847, as Davis faced the task of preventing confrontations between Britons and Chinese, behaviour which had sparked riots at Guangzhou in 1846, consuls were given additional powers to deport where they had reason to believe that a British subject was likely to commit a 'breach of the public peace' and the person in question could not find security for their good behaviour.[107] Deportation was used often for frequent minor offenders, despite the expense involved in deporting penniless British subjects which meant there was pressure from the FO to use the measure sparingly.[108] Orders for deportation from the treaty ports were often made to Hong Kong, the nearest British territory to China, but this eventually provoked a protest from the Hong Kong Government. Under the 1904 OIC it was made more difficult for the consuls or courts in China to deport British subjects to Hong Kong without the colony's consent.[109] Disagreements later broke out between Hong Kong and Shanghai over deportation of Indians to the colony from Shanghai.[110] The view from the colony was therefore often far from being one wherein Britain's China world was conceptualised as part of a larger project with common aims shared by the colony and agents of the British presence at the treaty ports. Instead, the colony's interests were viewed more narrowly and given priority by its government.

Deportation remained a tool for dealing with small-scale career criminals and vagrants through the nineteenth century and beyond, but it was also

105 The power was first conferred by section 9 of Davis' ordinance No. 7 of 1844, *HCoT*, vol. 7, p. 190.

106 Davis' circular in Tuson, *The British Consul's Manual*, p. 232.

107 Davis' Ordinance No. 2 of 1847 in *HCoT*, vol. 8, p. 115.

108 TNA FO 656/53: Judge George French to FO No. 14, 14 October 1880.

109 TNA FO 656/106: Judge de Sausmarez to Satow, 27 June 1905.

110 TNA FO 671/437: Charles Denham to HK Captain Superintendent E. D. C. Wolfe, 22 October 1922.

adopted for use against different kinds of threats in the early twentieth century. In 1904, the Tianjin consul ordered the deportation of the British proprietor of *The China Times*, John Cowen, who had failed to give security for good behaviour for twelve months for having published an article likely to cause a breach of the peace (the article concerned the alleged cruelty of Russian troops in China).[111] In 1906 a number of Indian members of the Shanghai Municipal Police were deported following their participation in a strike.[112] Indians found guilty of sedition in the 1910s and '20s were also generally deported after serving their sentences.[113]

An additional means available to consuls to control the activities of British subjects was the passport for travel in the interior of China. From 1842 to 1860, British and other foreign nationals were only allowed to travel a short distance from the open ports. In the case of British subjects this distance was defined in the general regulations published by the British authorities. Following the ratification of the Treaty of Tianjin, consuls began issuing passports for British subjects to travel outside the immediate environs of the treaty ports for the first time. The passport documents issued by consuls in the 1860s contained a declaration by the consul that the holders were 'persons of known respectability', and consuls were warned by Bruce, in a circular which was also published in *The North-China Herald* (*NCH*), to be highly selective in issuing passports:

> I have to impress particularly on you the necessity of not issuing passports to any British subjects who are not persons whose character, position, and antecedents afford reasonable guarantees for their good conduct.[114]

This approach left marginal British subjects wanting to exercise the new freedom of movement under the Tianjin Treaty in a difficult position. Consul Robert Swinhoe in 1866 required Chinese British subjects who sought passports to give security for their good behaviour, which had the effect of deterring such applicants from going through with their applications.[115]

111 *NCH*, 11 March 1904, p. 473; *NCH*, 10 June 1904, pp. 1229–32. The judge of the SCC reversed the order since Cowen had not repeated the offence, but was careful not to criticise the decision of the consul in the case.
112 TNA FO 656/263: Judge Sausmarez to Consul Fulford at Tianjin, 16 October 1916.
113 See for example, TNA FO 676/34: 'Report of proceedings in HM Consular Court Beijing in the matter of R. v. Fouje Khan, 9, 10 and 17 February 1917'. Also 'Year's Sentence Given 3 Indians in Sedition Case — Hard Labor, Deportation Ordered in Supreme Court,' *The China Press*, 6 July 1927, p. 1.
114 TNA FO 228/405: 'Consular Notification', *NCH*, 5 January 1861, p. 2.
115 TNA FO 228/405: Swinhoe to Hornby, 15 June 1866.

In the twentieth century, consuls were issued with a series of rules and restrictions regarding the issue of passports to British Indians, as part of the surveillance and control of that group, which is covered in Chapter 4.[116]

From 1844, a basic tool for exercising control over British subjects was put in place with the requirement to register at the consulate. This was not at first rigidly enforced, since Davis gave instructions that 'respectable parties' need not be troubled excessively by demands to register themselves.[117] The requirement to register was retained in the first principal OIC of 1853, and was included in subsequent principal orders. Under the 1865 OIC, an annual fee for registration, the level of which varied according to whether the registrant was a 'gentleman' or an 'artisan', was introduced and the requirement was more generally enforced.[118] For the consul, having an accurate list of the British subjects in his district was useful for a number of reasons, including monitoring and controlling the growth of populations of discharged seamen and other potential undesirables, facilitating service of warrants and summonses, assisting in drawing up lists of assessors or jurymen, establishing the nationality of a person alleged or claiming to be British (and thus under his jurisdiction or protection in any legal action or wrangle with Chinese or other foreign authorities), and to ensure that notifications and circulars were seen by all members of the community. Many British subjects were fined for non-registration after 1865 when it began to be more strictly enforced, and there was considerable opposition vented in the press, against what was regarded by some as an unjust 'poll tax'.[119] Registration 'campaigns', when those failing to register were summoned before the courts, were undertaken periodically at Shanghai throughout the nineteenth century and into the twentieth. Consuls were also informed in 1916 that it was 'of the greatest importance that all British Indians should be registered' and were told to bring proceedings against any who did not register.[120] As well as ensuring that those who should register did register, the consuls also had to ensure that those who sought to register were in fact entitled to do so, a particularly difficult question in the case of many Eurasians and Chinese British subjects (the latter mostly from Hong Kong

116 Major, *A Compendium of Instructions to H.M. Consular Officers in China*, (London, 1927), p. 109.

117 John Francis Davis, 'Circular respecting consular jurisdiction', 22 November 1844, reprinted in Tuson, *The British Consul's Manual*, pp. 229–32.

118 Coates, *The China Consuls*, p. 160.

119 See, for example, editorial in *NCH*, 8 April 1867, p. 4; letter from 'A. Hartizan' *NCH*, 24 December 1867, p. 426.

120 Major, *A Compendium of Instructions to H.M. Consular Officers in China*, p. 25.

and the Straits Settlements), whose requests for registration and protection prompted a large correspondence at all levels of the British state hierarchy.

Another administrative function carried out by consuls was land registration. This seemingly mundane role is easily overlooked, but it was a highly important means by which the institution of the consulate underpinned the British commercial presence. Consular registration effectively guaranteed the title of British landholders to their land in concessions and settlements in China, and it was thus a more low-key way than the gunboats, so often prominent in histories of the treaty ports, through which the British state ensured that the latter were 'safe and secure bridgeheads' for British expansion.[121] The right to register land at the British consulate was a valuable one, which consuls sometimes denied to British Eurasians and Chinese British subjects.[122] It was arguably the state-backed guarantee of secure title to property which gave British and other foreign businesses the sense of stability and certainty they needed to risk investing substantial capital in building extensive and long-lasting enterprises, most notably those which were housed in the giant temples to commerce which lined places like Shanghai's Bund. Foreign-held property in China was easily mortgageable and transferable and indeed it became highly valuable — many fortunes in Shanghai were founded on property more than trade.[123] All this would most likely not have occurred to anything like the same degree without the security provided by British or other foreign state institutions, in particular without the consulate as a trusted registrar and the foreign — and especially the British — courts as a forum for settling property disputes.

The importance of this role was magnified during the numerous periods of upheaval in governance which China went through in the nineteenth and especially the early twentieth centuries. Consuls were told in 1920 to

121 This is Robert Bickers' expression. Bickers, *Britain in China*, p. 9. There were legal differences between leases in concessions and settlements but the role of the consulate in land transactions was, at least from the point of view of augmenting trust in the system, substantially the same. For a clear explanation of the detailed differences between concessions, settlements and other places of foreign residence, see Bickers, 'British Concessions and Chinese Cities'.

122 In regard to Chinese British subjects, an important case was successfully brought in the Supreme Court for China against the Guangzhou consul general by the Bank of East Asia, a Hong Kong Chinese bank controlled by Chinese British subjects, seeking to reverse the decision of the consul who had, with the backing of the FO, refused to register the bank's title to property in the British concession in Guangzhou. See 'The Shameen Land Transfer Dispute', *NCH*, 13 December 1924, p. 459.

123 One of the most obvious examples is Thomas Hanbury, who went to China as a fairly small trader but left as an extremely wealthy landowner. See Moore, *La Mortola: In the Footsteps of Thomas Hanbury* (London, 2004).

take care to ensure that they upheld the 'indefeasibility of a Title Deed [...] otherwise the officials could upset the whole system of land registration in China'.[124] Security of foreign property was of course ultimately backed up by military power, a factor which has often been noted in studies of British involvement in China, but it is important not to overlook the role of state administrative institutions, the infrastructure they created, and the practices of officials within them in creating the basis for British commercial expansion of the nature, and on the scale, which occurred in China, and especially at Shanghai, where in 1911, the British Consulate was responsible for more than three quarters of the total number of registrable land transactions.[125] Many transactions registered in the name of British subjects were done by British proxies acting on behalf of Chinese or other nationalities, and thus the influence of guarantees of British law and institutions on the development of the treaty ports extended beyond British subjects or corporate entities.

British Consuls and Mixed Courts

British consuls at some of the larger treaty ports were involved in overseeing legal proceedings in 'mixed courts', which generally handled legal cases against Chinese where there was a foreigner involved in the case, often but not always in the role of plaintiff.[126] There were mixed courts at Shanghai, Xiamen and Hankou, but the Shanghai Mixed Court was by far the most significant of these institutions, and handled a large volume of cases, including cases between Chinese subjects in the International Settlement, as well as mixed cases where a foreign individual or body was a party to proceedings.[127] The mixed court at Shanghai came into being, like so many of the structural arrangements for governance located in the Shanghai International Settlement, as part of attempts to restore order in the 1860s following the unrest caused by the Taiping Rebellion, which had led to the suspension for a time of Chinese government authority in Shanghai and the region around it, and had also resulted in a huge influx of Chinese into the safety of the International Settlement.[128] While the power vacuum had been

124 Teichman, *Vade-Mecum*, p. 18.

125 *Minutes of the SMC*, vol. 18, 27 December 1911, p. 178.

126 There were mixed courts in other parts of the world where Britain or other imperial powers wielded strong influence, for example Egypt. See Brown, 'The Precarious Life and Slow Death of the Mixed Courts of Egypt'.

127 Keeton, *Extraterritoriality in China*, vol. 1, pp. 404–05.

128 Cassel, *Grounds of Judgment*, p. 66.

partially filled in the past in the way outlined above, through the arrogation of powers of summary judgment over Chinese by the British or United States consuls at Shanghai, this was not deemed acceptable in the early 1860s, and a system more aligned to the contents of the treaties was briefly adopted, whereby Chinese offenders were sent to the Chinese City to be dealt with by Chinese officials, following a preliminary hearing before the British or United States consul. This was soon found to be unsatisfactory, since it was said that many Chinese offenders were not punished or were inadequately punished (in British eyes) by the Chinese authorities.[129] Both the consuls and the SMC, with its police force representing the front line of law and order in the International Settlement, desired a greater degree of control over the trial and punishment of Chinese offenders, and this was provided by the creation of the Shanghai Mixed Court, which was founded in 1864, and until its closure in 1927 played an important role in the government of the International Settlement.[130]

The degree to which the Shanghai Mixed Court can be said to have involved the integration of treaty power governments, and the British state in particular, into a joint form of governance in the International Settlement, has not received enough attention in histories dealing with treaty era Shanghai, leading to an insufficient appreciation of the role of the British state in the everyday governance of Shanghai.[131] The role of the SMC in the court has been emphasised by some writers, but since the key foreign official in the court was the assessor, a foreign consular employee, and most often a British one, the role of foreign states, and in particular the British state, in the development and operation of the Shanghai Mixed Court was central. In 1864 British consul Harry Parkes prompted the establishment of the court in the form in which it was ultimately realised, by proposing to the local Chinese authorities and the Municipal Council a scheme whereby a Chinese official and a foreign assessor would sit together to decide cases.[132] The Council had wanted to create an institution in which a municipal employee would sit as

129 Kotenev, *Shanghai: Its Mixed Court and Council*, p. 46.

130 The Shanghai Mixed Court was succeeded by the Shanghai Provisional Court. See Wakeman, *Policing Shanghai*, pp. 70–72.

131 For example, in building an argument for the SMC's autonomy in the realm of policing Isabella Jackson places insufficient emphasis on the role of the British and other consuls in the operation of the Mixed Court. See Jackson, *Shaping Modern Shanghai*, especially p. 115 where she refers to 'the Council's loss of judicial control in the Mixed Court' in the late 1920s. This is somewhat misleading, since although the SMC's influence grew post-1911, judicial control of the Mixed Court was always ultimately in the hands of the consuls.

132 *Minutes of SMC*, vol. 2, meeting of 13 April 1864, p. 47; Thomas B. Stephens, *Order and Discipline in China: The Shanghai Mixed Court, 1911–27* (Seattle, 1992), p. 44.

foreign assessor, but Parkes rejected this at a meeting of the land renters, of which he was chair and in which the new court was discussed, and he asserted that this would contravene the treaties with China. He furthermore commented, as an additional justification for his stance, that the Chinese authorities viewed the SMC as 'politically speaking, irresponsible'.[133] The SMC was therefore placed in a subordinate position to consular authority as far as the court's judicial decision-making was concerned.

The Mixed Court was initially located in a building in the British consulate compound at Shanghai, but members of the SMP were tasked with arresting and delivering Chinese accused of offences to the court for trial.[134] Later, separate premises were found for the court. The development of the court can best be dealt with in two stages, since the court changed substantially after 1911 when the Qing Dynasty was overthrown. Before 1911, the court was formally a branch of the Qing government's bureaucracy, and its Chinese judges were appointed by the latter government. After 1911, the court was placed under the control of the Consular Body, who appointed the court's Chinese magistrates.[135] Although SMC input and influence increased considerably from 1911, most notably in the operational administration, including financial management, of the court and the prison for Chinese, it is important to note that throughout both periods the court relied on the participation of foreign consuls as assessors, who were responsible for deciding cases with the Chinese magistrate, and could decide cases in ways which went against the wishes of the SMC.[136] It is furthermore possible to state with a high degree of confidence that the British consulate supplied the foreign assessor in a far greater number of cases than that of any other foreign power, since British interests were by far the largest part of the foreign presence in Shanghai, and it therefore follows that more cases would involve British plaintiffs or in other ways be held to be of concern to British interests. For at least a part of the period of its operation there was a settled arrangement as to the deployment of assessors, which resulted in British assessors dominating the

133 *NCH*, 29 April 1865, supplement (no page number).

134 *Minutes of SMC*, vol. 2, meeting of 5 April 1865, p. 140.

135 Teichman, *Vade-Mecum*, p. 5; Kotenev, *Shanghai: Its Mixed Court and Council*, pp. 170–76; Stephens, *Order and Disciple in China*, p. 49; Cassel says the SMC appointed the Chinese judges after 1911 but gives no source, and it appears that this may be an error: Cassel, *Grounds of Judgment*, p. 177. In 1912, the senior consul sent a note to the Council informing them of the appointment of the third assistant magistrate of the Mixed Court: *Minutes of the SMC*, vol. 18, meeting of 24 July 1912, p. 297.

136 For example, in 1912, the German assessor released a Chinese prisoner against the Council's wishes; the captain superintendent reportedly described the action as 'a severe blow to Gaol discipline'. *Minutes of the SMC*, vol. 18, meeting of 11 December 1912, p. 346.

work of the court: in civil cases, the assessor was usually the consul of the nation interested in the case; in all other cases, a British assessor sat three times a week, a US assessor twice, and a German assessor once.[137]

British state officials were thus central to the operation of the Shanghai mixed court throughout its history. However, although the SMC was not trusted to take control of the court, British and other consular officials frequently exercised their powers in the court in ways which supported the SMC's overall aims with regard to the governance of the International Settlement. For example, they saw that the court enforced municipal by-laws against nuisances such as noise and punished Chinese government employees from outside the settlement who attempted to extract debts or taxation from Chinese residing within the settlement.[138] British officials also showed the degree to which they were able to import British practices into the governance of the settlement through their dominant position in the court. From 1865, this was British policy, sanctioned by London: when the FO sent Edmund Hornby to China as the first British judge of the SCC, he was instructed to advise consuls in working towards the aim 'of securing, not only uniformity of action in the settlement of cases in which a British functionary takes part, but uniformity of practice in awarding for similar offences in the Mixed Court the like degree of punishment that would be awarded in a purely British Court'.[139] The procedure which developed in the Mixed Court broadly followed practices in English courts, and furthermore, British assessors were prepared to base their rulings on English case law.[140] In a case from as early as 1871, which concerned nuisance caused by a Chinese club and its associated brothels in a neighbourhood near to the French Settlement, the British assessor, Vice Consul Arthur Davenport, gave his opinion that the defendants were guilty in part based on a finding of Lord Ellenborough in an English case which Davenport used as a precedent.[141] This kind of everyday judicial and administrative practice built the British character of the International Settlement in a way that must have affected the perceptions of those who came into contact with the court and which moreover dovetailed with SMC objectives in creating a space, embodying British socio-cultural norms, deemed suitable for foreign habitation in the International Settlement.

137 Giles, *A Glossary of Reference on Subjects Connected with the Far East*, p. 181.

138 See, for example, cases described in the SMC *Annual Reports*, 1896, p. 46; 1900, p. 323; 1902, p. 37.

139 TNA FO 17/433: FO to Hornby, 16 May 1865.

140 Kotenev, *Shanghai: Its Mixed Court and Council*, p. 61.

141 'Re Lao-Ke-Chong', *NCH*, 7 August 1871, pp. 612–13.

Even more than their counterparts elsewhere in the world, consuls in China were 'jacks of all trades'. They were constantly faced with novel and complex situations and needed to try to understand how to apply English law, the superintendent's regulations, and also circulars and directives from the FO and minister to their varied workload. There was ample room for consuls' own prejudices to influence British official practices in the treaty ports, and this will be evident in the chapters of this book which deal with the particular groups of marginal British subjects which grew up at the treaty ports and whose trajectories intersected with British officialdom in various ways. The other British official institution which engaged most closely with British subjects in China — and also had an impact on the lives of Chinese in various ways — was a more specialised one: the Shanghai-based Supreme Court for China.

The 1865 Order in Council and the new British court

A new Order in Council which set out the legal framework for the creation of the Supreme Court for China and Japan based at Shanghai was passed in 1865.[142] The new system of legal governance thus created was modelled on a formula already in existence in the Ottoman Empire, said to have been prompted in that region by a desire to control lawless British subjects or protected persons from Malta and the Ionian Islands.[143] The FO and superintendent had drawn on policy and practice in the Ottoman Empire in the past in framing ordinances for China and now the FO again drew deeply on experience from that region: the OIC which provided for the establishment of the court was drafted by the same lawyer, Francis Reilly, who had been employed to draft the recent Turkey OIC; and Sir Edmund Hornby, who was judge of the British Supreme Consular Court at Istanbul, the principal British court in the Ottoman Empire, from 1857 to 1864, was appointed as the first judge of the new court at Shanghai.[144] While in London, Hornby

142 Here I will for obvious reasons focus on the court's role in China. For Japan, see Roberts, *The British Courts and Extra-Territoriality in Japan*. The court was from 1865 to 1899 officially entitled Her Britannic Majesty's Supreme Court for China and Japan. After the abolition of extraterritoriality in Japan, the court was styled Her Britannic Majesty's Supreme Court for China and Corea until 1911, when following Japan's annexation of Korea, it became simply Her Britannic Majesty's Supreme Court for China until Britain relinquished extraterritorial rights in China and the court was closed in 1943. For simplicity, it is referred to in this book as the Supreme Court for China (SCC).

143 HL Deb. (3rd series), 17 August 1843, vol. 71, cols. 906–07.

144 The Ottoman Empire was used as a model as early as 1847 — see Davis' Ordinance No. 2 'for the better maintenance of order and the repression of crimes among British subjects in China',

also assisted in the drafting of the new China OIC.[145] The choice of Hornby was made by the FO precisely because of his experience in the Ottoman Empire, and he was offered an exceptional salary (£3500 per year), higher than that of the chief justice of Hong Kong, in order to secure his services. In the correspondence between Hammond of the FO and Bruce (Minister for China) over the establishment of the court it was, somewhat surprisingly, Hammond in London who pushed for more generous terms for the judge, arguing that Bruce had underestimated the remuneration Hornby would require in China, and stressing the value of Hornby's experience: 'Hornby's case should be dealt with specially, as it is of great consequence to have the new system in China well started, and he has seven years experience of it.'[146]

It is worth considering the way in which the FO approached the creation and management of this new institution in China within the context of the existing circulation of ideas and practices to and from China across British imperial networks. In addition to their naturally strong ties to Great Britain, the British in the Chinese treaty ports were closely linked to British India through commerce, especially the opium trade, and also through the circulation of personnel, business practices and certain cultural characteristics, such as language, architecture and organisation of social life.[147] Linkages of all kinds between the colony of Hong Kong and the treaty ports were naturally also very strong. However, connections based on official channels clearly could, through policy, be directed or changed when it was thought expedient to do so. In the case of British justice in China, the FO very deliberately chose to drastically reduce the strength of links to Hong Kong and to transfer practices and personnel from another area, the Ottoman Empire, where Britain had operated a consular court system with its own supreme court for a number of years. Pär Cassel has argued that both the SCC and the Shanghai Mixed Court were 'products of a peculiar institutional environment that owed much to Chinese concepts of law and legal institutions'.[148] While there may be some truth in this statement in the case of the Mixed Court, in which Chinese and foreign officials together presided over cases involving Chinese defendants in Shanghai, in relation to the SCC it is difficult to reconcile this claim with the lack of evidence

in *HCoT*, vol. 8, pp. 115–17; Reilly — see TNA FO 83/2251: FO to LOs, 18 July 1864; Hornby — see Berridge, *British Diplomacy in Turkey*, p. 82; Kayaoglu, *Legal Imperialism*, p. 124.

145 Hornby, *Autobiography*, p. 193.

146 TNA FO 17/406: FO (Hammond, private) to Bruce 23 September 1864 and FO (Hammond, private) to Bruce, 23 October 1864.

147 Bickers, *Britain in China*, pp. 76–77.

148 Cassel, *Grounds of Judgment*, p. 63.

in the British archive to support it. The only official closely involved in the creation of the SCC who had any experience of China was Minister Frederick Bruce, and although he was consulted by the FO his influence was not great. Nor is it clear how the SCC can be said to have subsequently been shaped to a significant degree by an institutional environment of the kind suggested by Cassel. British experiences in the Ottoman Empire were by far the most influential factors which shaped the OIC through which the court was created, and later principal OICs did not depart from it in any fundamental way.

After Hornby, subsequent judges would also be transferred from the Ottoman Empire, from other parts of the world where the FO oversaw extraterritorial courts, such as Siam, or indeed from British colonies, such as Sierra Leone, but not from Hong Kong.[149] Some judges were previously lawyers who had made their careers at the Shanghai bar, showing that there was no consistent policy of bringing personnel in from outside China, while others had worked their way up through the ranks of the consular service; but neither the Shanghai bar nor the consular service were workplaces where Chinese concepts would realistically have projected much influence on the professional lives of those who became judges, and in any case it was more common for judges to be transferred from outside China.[150] There is evidence of the influence of attitudes and practices from British India, which is discussed further in Chapter 4, but this was not transmitted through formal institutional connections. Britain's China and India worlds were not closely linked in any formal sense through law, unlike in other areas, such as the military and policing, where connections were stronger.[151] Whereas British India had its own distinct legal system, comprising various unique measures including the Indian Penal Code and also various mechanisms providing for legal pluralism, British law in China was, at least on paper, far more closely tied to English law, with comparatively little formal modification.[152] There

149 For example: Judge George French from Sierra Leone (see *NCH*, 20 December 1877, p. 574), Judge Havilland de Sausmarez from the Ottoman Empire (see, 'The Supreme Court', *NCH*, 30 December 1904, p. 1492), Judge Skinner Turner from Siam (see, 'The New Assistant Judge', *NCH*, 4 December 1915, p. 693).

150 For example, Nicholas Hannen, former barrister ('Death of Sir Nicholas J. Hannen', *NCH*, 2 May 1900, p. 766). Hiram S. Wilkinson started his career in the Japan consular service but became chief justice of the SCC in 1900. 'The Retirement of Sir Hiram S. Wilkinson', *NCH*, 7 April 1905, p. 9.

151 Metcalf, *Imperial Connections*, pp. 130–33.

152 For law in British India, see Kolsky, *Colonial Justice in British India*. Practice was a different matter. See Chapter 4 in particular for the ways that judges adapted the law to deal with Indian British subjects in China.

was no movement of judicial personnel from India; in addition to the lack of institutional ties, the pay on offer in China was probably insufficient to entice anyone, since even Hornby's attractive salary was less than that of a puisne judge in India.[153]

The new judicial system created by the 1865 OIC, with the SCC at Shanghai at its head, would endure basically unaltered for the rest of the treaty century. It established, at least in theory, a parallel British hierarchy in China under which consuls at the treaty ports were, in their judicial role, subordinate to the judge at Shanghai. The judicial role of the minister was limited to confirming or commuting capital sentences, and mitigating or remitting punishment in other cases where the judge recommended he do so.[154] The great practical change brought about by the establishment of the court at Shanghai was that serious crimes and important civil cases could now, in most cases, be tried closer to the places where they were committed or where the parties to the proceedings were based. The new court exercised all first instance jurisdiction for the port of Shanghai and judges of the court could also hear important cases in the other ports when necessary. It was the court of appeal from the consular courts — now styled provincial courts — in the other treaty ports and the chief judge heard appeals from first instance decisions in Shanghai made by the assistant judge.[155] Since Shanghai was the most important centre of British settlement in China, most cases would arise there anyway, but if necessary, the judge went to the other ports to try cases, for example if a British subject was accused of murder. Appeals from the SCC lay to the Privy Council in London. Cases arising in China would only be tried at Hong Kong if the judge of the SCC at Shanghai decided that the case should be transferred to the colony for trial; otherwise, it was specifically decreed that 'all jurisdiction, power, and authority' of the Hong Kong court ceased in China and Japan from the commencement of the new OIC.[156]

In addition to the new judge, other senior personnel of the court were provided for in the OIC of 1865. There was to be an assistant judge and a law secretary who would both be able to preside alone over cases. The law secretary was the court registrar, sat as a summary judge in cases of minor criminal charges, and could also hear civil cases. The first holders

153 TNA FO 17/406: FO Hammond (private) to Bruce, 23 October 1864.

154 TNA FO 17/944: FO (Russell) to Wade, 16 May 1865.

155 Until 1925, when the Shanghai Full Court was established to hear such appeals, for which the chief justice of Hong Kong was brought to sit on a panel with the Shanghai judges.

156 OIC of 1865, section 160, *BaFSP*, vol. 55, p. 172.

of these roles were selected by Hornby and brought to Shanghai. The first assistant judge was Charles Goodwin, a barrister and a noted scholar, who had contributed to the influential publication *Essays and Reviews*, but had no prior foreign official experience.[157] The law secretary, John Fraser, was formerly employed at a consular position in the Ottoman Empire, where he had come to Hornby's attention.[158]

The OIC of 1865 called for male British subjects resident in mainland China to act as jurors for the first time since the opening of the treaty ports.[159] The SCC was required to sit with jurors in important cases, whether proceedings were held at Shanghai or at another port, but the old rule whereby consuls sat with assessors in their courts hearing lesser cases was not altered. Under the 1865 OIC, only five jurors were required (it was usual in England for a jury to comprise twelve members; the Turkey OIC of 1857 specified six).[160] Under the 1904 OIC, the number of jurors was increased to twelve in cases where the case concerned a capital offence.[161] To qualify to serve on a jury in 1865 a British subject had to earn a gross annual income of $250 or more, be able to speak and read English, and be free from conviction for any serious crime. The *NCH* considered these qualifications to be rather low, and this was presumably done deliberately, in view of the relatively small size of the British population in China, to ensure that there were enough names on the jury list.[162] To put the jury qualifications into context, in 1869 British consular constables, who were considered by consuls to be very poorly paid, typically earned about $50–70 per month, and the lowest class of European working in the Chinese Maritime Customs was reported to earn $76.50.[163] Both would therefore have easily qualified for jury service on grounds of income.

The new system clearly allowed for greater oversight by the FO of the judicial body responsible for China, and so made possible a tightening of

157 Shea and Whitla (eds.), *Essays and Reviews*.

158 Hornby, *Autobiography*, p. 193.

159 Important cases relating to crimes or civil disputes in China had however been tried by juries at Hong Kong. Juries were also provided for under the rules governing the court at Guangzhou in the pre-treaty era.

160 Section 30 of the 1865 OIC; Oldham, 'Special Juries in England: Nineteenth Century Usage and Reform', p. 157; Great Britain. 'Order in Council providing for the more efficient exercise of power and jurisdiction over British subjects within the Dominions of Turkey, by the judge of the Supreme Consular Court at Constantinople', 27 August 1857, in *BaFSP*, vol. 47, (London, 1857), p. 575.

161 Section 27 of the 1904 OIC, *HChT*, vol. 2, p. 905.

162 *NCH*, 29 July 1865, p. 118.

163 British Parliamentary Papers, House of Commons, *Reports on Consular Establishments in China, 1869*, p. 49.

British governance which could, in theory at least, bring consular jurisdiction more into line with executive priorities and policies; in particular it could assist in maintaining the cooperative approach to relations with the Chinese government which was in the ascendant in the 1860s. Hornby was sent out to Shanghai with instructions from the Foreign Secretary which tend to support this interpretation: he was to act as a legal advisor to British government representatives in China, as the law officers did for the British government in London; he was also to 'be guided by' the opinion of the minister with reference to any course of action which could influence relations between Britain and China. The FO also gave Hornby instructions which suggest that an element of the civilising mission existed alongside the new emphasis on cooperation: as already mentioned, he was ordered to assist consuls in bringing the Shanghai Mixed Court's practices closer to those practiced in British courts.[164] Hornby was granted the privilege of communicating directly with the Secretary of State whenever he felt necessary, and was told that if at any time he should believe that a new OIC were required, he should prepare a draft and send it to the FO.[165] The judge was in this way placed in a position of some autonomy in relation to the Legation, with a clear means open to him, not only to decide cases independently, but also to influence the direction of British governance in China.

In many ways it seems that the court was seen as a success from the point of view of the Legation and the FO. The fact that no major reform altering its role was made in the years following its opening, right up to the abolition of extraterritoriality in 1943, points to this conclusion, as well as suggesting that the FO recognised the usefulness of the court over the longer term. The new institution did put an end to some of the problems associated with the Hong Kong court, in particular its tendency to overturn consular decisions on legal technicalities. This mitigated a source of tension with the Chinese authorities and the court was also more effective in dealing with criminal cases involving British problem populations, especially 'rowdies' against whom Hornby launched a crackdown early on in his tenure.[166] However, the introduction of another, independently minded, power holder into the British system of governance, and based at Shanghai rather than Beijing, meant that there continued to be scope for disputes to emerge between the executive and judicial branches in China. Hornby claimed that the flexibility he allowed himself to deal with issues brought before

164 TNA FO 17/433: FO to Hornby, 16 May 1865.
165 TNA FO 17/433: FO to Hornby, 16 May 1865.
166 See the following chapter for a full discussion of these actions.

him was overtly sanctioned by the FO, presumably because the necessity of greater powers being exercisable by men on the spot, as had repeatedly been called for by Minister Bruce, had been recognised, and it was probably assumed that it was safe to confer wider powers on a legally qualified official of Hornby's experience.[167] But this flexible and independent approach, while useful in dealing with crime and disorder, could be at odds with the emphasis on correctness, following international law and respecting the treaties in dealing with the Chinese government, which was called for by the proponents of the cooperative policy espoused by British ministers in the 1860s. In a despatch on the subject of the extension of the Hong Kong authorities' jurisdiction over the waters and islands in the vicinity of the colony, Hornby told Alcock:

> Your Excellency is already in full possession of my views of the inexpediency of treating with the Chinese government, as if that government was conducted upon the same principles as those of civilized states and furnished the same guarantees of good faith and reciprocal action as the governments of Western nations furnish.[168]

Hornby also disagreed vehemently with arguments from Minister Alcock that the Chinese had a right under the treaties to demand joint trials presided over by both a Chinese official and the British judge in civil cases where one party was Chinese.[169] The aims of improved relations with the Chinese, and of promoting dealings with the Chinese state in a manner more closely aligned with the treaties and international law, were thus hindered in many ways by the creation of the SCC at Shanghai, despite the crackdown on 'the rowdy class'.

The establishment of the SCC at Shanghai and the embedding of its staff in the Shanghai British world had other consequences, of a perhaps less immediately obvious kind, for the nature of the British state's project of governance in China. Hornby and subsequent judges were supportive of the Shanghai Municipal Council (SMC), and closely involved with it in various ways. Hornby was elected Commandant of the Council's Shanghai Volunteer Corps, described by Robert Bickers as 'a key element in the theatrical colonial

167 Hornby, *Autobiography*, p. 260.

168 TNA FO 656/23: Hornby to Alcock (draft) No. 21, 28 December 1868.

169 TNA FO 228/484: Hornby to Clarendon, 27 July 1869. The copy in the Legation file is annotated with numerous exasperated comments by Alcock written in response to Hornby's assertions. See also Cassel, *Grounds of Judgment*, p. 70, for a discussion of this disagreement.

posturing of the Shanghailanders', shortly after arriving at Shanghai.[170] His prejudice against the Chinese government meant it was natural for him to support the SMC at a crucial moment in the development of the Shanghai International Settlement, when the new Land Regulations (which provided the legal basis for the SMC's existence and functions) were being considered in 1866. Hornby assisted in drafting the new Regulations, and urged the FO to approve them, warning that since the Chinese government was 'unable, as well as under the circumstances utterly unfit' to oversee law and order in the International Settlement, the British government would be required, at great expense, to undertake a large-scale policing role if the SMC was not given adequate support.[171] This highlights the fact that the SMC was already in the 1860s providing services which complemented the British state's own project of governance to a considerable degree. It was clear that Hornby's sympathies and outlook on the issue of the SMC lay more with the Shanghai British commercial community who controlled the council than with the consuls and the Legation. Hornby went as far as to write privately in April 1866 to Reilly and Hammond at the FO in London, introducing James Hogg, recently retired Vice-Chairman of the SMC, in a clear attempt to ensure that the SMC viewpoint was heard by the FO when considering the new regulations. Hornby told Reilly he had given Hogg a note to Hammond, 'as I am most desirous that both he and you should get a non-official view of the questions here'.[172] Hornby's note was written at a time of great tension between the Shanghai consul, Charles Winchester, and the SMC. In April 1866, only a few weeks before Hornby's supportive letter about Hogg, Winchester was so outraged by the SMC seeking to prevent the Chinese government taxing Chinese residents in the Settlement that he walked out of a meeting of the land renters of which he was the chair and suggested that it might be necessary to call for the intervention of British naval forces to prevent a breach by the SMC of British treaty obligations.[173] When Winchester asked him for advice on the issue, Hornby supported the

170 'Volunteer Meeting', *NCH*, 29 July 1865, p. 118. Bickers, 'Shanghailanders: The Formation and Identity of the British Settler Community in Shanghai 1843–1937', p. 197. Other aspects of the history of the Shanghai Volunteer Corps (SVC) also support the argument that the British state supported the SMC in many ways. For example, the British government supplied ammunition for practice purposes to the SVC free of charge, and senior army officers were sent from Hong Kong to inspect the force to assure its capability: *SMC Annual Report for 1900*, pp. 3–4.

171 TNA FO 17/944: Note by committee of land renters, 22 January 1866; Hornby, *Autobiography*, p. 205; TNA FO 17/453: Hornby to FO No. 5, 8 February 1866.

172 TNA FO 17/944: E. Hornby to F. Reilly 17 May 1866.

173 TNA FO 656/12: C. Winchester to E. Hornby, 19 April 1866.

SMC's desire to keep Chinese authority out of the Settlement by suggesting that the best course would be for the SMC to collect any taxes on the Chinese government's behalf.[174]

After Hornby retired in 1876, the FO downgraded the post of judge somewhat by reducing the pay and, in 1891, amalgamating the position of chief justice of the SCC with that of Shanghai consul general, although this latter move was deeply unpopular with non-official Britons and was reversed after only six years.[175] No subsequent judge seems to have had quite the influence or status that Hornby held as the inaugural office holder, or was prepared to put himself so much at odds with the minister and consuls as Hornby. His inbuilt sense of his own importance and abilities, so evident in his autobiography, no doubt contributed to this. In the longer term it appears that the court and judge's place in the British state hierarchy in China was a little more firmly situated beneath that of the Legation and minister, but relations between the judges and the Shanghai commercial community and the SMC were often still very close. Judges Rennie and Hannen had practised at the Shanghai bar before obtaining judicial appointments, so were fully embedded in the Shanghai commercial world before becoming British officials. Later judges worked closely with the SMC in ways which increased the entanglement of the project of governance of the British state with that of the SMC. Chapter four, dealing with Indians, describes in detail the way in which the SCC in the early twentieth century, and especially Judge de Sausmarez, worked with the SMC to discipline Indian policemen, often in ways which were improvised to meet the particular needs of the Council and involved the stretching and adaptation of the judge and the court's role. Contrary to the intentions of British policy in the 1860s under Ministers Bruce and Alcock, it is clear that the establishment and development of the court as a state institution at Shanghai contributed to the emergence of the International Settlement as a colonial space governed through a set of closely collaborating structures, dominated by the SMC and British state institutions until at least the 1920s.

Other major foreign powers in China set up their own courts, including the United States, which established its court for China much later, in 1906.[176] Expertise was transferred from other colonial jurisdictions to do so: the

174 TNA FO 656/13: E. Hornby to C. Winchester, 19 April 1866. The issue of Chinese tax collection in the Settlement arose again in later years, with the SMC continuing to resist attempts by Chinese officials to tax Chinese residents. See Bickers, *Britain in China*, pp. 126–67.

175 'The Changes at the Consulate', *NCH*, 3 April 1891, p. 389.

176 The other noteworthy example is Japan. See Brooks, *Japan's Imperial Diplomacy: Consuls, Treaty Ports, and War in China.*

first judge of the US Court for China, Lebbeus Wilfley, was moved to China from Manila, where he had served as Attorney General for five years. The US court was established on similar lines to the British in that its decisions were made based on a combination of US federal law and edicts of the US minister in China. On his arrival, the first US judge engaged in a crackdown on disreputable American elements somewhat similar to Hornby's, although more severe, and with less support from the consular body. In contrast to the warm relations which generally existed between the British judge and local British commercial interests, the US interests in China which were targeted by the court were sometimes influential ones, and they counter-attacked, and made considerable trouble for Judge Wilfley, resulting in his resignation in 1909.[177] Because of the later development of the structures of other major foreign powers, and because the dominant culture of the SMC was British (following from the nationality of most of its senior- and middle-ranking staff), and also because British interests in Shanghai were much greater — whether measured financially or in terms of population size — no other foreign power's court or officials were bound up so closely in the work of the SMC and the governance of the Shanghai International Settlement as the SCC and British officials were.

Conclusion

Complex, costly and long-lasting British state institutions were built in China, within a context often characterised as 'informal empire', which were comparable in many ways to those created in parts of the world governed directly from the Colonial Office and famously coloured pink on world maps.[178] Alongside, and crucially important for, British commercial, settler and missionary expansion into China, the state was a key part of Britain in China in multiple ways that go beyond the high-level interactions of foreign ministries or gunboats sailing up the China coast. The Opium Wars and the treaties which followed did not merely open China to foreign trade, they also meant that China was opened to the intrusion of the British state, its institutions and agents.

British state agents gradually created a large and complex structure of laws and institutions aimed at regulating, surveilling and punishing

177 Scully, *Bargaining with the State from Afar*, pp. 110–24.
178 There is in fact plentiful evidence of the minimal colonial state which existed under 'formal' empire in many parts of Africa. See Young, *The African Colonial State in Comparative Perspective*.

British subjects in China and which also served the important roles of supporting British commercial undertakings as well as other institutions of empire in China, such as the British municipal councils and the SMC. An analysis of British involvement in China which gives these institutions due weight draws attention to the potentially unsatisfactory aspects of the term 'informal empire', or at least makes clear that that term needs careful handling if we are not to lose sight of the important, wide-ranging and long-lasting role of governance undertaken by the British state, and the important implications of that role. The case of treaty port China, and perhaps also that of other countries where extraterritoriality was practised, suggests the need for ways to conceptualise empire which do not push us towards thinking in terms of mutually exclusive alternatives. If we keep the concept of space based on imperial networks firmly in the foreground this is more easily done, since it allows us to move away from a fixation with sovereignty over bounded entities, and to give due weight to the 'proliferation of geopolitical ambiguities', which were empirically a not uncommon feature initiated, facilitated and perpetuated by the British state in this period.[179]

Personnel, ideas and practices circulated throughout the British empire world to the fringes of empire through 'multiple, co-existent connections'.[180] This was true for British institutions in China and their interaction with institutions elsewhere. In examining these connections, we can see how they were created, shaped and broken, sometimes in a contest, sometimes in a collaboration, between both official and unofficial actors distributed across a variety of imperial spaces. Although connections through commerce and the military, especially with British India, are fairly well-known, the creation and reform of British state institutions in China led to the development of connections between British state structures in China and British institutions in different parts of the world, such as the Ottoman Empire.[181] Such linkages, since they were not found in other aspects of the British presence in China, such as the commercial or military spheres, have been little explored. Furthermore, institutional connections were sometimes absent or were severed between the British state in China and state bodies and officials in parts of the British empire which were otherwise closely

179 The words are those of Ann Laura Stoler and Carole McGranahan: Stoler and McGranahan, 'Refiguring Imperial Terrains', p. 26.

180 These are Alan Lester's words: Lester, 'Imperial Circuits and Networks', p. 129. See also, Lambert and Lester (eds.), *Colonial Lives across the British Empire*; Metcalf, *Imperial Connections*.

181 For a summary of connections between the treaty ports and India (albeit with relatively little on official connections), see Bickers, 'Britain and China, and India, 1830s–1947'.

connected to Britain in China. Giving the British state a larger place within studies of British expansion in China therefore provides a more accurate picture of the interconnections between the treaty ports and other parts of the British empire.

The existence of many of the connections between the British state and the SMC discussed in this chapter has been underappreciated, which can lead to the impression that the British state had only limited interest or involvement in the running of the International Settlement, tolerating it but neglecting it, at least until the moment of retrenchment and modernisation of Britain's China policy beginning in the later 1920s, when steps were taken to rein in the activities of British settlers.[182] The British state provided the legality relied upon by the SMC and the International Settlement in many areas: in land registration, through the creation and operation of the Mixed Court, through port regulations and by providing the means to control the SMC's police force. This was a deep engagement, through institutional connections which developed in their extent and importance at least into the first decade or two of the twentieth centuries, and which could be described as constituting a hybrid colonial state, since these connections went to the heart of the exercise of foreign power at Shanghai. The following chapter looks more closely at the reasons behind the founding of the key British institution located at the latter place, the Supreme Court for China, which was created primarily to deal with British violence perpetrated by a particular problem population, but developed to influence the treaty ports, and especially Shanghai, in a number of ways.

Bibliography

Berridge, G. R., *British Diplomacy in Turkey: 1583 to the Present; a Study in the Evolution of the Resident Embassy* (Leiden: Martinus Nijhoff Publishers, 2009).

Bickers, Robert, 'Shanghailanders: The Formation and Identity of the British Settler Community in Shanghai 1843–1937', *Past & Present*, 159, 1 (1998), 161–211.

Bickers, Robert, *Britain in China: Community, Culture and Colonialism, 1900–49* (Manchester: Manchester University Press, 1999).

Bickers, Robert, 'Purloined Letters: History and the Chinese Maritime Customs Service', *Modern Asian Studies*, 40, 3 (2006), 691–723.

Bickers, Robert, *The Scramble for China: Foreign Devils in the Qing Empire, 1832–1914* (London: Allen Lane, 2011).

182 For that process, see Bickers, *Britain in China*, Chapter 4.

Bickers, Robert, 'British Concessions and Chinese Cities, 1910s–1930s', in Billy K. L. So, and Madeline Zelin (eds.), *New Narratives of Urban Space in Republican Chinese Cities* (Leiden: Brill, 2013), 296.

Bickers, Robert, 'Britain and China, and India, 1830s–1947', in Robert Bickers and Jonathan J. Howlett, (eds.), *Britain and China, 1840–1970: Empire, Finance and War* (Abingdon: Routledge, 2016), 58–83.

Brooks, Barbara, *Japan's Imperial Diplomacy: Consuls, Treaty Ports, and War in China, 1895–1938* (Honolulu: University of Hawai'i Press, 2000).

Brown, Nathan J., 'The Precarious Life and Slow Death of the Mixed Courts of Egypt', *International Journal of Middle East Studies*, 25, 1 (1993), 33–52.

Bruce, John, *Annals of the Honorable East-India Company, Vol. 3* (London: Cox, Son and Baylis, 1810).

Cassel, Pär Kristoffer, *Grounds of Judgment: Extraterritoriality and Imperial Power in Nineteenth-Century China and Japan* (Oxford: Oxford University Press, 2012).

Coates, P. D., *The China Consuls: British Consular Officers, 1843–1943* (Hong Kong: Oxford University Press, 1988).

Chappell, Jonathan, 'Maritime Raiding, International Law and the Suppression of Piracy on the South China Coast, 1842–1869', *The International History Review*, 40, 3 (2018), 473–92.

Chen, Li, 'Law, Empire, and Historiography of Modern Sino-Western Relations: A Case Study of the "Lady Hughes" Controversy in 1784', *Law and History Review*, 27, 1 (2009), 1–53.

Chow, Phoebe, *Britain's Imperial Retreat from China, 1900–1931* (London: Routledge, 2017).

Day, Jenny Huangfu, *Qing Travelers to the Far West: Diplomacy and the Information Order in Late Imperial China* (Cambridge: Cambridge University Press, 2018).

Edwards, R. Randle, 'Ch'ing Legal Jurisdiction Over Foreigners', in Jerome Alan Cohen, Fu-mei Chang, and R. Randle Edwards (eds.), *Essays on China's Legal Tradition* (Princeton, NJ: Princeton University Press, 1980), 222–69.

Esselstrom, Erik, *Crossing Empire's Edge: Foreign Ministry Police and Japanese Expansionism in Northeast Asia* (Honolulu: University of Hawai'i Press, 2009).

Fairbank, John King, *Trade and Diplomacy on the China Coast: The Opening of the Treaty Ports, 1842–1854* (Stanford, CA: Stanford University Press, 1953).

Feuerwerker, Albert, *The Foreign Establishment in China in the Early Twentieth Century* (Ann Arbor: Center for Chinese Studies, University of Michigan, 1976).

Giles, Herbert Allen, *A Glossary of Reference on Subjects Connected with the Far East* (Shanghai: Kelly & Walsh, 1900).

Greenberg, Michael, *British Trade and the Opening of China 1800–1842* (Cambridge: Cambridge University Press, 1969).

Hevia, James L., *English Lessons: The Pedagogy of Imperialism in Nineteenth-Century China* (Durham, NC: Duke University Press, 2003).

Hornby, Sir Edmund, *Sir Edmund Hornby: An Autobiography* (Boston, MA: Houghton Mifflin, 1928).

Jackson, Isabella, 'The Raj on Nanjing Road: Sikh Policemen in Treaty-Port Shanghai', *Modern Asian Studies*, 46, 6 (2012), 1672–704.

Jackson, Isabella, *Shaping Modern Shanghai: Colonialism in China's Global City* (Cambridge: Cambridge University Press, 2017).

Kayaoglu, Turan, *Legal Imperialism: Sovereignty and Extraterritoriality in Japan, the Ottoman Empire, and China* (Cambridge: Cambridge University Press, 2010).

Keeton, George Williams, *The Development of Extraterritoriality in China*, Vol. 1 (London: Longmans, Green & Co., 1928).

Koo, V. K. Wellington, *The Status of Aliens in China*, (New York: Columbia University Press, 1912).

Kolsky, Elizabeth, *Colonial Justice in British India* (Cambridge: Cambridge University Press, 2010).

Kotenev, Anatol M., *Shanghai: Its Mixed Court and Council* (Shanghai: North China Daily News & Herald Limited, 1925).

Lambert, David and Alan Lester (eds.), *Colonial Lives across the British Empire: Imperial Careering in the Long Nineteenth Century* (Cambridge: Cambridge University Press, 2006).

Lane-Poole, Stanley, *Sir Harry Parkes in China* (London: Methuen & Co., 1901).

Lester, Alan, 'Imperial Circuits and Networks: Geographies of the British Empire', *History Compass*, 4, 1 (2006), 124–41.

Leung, Yuen-sang, *The Shanghai Taotai: Linkage Man in a Changing Society, 1843–90* (Honolulu: University of Hawai'i Press, 1990).

Lovell, Julia, *The Opium War: Drugs, Dreams and the Making of China* (Basingstoke: Macmillan, 2011).

Major, A. G., *A Compendium of Instructions to H.M. Consular Officers in China* (Beijing: British Embassy, 1927).

Metcalf, Thomas R., *Imperial Connections: India in the Indian Ocean Arena, 1860–1920* (Berkeley, CA: University of California Press, 2008).

Moore, Alasdair, *La Mortola: In the Footsteps of Thomas Hanbury* (London: Cadogan Guides, 2004).

Morse, Hosea Ballou, *The International Relations of the Chinese Empire: Vol. 1, The Period of Conflict, 1834–1860* (London: Longmans, Green, 1910).

Morse, Hosea Ballou, *The International Relations of the Chinese Empire: Vol. 2, The Period of Submission, 1861–1893* (London: Longmans, Green, 1918).

Morse, Hosea Ballou, *The Chronicles of the East India Company, Trading to China 1635–1834*, Vol. 1 (Boston: Harvard University Press, 1926).

Munn, Christopher, *Anglo-China: Chinese People and British Rule in Hong Kong, 1841–1880* (Richmond: Curzon, 2001).

Norton-Kyshe, James William, *History of the Laws and Courts of Hongkong*, Vol. 2 (London: T. Fisher Unwin, 1898).

Osterhammel, Jürgen, 'Semi-Colonialism and Informal Empire in China: Towards a Framework of Analysis', in W. Mommsen and J. Osterhammel (eds.), *Imperialism and After: Continuities and Discontinuities* (London: German Historical Institute, 1986), 290–314.

Osterhammel, Jürgen, 'British Business in China, 1860s–1950s', in Davenport-Hines, R. P. T. and Geoffrey Jones, (eds.), *British Business in Asia since 1860*. (Cambridge: Cambridge University Press, 1989), 189–216.

Parry, Clive (ed.), *Law Officers' Opinions to the Foreign Office, 1793–1860: A Reproduction of the Manuscript Series with Index and Commentaries*, Vol. 19 (Farnborough: Gregg International Publishers, 1970).

Roberts, Christopher, *The British Courts and Extra-Territoriality in Japan, 1859–1899* (Leiden: Global Oriental, 2013).

Scully, Eileen P., *Bargaining with the State from Afar: American Citizenship in Treaty Port China, 1844–1942* (New York: Columbia University Press, 2001).

Stephens, Thomas B., *Order and Discipline in China: The Shanghai Mixed Court, 1911–27* (Seattle: University of Washington Press, 1992).

Stoler, Ann Laura, and Carole McGranahan, 'Refiguring Imperial Terrains', *Ab Imperio*, 2 (2006), 17–58.

Teichman, Eric, *The Consular Officer's Vade-Mecum* (Tientsin Press, 1920).

Tuson, E. W. A., *The British Consul's Manual: Being a Practical Guide for Consuls, as Well as for the Merchant, Shipowner, and Master Mariner, in All Their Consular Transactions* (London: Longman and Co., 1856).

Van de Ven, Hans J., *Breaking with the Past: The Maritime Customs Service and the Global Origins of Modernity in China* (New York: Columbia University Press, 2014).

Wakeman, Frederic E., *Policing Shanghai, 1927–1937* (Berkeley, CA: University of California Press, 1996).

Ward, A. W. and G. P. Gooch (eds.), *The Cambridge History of British Foreign Policy, 1783–1919: Volume III: 1866–1919* (Cambridge: Cambridge University Press, 1923).

Wright, Mary Clabaugh, *The Last Stand of Chinese Conservatism: The T'ung-Chih Restoration, 1862–1874* (Stanford, CA: Stanford University Press, 1957).

Young, Crawford, *The African Colonial State in Comparative Perspective* (New Haven: Yale University Press, 1994).

3 Sailors, destitutes and the 'rowdy class': British crime and violence in China

Abstract
The impulse to control deviance in the form of crime, largely by lower class Britons, resulted in the creation of early state institutions following the opening of the treaty ports in 1842 and led to the expansion of state structures in various ways over the ensuing quarter century. The key institution created by the Foreign Office to control 'rowdy' Britons, the Supreme Court for China, became a key element of the British state presence in China, influencing in particular the development of Shanghai. British governance over British subjects in China, especially through the courts, constituted the treaty ports as colonial spaces, so that both foreigners and also the many Chinese in the ports experienced colonial relations in their everyday lives.

Keywords: Sailors, courts, white violence, crime, Frederick Bruce, Edmund Hornby

> The foreigner becomes more audacious, and the scum of the earth are attracted to a country where they can commit excesses without restraint.[1]
> Frederick Bruce, 1858

The previous chapter summarised the institutional expansion of the British state into China from 1842 onwards. It showed that the state was present in China, by virtue of various institutions, personnel and practices, in a far more complex and extensive form — and beyond diplomatic or military spheres — in a way that has not generally been recognised. This chapter

1 Frederick Bruce to sister, quoted in Gerson, *Horatio Nelson Lay and Sino-British Relations*, p. 211.

Thompson, Alex: *British Law and Governance in Treaty Port China 1842-1927. Consuls, Courts and Colonial Subjects.* Taylor & Francis Group, 2024
DOI: 10.5117/9789463720397_CH03

will turn to examine why a large part of that institutional apparatus was thought necessary in the first decades of the opening of the treaty ports. The need to control crime and criminals, particularly those responsible for violent crime inflicted on the Chinese, not only shaped the initial state institutions which were created following the opening of the treaty ports in 1842, but also prompted the expansion and development of state structures in various ways over the ensuing quarter century, and especially in the 1860s, the period of the most important changes in British state structures in China.

In some respects, the focus outlined above offers an alternative view of the British state to that of an imperial aggressor, responsible only for inflicting war, upheaval and imperial domination on the Chinese state. Such a narrative overlooks certain aspects of the role played by the British state in China. Consular jurisdiction over British subjects under the extraterritorial rights granted by treaty was a key aspect of the British state's expansion into China, but it remains understudied. Although work has been done recently to add to our understanding of extraterritoriality as more than a tool of imperial control imposed on China from outside, there remains a lack of material which examines in detail British aims in establishing the system of consular jurisdiction, and which assesses the outcomes of the structures which were put into place for that purpose.[2] As already indicated, the state did not just force China open through violence and then withdraw to leave expansion in China as a private enterprise venture — British state actors clearly saw it as being in Britain's interests to exercise a degree of control and prevent individual Britons from disrupting treaty port life and triggering conflict with the Chinese. Both Eileen Scully and Robert Bickers have shown how tensions between metropolitan governments and settlers in China emerged and prompted state actions, focussing largely on the early twentieth century.[3] This chapter will develop similar themes, but focus on an earlier time period, and in addition will point out that serious tensions and conflicts of interest emerged also between different agents of the British state involved in treaty port China. We can thereby better understand some of the complexity of the British state's involvement in China.

Despite the shift of emphasis from state-initiated violence and aggression, the aim here is not to argue that the British state's presence in China was therefore somehow less 'imperial'. In expanding its institutions in China, albeit often with the principal aim of controlling British violence and other crime, and often in order to mitigate the effect this had on relations

2 In particular Cassel, *Grounds of Judgment*.

3 Scully, *Bargaining with the State from Afar*; Bickers, *Britain in China*.

with Chinese officials (and ordinary Chinese people), the institutions and practices of the British state will nevertheless be seen to have contributed to the development of colonialism in the particular form which it took, and in which it was experienced, in China in the treaty port era.[4] The work presented in this chapter is therefore positioned in close relationship to writing which views the British involvement in China as a part of the wider phenomenon of British colonial expansion elsewhere in the nineteenth and early twentieth centuries, by addressing colonial relations and the way they shaped the places where they were enacted.[5] Many scholars working on nineteenth- and twentieth-century colonialism have produced work which has complicated our notion of the colonisers, and made clear that the latter were most certainly not a homogenous group in various settings, with factors including conceptions of race, class and gender all serving to differentiate among them, often in a complex and interwoven fashion which was intimately connected to the management of relations between colonisers and colonised.[6] Here I show that a project of governance aimed at disciplining largely lower class British subjects nevertheless played a part in ordering treaty port China as a colonial space, in which asymmetrical relations were predicated also to a large extent on notions of the racial difference between Europeans and Chinese.

Most of the British subjects whose violence or destitution in the 1840s to the 1860s earned them the status of problem population, and labels such as 'rowdy', 'scum', 'blackguard' or 'bad character', were non-élite 'white' Britons from the British Isles, often with a seafaring or military background.[7] There were of course also cases of violence and other crime perpetrated by Britons who were more prosperous or socially less marginal in relation to official élites. Individual cases involving such people sometimes prompted official responses but did not generally create the same levels of alarm. Whiteness was rarely commented on or made an issue of in the early decades of the

4 In some ways, this echoes the work of James Hevia, who refers to 'deterritorialising' and 'reterritorialising' practices conducted by British actors in China. See Hevia, *English Lessons*.

5 Those who examine British expansion in China within a British colonial context include Robert Bickers, James Hevia and Jürgen Osterhammel. See Bickers, *Britain in China* and *Empire Made Me*; Hevia, *English Lessons*; Osterhammel, 'Britain and China, 1842–1914'.

6 For China, see Bickers, *Empire Made Me*; more generally, see Cooper and Stoler, *Tensions of Empire*; much work has focussed on India, especially Fischer-Tiné, *Low and Licentious Europeans*.

7 No aggregated statistics are obtainable but this conclusion is drawn from records of deportations in the archives (especially FO 656) and court cases published in *The North-China Herald*, based on the assumption that names can generally be relied on as broadly indicative of geographical origin, and also resting on the tendency of officials and reporters to comment on the skin colour, origin or religion of subjects who were not 'white'.

treaty century. The concept of race was largely unexpressed in discourses concerning those committing violence and criminality, but that does not suggest it was irrelevant as an organisational category in official minds — whiteness was the default, or norm — and it is clear in the following chapter dealing with another marginal group ('martial' Indians), where the idea of race played an overt part in official discourses, that the members of other, non-white, groups were inherently viewed as problematic based in part on notions of racial difference. 'White' was a term which was less commonly used than today, but we can reasonably assume that when British officials in this context referred to men as 'European', or indeed often when they failed to label a British subject's ethnicity at all, they did so because they held mental conceptions of a category of shared ethnicity which corresponds fairly closely to the present-day category usually designated by the word 'white'. Ideas of race were clearly relevant in court cases where British subjects were accused of violent crimes towards Chinese, as is discussed towards the end of this chapter.

The chapter is focussed on the period 1842 to around 1870, and proceeds broadly chronologically. It begins with an examination of the basic framework deployed from early on to maintain order over the population of lower-class Britons in China, especially seamen, who were the group most often subjected to measures designed to deal with violence or other crime. It then moves on to show how, in the midst of disorder and upheaval in China caused by war and rebellions, major changes were made in the 1850s and 1860s to the means of dealing with the criminal behaviour of British subjects. These changes took place under Minister and Chief Superintendent of Trade Frederick Bruce and culminated in the creation of the new institution of the Supreme Court for China (SCC) at Shanghai in 1865. Concerns about controlling groups of 'rowdy' British subjects, who at this point became identified more clearly as a distinct problem population situated in local conditions, played a key role in this crucial moment for the expansion and reorganisation of British state structures in China. I then examine the work of the SCC in connection with controlling the problem population of violent criminals and destitutes, and consider the relationship with the Shanghai Municipal Council (SMC), since collaboration with that body over crime and policing developed into a key relationship for the British state in China, in particular from the 1860s onwards through the attitude and practices of its first judge, Sir Edmund Hornby. This shows more clearly that ultimately the aims of improving British relations with China in accordance with the policy of the Foreign Office (FO) and ministers in the 1860s were not fully met by the structures established. Finally, I go on to explore the issue of race-based thinking in connection with the handling of the most serious violent crimes in the Court, to show how British judicial practices surrounding 'white violence' in China were similar to those found in colonial courtrooms elsewhere in the world. In this way, British official practices aimed at suppressing deviance in the form of serious crime were carried out by means of transactions involving unequal power relations, which in turn contributed to the making of the treaty ports into distinctively colonial spaces.

Avoiding collision and bloodshed: creation of the apparatus of control

British officials in the 1840s, tasked with creating new institutions of governance for the newly opened treaty ports, were clearly concerned by the crime and disorder which had caused friction under the previous regime when trade was conducted at Guangzhou prior to 1842.[8] They anticipated that increased numbers of British subjects, especially seamen, would prompt the need for a more substantial apparatus of control than had previously existed, as a Foreign Office memorandum on proposed legislation in 1843 makes vividly apparent:

> It can hardly be doubted that the utmost care will be required at all places in China opened to British Trade, to maintain the intercourse on a friendly footing. It will be necessary to consult, and as far as possible defer to, the wishes and prejudices of the Chinese authorities and People, and above all to take care that British Subjects either on shore or afloat should not commit excesses which may lead to collision and bloodshed.[9]

A combination of laws and regulations, together with the deployment of personnel at Hong Kong and in the treaty ports, constituted the early apparatus intended to meet the above aims. These have been discussed in general terms in the previous chapter, but here I provide details of specific provisions aimed at suppressing the particular kinds of crime and disorder perpetrated by British subjects in China, showing how and why they developed as they did.

In the nineteenth century, seamen on British ships throughout the world were subject to a strict regime of discipline and control, at the hands of the

8 See Morse, *International Relations*, vol. 1, Chapter 5, for a detailed narrative account.

9 TNA FO 17/76B: Memorandum: China Bill of 1843, 22 July 1843.

masters of vessels which was sanctioned by British law.[10] State intervention in regulating and disciplining seamen and in particular preventing desertion has generally been viewed as having been designed to protect commercial interests, to ensure that shipping could function in the interests of trade and also to avoid where possible state expenditure on repatriation if seamen were left behind at ports.[11] When British ships came into port, British consuls in places where there were no extraterritorial rights played a key part in upholding this system.[12] In China, as in the Ottoman Empire and other places where there was extraterritoriality, consuls' duties and powers were far greater, and their roles involved a larger degree of supervision over activities occurring on land, as well as more contact with the local authorities.

After the ratification of the 1842 Treaty of Nanjing, a set of controls to deal with British seafarers in the particular context of the China coast was laid down through a number of different provisions. The importance of such measures to Anglo-Chinese relations is indicated by the fact that specific details were included in the treaties made between the British and Chinese governments. In Article 6 of the Supplementary Treaty signed at Humen in 1843 (also sometimes called the Treaty of the Bogue), which set out the key framework for the operation of trade at the ports, it was stated that 'seamen and persons belonging to the ships shall only be allowed to land under authority and rules which will be fixed by the Consul, in communication with the local officers'.[13] Consuls issued their own rules to implement this provision, and Robert Thom demonstrated the ambitious aims some early British officials set for themselves in maintaining peace and order when he issued the regulations which would apply at his post at Ningbo in 1844:

> Masters of British vessels [...] will be required to be exceedingly strict and attentive as to the degree of liberty they allow their men while in port. No more persons will be allowed to go on shore from each ship than what are absolutely necessary for the carrying on of the lawful business of the ship, without being first duly reported at this Consulate and getting a special licence: and such special licences can only be granted when the men are under the care of an officer.[14]

10 Wiswall, *The Development of Admiralty Jurisdiction and Practice since 1800*, pp. 44–46.

11 Milne, *People, Place and Power on the Nineteenth-Century Waterfront*, p. 181.

12 Symons, *The Law Relating to Merchant Seamen.*

13 'Supplementary Treaty between Great Britain and China. Signed (in the English and Chinese languages) at Hoomun-Chae, 8th October, 1843', *Hertslet's Commercial Treaties* (*HCoT*), vol. 6, 1845, p. 264.

14 Tuson, *The British Consul's Manual*, p. 247.

By Article 10 of the Humen Treaty it was agreed that a British warship would be stationed at each of the open ports 'to enforce good order and discipline amongst the crews of merchant shipping, and to support the necessary authority of the consul over British subjects'.[15] The ultimate symbol of British imperial domination in the treaty ports, the gunboat, was therefore in fact also a vital component of the apparatus designed to control British subjects, especially seafarers, in China. While not of course forgetting that British gunboats were deployed in aggressive and violent actions against China on numerous occasions over the course of the treaty century, the stated reason for their presence — which was an obligation of the British government under the treaties — was governance over British subjects in China.

Various rules were made by the superintendents of trade in the 1840s and 1850s which specifically targeted seamen as subjects of control. Ordinance No. 3 of 1844 prohibited 'masters of merchant-vessels belonging to Her Majesty's subjects from leaving seamen and others in a destitute state in the dominions of the Emperor of China' without the consul's permission. This required masters to give a bond to consuls, declaring that they would not leave behind any crew members without permission, and also that they would agree to receive any distressed seamen (not just members of their own crew) at the ports if sent on board by the consul to be conveyed to Hong Kong or Great Britain.[16] In 1854, the superintendent issued consolidated and standardised regulations for the five ports.[17] By Article 3 of the 1854 regulations, masters had to deposit their papers (which would include a list of the crew) at the consulate within 48 hours of arrival, and these would only be returned on completion of formalities before departure. Under Article 13, the permission of the consul was required in order to leave behind any person belonging to a British ship at the port, and even if permission were given, security was demanded 'for his maintenance and good behaviour while remaining on shore'. If British seamen who had been left behind were subsequently found to require 'public relief' the vessel would be 'held responsible for the maintenance and removal of such British subject'. Article 16 dealt with facilities at the ports for sailors, and required any British subject wishing to open 'a boarding or eating-house' to apply for the consul's permission, and give security 'that he will not harbour any seaman who is a runaway, or who cannot produce his discharge accompanied

15 *HcoT*, vol. 6, 1845, p. 265.

16 *HCoT*, vol. 7, 1850, p. 171.

17 'General Regulations for British Trade', of 18 May 1854 in *BaFSP*, No. 47, pp. 594–98

by a written sanction from the Consul to reside on shore'.[18] Similar regulations were periodically reissued from then on by the superintendent, and generally imposed a number of requirements on ships' masters in order to control their crews in particular.[19] However, it was not always possible or desirable to keep the ports completely free of unemployed seamen through such means of control, particularly at Shanghai, where shipping grew rapidly (see Table 1 below), as did a demand for European labour in areas such as the customs, municipal works and commercial undertakings, which hired lower class British men, in particular in policing, security and other lower level supervisory roles at the front line of the colonial interface with local people. In 1867 Shanghai Consul Charles Winchester reported that it would be inadvisable to prevent all discharges at the port because ships needed to be able to form new crews there, and he added that 'the general character of the port makes it the point to which stowaways, runaways and deserters from vessels at other ports are attracted'.[20]

Table 1. Annual total of foreign and British ships entering Shanghai port (1844–55).[21]

Year	Number of foreign ships	Number of British ships
1844	44	no data
1849	133	94
1852	182	103
1855	437	249

The regulations aimed at trying to prevent seamen from causing difficulties at the ports were therefore both detailed and exacting, but the approach which developed to consular criminal jurisdiction over British subjects more generally was by contrast rather less well-defined. To accompany the Order in Council (OIC) and ordinance of 1844 which gave consuls jurisdiction over British subjects in China, Superintendent of Trade John Davis sent out to consuls what were probably the earliest general instructions relating to their role in British governance, in which he explained that it was the duty of consuls to ensure that the grant of extraterritoriality did not have any

18 'General Regulations for British Trade', of 18 May 1854 in *BaFSP*, No. 47, pp. 594–98.

19 For example, in 1869 — 'Port, Consular, Customs, and Harbour Regulations, applicable to all the treaty ports in China' (31 May 1869), p. 74 in *HChT*, 1908.

20 TNA FO 228/433: Winchester to Alcock, 27 December 1867.

21 Figures are taken from Morse, *International Relations*, vol. 1, p. 357.

'injurious effects resulting from it to the territorial Sovereign', in particular by maintaining order and punishing crime.[22] Davis stressed that a practical approach to consuls' judicial duties was called for: it was desirable that cases should be settled informally where possible; when proceedings were necessary and crimes were to be punished, 'certain and speedy, rather than severe, punishment is to be preferred'; it was 'unnecessary to deal with crimes according to the strict definition of English law'.[23]

A notable feature of the apparatus was the provision included in Davis' Ordinance No. 7 of 1844, to allow claims in assault cases to be settled through the payment of compensation: 'in case of assault, it shall be lawful for the Consular officer before whom complaint is made, to promote reconciliation and to suffer compensation and amends to be made, and the proceedings thereby to be stopped'.[24] This provision continued in force for some time, and it was included in the first principal OIC, of 1853, so clearly had the approval of officials at the FO, who were closely involved in drafting that instrument.[25] This flexible system was perhaps viewed as being the only way to create a system under conditions of limited resources which would enable consuls to balance the interests of shipping and trade with smoothing relations. As seamen were most likely to be responsible for cases of assault, compensation allowed quick settlement of cases, without the consequence of holding up shipping which would be likely if men were imprisoned as punishment. The practice further perhaps reflected a recognition that consular resources were stretched and that most consuls were not legally trained. There is also evidence that the practice was amenable to Chinese officials and Chinese victims and their families.[26] For example, in 1859 at Fuzhou, Consul Walter Medhurst settled the case of a Chinese girl who drowned following a violent incident by arranging the payment of compensation between the girl's family and the British subject accused of causing her death, instead of overseeing criminal proceedings against the man. Medhurst reported that the settlement of the case through compensation had been 'hinted at' as

22 'Order in Council relating to the trial and punishment at Hong-Kong, or in China, of Offences committed by British subjects', printed in *BaFSP*, vol. 32, p. 895–97; Ordinance No. 7 of 1844 'for the better administration of justice in the Consular Courts', 20 November 1844, *HCT*, vol. 7 (London, 1850), pp. 185–91; John Francis Davis, 'Circular respecting consular jurisdiction', 22 November 1844, reprinted in Tuson, *The British Consul's Manual*, p. 230.

23 John Francis Davis, 'Circular respecting consular jurisdiction', 22 November 1844, reprinted in Tuson, *The British Consul's Manual*, pp. 229–32.

24 Article 6 of Ordinance 7 of 1844.

25 Section 26 of the 1853 Order in Council (OIC), in *BaFSP*, vol. 42, p. 269.

26 Morse, *International Relations*, vol. 1, p. 101. Also see the case at Fuzhou referred to below, where Medhurst claimed that compensation was proposed as a solution by Chinese officials.

an appropriate response by the local Chinese authorities, and justified his action by declaring that the settling of the case had avoided the likely acts of 'blind and angry revenge' which an allegation of the murder of a Chinese by a foreigner would provoke.[27] In some ways, these practices represented a continuation of a long-standing approach to settling disputes between Chinese and foreigners on the China coast; in the years prior to the treaties, many cases of foreign violence against Chinese were settled this way.[28]

Consuls had three options in the formal handling of criminal cases under the 1844 Ordinance: a summary decision; a decision made with the aid of British assessors; and a referral of the case to the Hong Kong Supreme Court.[29] Consuls' powers of punishment were limited to sentences of imprisonment of 12 months or a 200 dollar fine, but Davis informed consuls that it was intended that only when British subjects had been charged with murder that they should be sent to Hong Kong for trial. Other than in this respect, Davis' circular and Ordinance did not address the role of the Hong Kong Supreme Court, and he appears to have envisaged its role in consular jurisdiction as being extremely limited. However, by an earlier Ordinance, the Hong Kong Supreme Court had been given very extensive supervisory powers, should it choose to exercise them: consuls were to report details of all decisions to the court; the court could decide to alter any decision 'as shall seem just and expedient'; and the OIC of 1844 also made clear that the chief justice of the Hong Kong Supreme Court had the power to try British subjects accused of crimes in China, beyond the colony.[30]

Overall, this was not an attempt by the early superintendents to establish an apparatus which would in practice conform closely to the system of criminal justice delivered in the courts in Great Britain. It was, however, a serious and pragmatic attempt to create a system which would allow the consuls, given their limited resources, to do the minimum necessary — in accordance with the wishes the FO had expressed in 1843 — to 'maintain the intercourse on a friendly footing'.[31] Resources were targeted at seafarers, who were assumed to be the group most likely to commit crime, especially crimes of violence, and the superintendents appear to have intended to allow

27 TNA FO 337: Medhurst to Bruce, 2 May 1860, enclosure in Bruce to FO, 22 May 1860.

28 Morse, *International Relations*, vol. 1 gives details: pp. 99–107.

29 Davis, 'Circular respecting consular jurisdiction', 22 November 1844, reprinted in Tuson, *The British Consul's Manual*, p. 231.

30 Pottinger's Ordinance No. 2 of 1844 — in *HcoT*, vol. 7 (1850), p. 168; 'Order in Council relating to the trial and punishment at Hong-Kong, or in China, of Offences committed by British subjects', printed in *BaFSP*, vol. 32, pp. 895–97.

31 TNA FO 17/76B: Memorandum: China Bill of 1843, 22 July 1843.

consuls flexibility to handle most cases speedily and economically, without recourse to the Hong Kong Supreme Court. However, despite these intentions, the Hong Kong court intervened on a number of occasions, causing friction between superintendents and the Hong Kong judiciary. An example of this clash in relation to cases arising from breach of the treaties has already been discussed in Chapter 2. There were also significant disagreements which arose over the handling of criminal cases, in particular where British subjects were accused of violent behaviour towards Chinese.

In 1846, for example, Charles Compton was convicted by the Guangzhou consul Francis McGregor of an offence involving an assault and false imprisonment. McGregor and Superintendent Davis attempted unsuccessfully to deny Compton an appeal against his conviction to the Hong Kong court, motivated it seems in large part by a desire to mollify the Chinese authorities.[32] They failed to do so, and the decision of the consul was overturned by Hong Kong Chief Justice Hulme, who described the sentence as 'unjust, excessive and illegal'. This triggered a set of actions on the part of Davis, including an unsuccessful campaign to discredit Hulme through accusations of drunkenness made to the FO.[33] Davis expressed his anger over the actions of the Hong Kong court, and explained the difficulties it caused him, when reporting to Palmerston:

> I hold the highly responsible office of preserving peace between the two countries, and therefore look to Your Lordship for a fair estimate of my motives in desiring to restrain the excesses of the English within the Chinese territories, where the inherent rights of the Government have been given up to us. Mr Hulme's argument [...] will operate, I fear, as a terrible encouragement to our people to be violent in a place like Canton, where the elements of mischief are rife.[34]

Davis also took steps to try to prevent a recurrence of this problem by issuing a new ordinance. In 1847 he removed the right of British subjects to appeal to the Hong Kong court from decisions in the consular courts.[35] However,

32 Keeton, *The Development of Extraterritoriality in China*, vol. 1, p. 218.

33 From the *China Mail*, 26 November 1846, quoted in Keeton, *The Development of Extraterritoriality in China*, vol. 1, p. 222; for Davis' attempt to discredit Hulme see Keeton, *The Development of Extraterritoriality in China*, vol. 1, pp. 225–26. Davis' successor Bonham also feuded with the chief justice, again over the role of the supreme court in consular jurisdiction — see John King Fairbank, *Trade and Diplomacy on the China Coast: The Opening of the Treaty Ports, 1842–1854*.

34 TNA FO 228/57: Davis to FO, 25 November 1846.

35 Keeton, *Extraterritoriality*, p. 224.

because the consuls were not empowered to inflict heavy punishments, the problem caused by the need to make use of the Hong Kong court in cases of serious crimes committed in mainland China or its waters was not resolved by this action. A case arose in 1848 which again triggered considerable dissatisfaction with the Hong Kong court on the part of the superintendent of trade, by then Samuel George Bonham. This involved a British ship which attacked a Chinese fishing boat, killing five men. The captain was prosecuted in Hong Kong, but was acquitted amidst suspicions that Chief Justice Hulme had behaved improperly in his directions to the jury, and also that the Chinese witness had been bribed or intimidated by the British captain's supporters in Hong Kong.[36]

Both Davis and Bonham wished to reform the system of consular jurisdiction by removing the ability of the Hong Kong court to participate in the handling of consular court cases, but were only partially successful in doing so. The most significant cases which prompted them to push for this outcome were not, however, ones involving the most marginal of British subjects: Compton was a merchant well able to afford the $200 fine initially imposed by the Guangzhou consul and with the resources to appeal his case to the Hong Kong court. The captain in the case which annoyed Bonham was equally able to marshal resources to mount a defence to his case in the courts, and possibly also to bribe the witness. Although cases such as these troubled successive Superintendents of Trade, and they in turn complained to the FO about the role of the Hong Kong court, the complaints do not seem to have been taken seriously enough in London to prompt major reform of the procedure in criminal cases. This would come only with the rise of a 'rowdy' problem population in the late 1850s, amidst the unrest of rebellions and war.

New responses to disorder: Frederick Bruce at Shanghai and Beijing

Frederick Bruce became superintendent of trade in 1859, when the British government was still engaged in the conflict with the Chinese government triggered by the 1856 Arrow War. His assumption of the position represented a new start for Britain in China in terms of practical issues of governance in one key way: he was the first British superintendent of trade based permanently on Chinese soil, rather than at the colony of Hong Kong, and thus was not only engaged more closely and directly with Chinese officials,

36 Munn, *Anglo-China*, p. 182.

but was also more intimately aware of the actions of British subjects in China, especially those forming the growing presence at Shanghai. Bruce's role in China's foreign relations has generally been explored in relation to the 'cooperative' policy which he is said to have initiated, in collaboration with US Minister Burlingame, at Beijing from the 1860s.[37] It will be shown here that his impact on British governance in China was significant, and that Bruce was clearly already thinking 'cooperatively' in one sense while at Shanghai in 1859, before the settlement of the Second Opium War was finally agreed late in 1860.

Bruce was based at Shanghai in the period 1859–60 after he had been barred by the Chinese from proceeding to Beijing to exchange the ratified Treaty of Tianjin. While there he was able to witness at first hand some of the misbehaviour perpetrated by violent British subjects, and see the effect it had on relations with the Chinese at Shanghai. He was clearly horrified by British behaviour in a number of areas, and this motivated his desire to reform the system in response. The situation presented to Bruce was one in which the British systems of law and order had been severely tested by a number of factors arising in the years shortly after the opening of the ports. Most obviously, the volume of British shipping had increased, in particular at Shanghai, and so too naturally had the work of the consuls in attempting to exercise the supervision outlined above. Furthermore, the trade in China had unique complicating features in that the technically-illegal opium trade played a huge part in it, and this produced particular challenges for consuls in dealing with crime and keeping order. The opium trade at Shanghai also expanded considerably in the period 1843 to 1855.[38] Seamen employed in the opium trade worked not only on ships sailing between places transporting cargo, but also at receiving stations, or opium 'hulks', which were moored semi-permanently at locations along the coast. These were really floating warehouses which made it possible to conduct the opium trade outside large ports and thus allow British consuls to officially feign ignorance of its existence much of the time.[39] The opium trade was made legal in 1858 but continued use was made of receiving stations. From the early days officials blamed the opium trade for fostering lawlessness among both foreigners and Chinese involved in the trade.[40] The crews of

37 Wright, *The Last Stand*, especially pp. 23–30.

38 Morse, *International Relations*, vol. 1, p. 358.

39 See Fairbank, *Trade and Diplomacy*, pp. 227–36.

40 James Hevia calls this set of circumstances 'opium anarchy', see Hevia, *English Lessons*, p. 53.

opium hulks were obviously further removed from official supervision than crews manning ships coming and going at the open ports with other cargoes, and this remoteness exacerbated the difficulty for officials of controlling the activities of such men. Denser, more established connections between the crews of opium hulks and local Chinese were also made more likely since these craft stayed in one location for longer periods of time than was usual with ordinary shipping. Following a trial for a robbery committed at Xiamen in 1846, Consul Temple Layton reported that British opium ships in the area employed a 'reckless, lawless and smuggling class of seamen', who were in contact with 'the lowest thieves and prostitutes in Amoy [Xiamen]'.[41]

A further factor which presented a challenge to British systems of control was the lack of any effective Chinese government at various places from the mid-nineteenth century onwards, as the Qing state struggled to recover from the effects of both foreign invasion and internal rebellion. This allowed for the growth of the interrelated activities of piracy and convoying, the latter a practice whereby foreigners were paid by Chinese ship-owners, and sometimes Chinese officials, to accompany their vessels to guard against attacks by pirates.[42] Rival groups of foreigners emerged who fought each other over supremacy in this activity, and also themselves engaged in acts of piracy, destruction or violence. In 1859, Minister Bruce blamed convoying for drawing large numbers of British 'bad characters' to certain places on the coast. He described the crew of the typical British convoy boat: 'The foreign sailing-master is generally a seaman of an ordinary class, allured by the prospects of indefinite gain, and of a roving life, with a crew of half-castes and Chinese — the latter little, if at all, better than the pirates they profess to attack'.[43] Ningbo and its environs was a chief locus of the practice, where it was said to be carried on by British-owned boats, 'sailing without papers or flag' and thus breaking mercantile regulations, in addition to bringing crime and disorder.[44] Similar activities took place on the rivers, especially near Shanghai, where foreigners were hired to sail on Chinese boats and bully Chinese officials into letting contraband pass through. In 1862, Consul Adkins at Zhenjiang (about 240km upriver from Shanghai) reported to Bruce that a gang of Europeans and Chinese had murdered the captain of a junk, and he issued the dramatic warning

41 TNA FO 228/70: 'Remarks by Consul', 8 January 1847, enclosed in Layton to Davis, 28 January 1847.

42 Fairbank gives a description of this practice in his *Trade and Diplomacy*, pp. 329–46.

43 TNA FO 17/314: Bruce to FO, 5 November 1859.

44 TNA FO 17/314: Bruce to FO, 5 November 1859.

that 'the river is likely to be overrun by foreign blackguards knowing no law and under no control'.[45]

The number of unemployed British 'blackguards' also grew as a result of the Second Opium War and the Taiping rebellion in China (1850 to 1864). By 1862, the SMC was reporting that the 'increase of the foreign population, more especially in the lower orders, within the last 12 months, has defied all the efforts of the Council to keep pace with it in police organisation.'[46] This growth occurred at least in part as a direct consequence of war and rebellion, since British soldiers who were discharged following the British military engagements in those events were sometimes left behind in China. In 1864, *The North-China Herald*, which reported 'an alarming increase in crime of every description' at Shanghai, attributed it in part to the fact that a large number of men of the British 31st Regiment, when on the point of returning to Great Britain following the war, had been allowed to join Gordon's Chinese government-backed force fighting the Taiping, without any arrangements being made for them to be repatriated once the unit was eventually disbanded. When the latter event took place, the paper declared, 'the country became flooded with foreigners of the very worst character'.[47] The SMC recruited a large number of soldiers from the same regiment to join its Shanghai Municipal Police at around the same time, but many were dismissed after serving for only a short time for offences including drunkenness.[48]

In 1864 it was reported by the Municipal Council that at Shanghai there were about 45 'white men' some of whom were said to 'eke out a precarious existence as watchmen at Gambling Houses', while others had no fixed abode and moved from Shanghai by boat for short periods inland from time to time.[49] The latter were probably engaging in 'creek piracy', which meant sailing up the smaller waterways in search of vulnerable Chinese targets to plunder and was another activity facilitated by the breakdown of government authority. Creek piracy and other crimes committed by gangs, often composed of both foreigners and Chinese, were a particular feature

45 British Parliamentary Papers, House of Commons, China No. 3 (1864) Papers relating to the Affairs of China, vol. 63, [c.3295], (1864), p. 8.

46 'Municipal Report for the Year 1862', *The North-China Herald* (*NCH*), 11 April 1863, p. 58.

47 'Summary of the Week', *NCH*, 23 January 1864, pp. 14–15.

48 In 1863 the SMC employed ninety-two men from the British 31st Regiment, which was no longer required in China following the end of the Arrow War: *Municipal Report for the Half year ending 30th September 1863*, p. 1. See also Bickers, 'Ordering Shanghai: Policing a Treaty Port, 1854–1900'.

49 Gould letter to Parkes, 30 September 1864, printed in Supplement to *NCH*, 22 April 1865.

of the period of the early- and mid-1860s, when the areas neighbouring Shanghai were subject to the greatest degree of unrest caused by the Taiping Rebellion. The typical *modus operandi* of the creek pirate was described by Judge Edmund Hornby in his autobiography:

> Their habits were to get a snake-boat, hire a Chinese crew of eight or ten scoundrels, and go up the creeks into the interior, plunder villages, levy blackmail, beat and sometimes murder the villagers, rape the women, and ill-use the children.[50]

Superintendent Bruce reported to the FO that it was impossible to convict foreigners involved in these kinds of violent acts, saying that Chinese witnesses were not prepared to give evidence against them.[51] It is not difficult to see how for a Chinese villager or shopkeeper, the prospect of being mixed up in the unfamiliar, confusing and potentially frightening world represented by British officials and institutions would be highly unattractive.

By the late 1850s, as Britain's relationship with China was being re-evaluated amidst the crisis of the Second Opium War, it was therefore already clear that consular criminal jurisdiction was fraught with difficulties, and the pressures on the system were increasing. A set of structures which had been designed to deal with violence and disorder on the part of seamen, focussed on keeping them on their ships as much as possible, and removing those left behind economically and quickly, was not workable in the context of the China coast as it had developed, amidst the expansion of commerce (especially trade in opium), dubious maritime activities and a general breakdown of Chinese government authority. The reasons outlined above had led to a fairly rapid growth in the population of British sojourners or settlers at the treaty ports, and especially Shanghai.[52] Resources were therefore strained. In 1857, the Shanghai consular jail was so crowded that men were released early after an outbreak of sickness.[53] Consuls asked for more resources in response to the increase in crime: Meadows at Shanghai in 1859 requested an additional constable and reported that the consular jail often had 40 prisoners in it.[54] Consul Robertson at Guangzhou reported that

50 Hornby, *Autobiography*, p. 254.

51 TNA FO 17/314: Bruce to FO, 5 November 1859.

52 The Shanghai International Settlement's British population grew from 91 in 1847 to 256 in 1851, and reached 894 by 1871. Source for 1847 figure — Morse, *International Relations*, vol. 1, p. 355; other figures from Bickers, 'Shanghailanders', p. 176.

53 TNA FO 97/106: Shanghai Police Sheets, 31 December 1857.

54 TNA FO 228/274: Meadows to Bruce, 14 November 1859.

'owing to various causes, a considerable number of unemployed Europeans, chiefly British subjects, find their way up here' and requested a European constable so he could 'keep something like order among a class whose proper residence is a prison'.[55] Consul Harry Parkes, at Shanghai in the 1860s, also complained of the increasing workload imposed on him by dealing with judicial matters, and the problem of 'foreign rowdies' became an issue of growing importance to the SMC, who asked the foreign consuls in 1864 to assent to the Council establishing a 'system of incarceration and enforced labour in the case of all persons, native or foreign, who failed to afford a satisfactory account of their presence'.[56] From February 1865, the SMC began collecting data about foreigners 'without known occupation' in Shanghai, which was sent monthly to the foreign consuls.[57]

As concern over disorder and criminality increased, British officials began to view certain foreigners, a significant number of them British subjects, whose livelihoods in China were based on engaging in violent crimes ranging from murder and piracy to assaults and petty theft, as a distinct problem population. They were most often referred to as 'the rowdy class', and officials increasingly turned their attention to dealing with this group, who they viewed as a clear threat to British interests. Superintendent of Trade Bruce attempted reforms aimed at securing greater powers for himself and the consuls in 1859. In a lengthy despatch addressing both the issues of the convoying system and British 'bad characters' more generally, Bruce argued that there were many failures in British justice in China as it was then practised, and that to solve them required that the powers of the superintendent and consuls be increased to enable them to act preventively, by deporting those with no visible means of subsistence and unable to find security for their good behaviour, without the need first to prove the commission of an illegal act. Without such new powers, Bruce predicted that 'we shall certainly alienate from us the goodwill of the Chinese population' and he argued they were needed for 'justice to the Chinese, and not less a regard for our own interests and reputation'.[58] The FO referred Bruce's request to the law officers of the Crown, who criticised the proposal, calling it an 'extreme measure', and the FO informed Bruce that they would not grant the additional powers to consuls.[59] The law officers insisted that existing

55 TNA FO 228/305: Robertson to Bruce, 7 January 1861.

56 Lane-Poole, *Harry Parkes*, p. 475; *Minutes of the SMC*, vol. 2, 28 September 1864, p. 95.

57 *Minutes of the SMC*, vol. 2, 1 February 1865, p. 127.

58 TNA FO 17/314: Bruce to FO, 5 November 1859.

59 TNA FO 83/2251: Law Officers (Queens Advocate Harding) to FO, 13 February 1860; and FO to Queens Advocate Harding, 11 October 1860.

powers had not been sufficiently tested, and that Bruce and his consuls should attempt to exert greater control without any augmentation to the tools at their disposal.

Bruce's focus was very clearly fixed on removing factors which provoked Chinese hostility at the ports towards foreigners. Despite the fact that these actions — taking place in a pause of the military actions instigated by Britain in the second opium war — were aimed at reducing certain kinds of conflict, they should not be misconstrued as evidence of Bruce and other British officials being risk-averse or conciliatory towards China. We should draw a distinction between their attitude towards Chinese at the ports and their approach towards the Chinese government — Bruce was especially concerned that *local* populations would not protest or turn against foreigners — since such action could create enormous practical problems for the British, who were reliant on local Chinese assistance in most aspects of business and everyday life at the treaty ports. In 1859, Bruce reported to the FO while pressing for greater powers for consuls that he had witnessed a riot of local Chinese outraged by the behaviour of discharged seamen at Shanghai.[60] There is also evidence (see the quote above) that a further motivation for Bruce was concern for Britain's reputation as the leading colonial power in China (and China's key 'teacher').

In addition to calling for stronger powers for consuls, Bruce made changes to the way that consuls were to handle the issue of violence against Chinese, going against previous arrangements and signalling something of a change of direction. He insisted that past practices involving conciliation and compensation in settling cases of violence should be abandoned. He reported to the FO that the existing practices neither discouraged abuse, nor satisfied the obligations in the treaties, and moreover they created 'prejudicial results on the disposition of the native inhabitants' towards foreigners.[61] Bruce wrote to Consul Walter Medhurst at Fuzhou, who had brokered compensation in the case where a Chinese woman drowned following a violent incident perpetrated by British subjects, and wrote also to Consul William Gingell at Xiamen, where he had learned of similar practices, reminding the latter that 'the lives and property of Chinese are under treaty as sacred, as those of an Englishman in England'.[62] He ordered Medhurst and Gingell to ensure in future that crimes against Chinese were punished in such a way as to ensure that British subjects would be deterred from committing such acts.

60 TNA FO 17/314: Bruce to FO, 5 November 1859.

61 TNA FO 17/337: Bruce to FO, 22 May 1860.

62 TNA FO 228/285: Bruce to Gingell, 17 May 1860.

As well as expressing a difference of opinion with past approaches over the practical means to maintain good order, Bruce was also making an argument for official actions to be strictly correct in a more abstract sense; he emphasised equality and universal values, and there was a clear moral tone evident in his choice of words, in particular his assertion that Chinese lives and property were 'sacred'.

Bruce continued to focus on the reform of consular jurisdiction, pushing for the power to remove 'notorious characters' from the treaty ports, and also raising the problems arising from the need to send serious criminal cases to Hong Kong for trial: consuls still could not inflict heavy sentences, and there were serious problems with the Hong Kong courts, especially when it came to deciding cases arising from crimes committed in China, outside the colony. In 1860 a man named McCodd was acquitted of murder by a Hong Kong jury, and the law officers in London acknowledged that this had been done 'perhaps somewhat unreasonably', but they once more stopped short of accepting that serious reform was needed, arguing that to give consuls greater powers would endanger 'public and private rights'.[63] Former Hong Kong official Norton-Kyshe, in his history of the courts of Hong Kong written at the end of the nineteenth century, summed up the situation which existed prior to 1865, chiefly as a result of the problems of biased juries and getting Chinese witnesses to the colony to testify:

> A fine of a thousand dollars or twelve months imprisonment was no fitting punishment for murder or arson, and yet it was the only one that could with any certainty be applied. To send a criminal for trial to Hong Kong was, as a general rule, to ensure his acquittal and release.[64]

The US consul at Shanghai, by contrast, was at this time not impeded in the way his British counterpart was, and in 1863–64, US Consul George Seward launched a crackdown on his own nationals by prosecuting and sentencing to death three US citizens, all for crimes of violence, one of whom, David Williams, had killed three Chinese while involved in creek piracy.[65]

Although earlier reforms to the interrelationship of consular jurisdiction with the Hong Kong court had removed the problems surrounding cases involving the treaties (see Chapter 2), the different arms of British governance charged with dealing with British criminals in China did not

63 TNA FO 83/2251: Law Officers to FO, 8 November 1860.

64 Norton-Kyshe, *History of the Laws and Courts of Hong Kong*, vol. 2, p. 78.

65 Scully, *Bargaining with the State*, pp. 68–69. *NCH*, 20 February 1864, p. 30.

work well together and produced a dysfunctional apparatus of control. *The North-China Herald* (*NCH*) called for reforms to the system following the case of a seaman who had shot a Chinese woman and had been given a sentence of only three months' imprisonment and deportation:

> In Shanghai, where the number of low class foreigners is every day increasing we want either a magistrate entrusted with far higher powers than those wielded by our present energetic Consul, or a judge of assize who should at stated intervals go a circuit of the ports, and enjoy the same authority as is vested in the Supreme Court of Hong Kong.[66]

All of the above issues — the rising concern over a British criminal problem population, especially at or near Shanghai (witnessed first-hand by Britain's senior official), the inadequacy of consular powers and legal knowledge, the problems of the Hong Kong court — contributed to a distinct sense of crisis in Bruce's despatches to the FO concerning the state of British law and order at the treaty ports in the later 1850s and early 1860s. At the same time, the FO and especially Bruce were committed in the early 1860s to the opening of a new chapter in relations with China, and to pushing the Qing state to expand its governance in a form more alike that exercised by European states, in order to create the kind of orderly conditions that they hoped would allow trade to flourish.[67] Bruce explicitly connected this project with the requirement to take steps to control British crime and violence when writing to Consul Parkes about municipal government at Shanghai:

> I look forward to increased confusion and difficulty if we cannot make the Chinese exert themselves to do their duty, and if we cannot keep our own blackguards in order. We must work with the Chinese officials, and not be perpetually in antagonism, if we wish to found anything permanent.[68]

The need was therefore seen for a major reordering of British approaches towards crime in China, and the FO by 1864 accepted the case for major reform. This was achieved through an expansion of the British state's institutions in China by means of the 1865 OIC and the founding of the Supreme Court for China at Shanghai. This institution, already described in general terms in Chapter 2, naturally played an important part in subsequent British

66 *NCH*, 4 February 1865, p. 18.

67 Wright, *The Last Stand*, pp. 23–30.

68 Bruce to Parkes, 29 March 1864, quoted in Lane-Poole, *Harry Parkes*, p. 482.

actions to deal both with crime generally, and 'the rowdy class' as a particular problem population, especially at Shanghai.

Violence and the 'rowdy class' under the British Supreme Court at Shanghai

As described in Chapter 2, the FO brought Sir Edmund Hornby to China from the Ottoman Empire in 1865, to head up the new judicial system as chief judge, based at Shanghai. Hornby continued Bruce's work in an important respect by immediately turning his attention to the question of violent British subjects. In February 1866 he made a lengthy report to the FO reviewing the work of the new judicial system since its commencement, in which he reported in some detail on the question of dealing with violence towards Chinese at the treaty ports. From Hornby's autobiography and his despatches in the archives, it is plain that he was no moralising progressive, influenced by either religious views or egalitarian ideals, and he clearly believed in British superiority over 'Asiatics' and the naturalness of colonial hierarchies.[69] Nevertheless, Hornby found the level of violence at the treaty ports unacceptable. He explained that 'Chinese servants, labourers and even small native merchants were constantly assaulted and severely beaten upon the slightest provocation or suspicion' by British subjects, whose behaviour 'exasperated the natives against foreigners'.[70] One way he addressed the problem of violence was by making an example of a British master of a ship who had flogged some Chinese workers suspected of stealing opium. Hornby punished the master, George Bennet, by inflicting on him a sentence of imprisonment.[71] Bennet was said to be 'very much surprised at the Court's interference', and Hornby explained that he had received a large number of complaints and two petitions from the British community about the handling of this case.[72] The petitioners argued that Bennet had 'acted according to a custom of the port', and that such practices had long been accepted by the Chinese authorities, who had 'absolutely deputed to shipmasters the power of punishing Chinese for offences'.[73]

69 Hornby, *Autobiography*. Very many examples could be cited from this text. See pp. 235–37 for a typically disdainful description of Chinese officials.

70 TNA FO 17/453: Hornby to FO, 8 February 1866.

71 TNA FO 17/453: Hornby to FO, 8 February 1866.

72 TNA FO 17/453: Hornby to FO, 8 February 1866.

73 TNA FO 17/453: memorial enclosed in Hornby to FO, 8 February 1866.

Both Hornby's actions in the Bennet case, and Bruce's earlier move to stop compensation in lieu of punishment, were said to be taken to improve relations with the Chinese. And yet both measures involved overturning practices which were said to have existed at the treaty ports for some time with the complicity of Chinese officials, suggesting the complicated nature of this issue. It was perhaps almost instinctive for Hornby as a trained British judge to admonish British subjects for taking the law into their own hands, having been sent out to China, just as he had also been sent to the Ottoman Empire, to organise and rectify a confused judicial system. But this move away from a kind of improvised co-operation at the local level, especially in the case of Bruce's actions, also serves as a reminder that the British 'cooperative policy' in China was part of a new approach which meant more than propping up the Qing regime or smoothing over conflicts which arose: it involved a moralistic and a pedagogical aspect too, aimed at shaping the Chinese state into a polity more similar to Western nations in its structures and actions.[74] Hornby claimed that this aspect was made clear to him by the FO in advance of both his extraterritorial judicial appointments:

> I may mention that while both Lord Clarendon and Mr. Hammond desired to put the English judicial service in Turkey — and afterwards the same service in China — on a better footing, they both desired to set an example to the Governments of those two countries.[75]

This was then a reassertion and strengthening of British state authority at the treaty ports, which fitted in with the British call for the Chinese state to also assert its authority in China. The SCC was intended by the FO simultaneously to be both a means of smoothing relations with officials as well as ordinary Chinese and a projection of British power. Hornby's early actions may have aligned with both aspects of this policy, but as time went on he can be seen to have strayed considerably from the cooperative line taken by the Legation, as he became closer to British mercantile interests and grew increasingly scornful and dismissive of Chinese officials.

The advent of the SCC under Hornby in this way represented, at least initially, a continuation of the course Bruce had set. Hornby was also early on able to further another of Bruce's goals, when he took a tough stance against members of the problem population he identified as the 'rowdy

74 James Hevia has described a variety of other ways in which the British adopted a pedagogical approach towards China: Hevia, *English Lessons*.

75 Hornby, *Autobiography*, p. 94

class' of British subjects, a group which Bruce had in 1859/60 tried but failed to obtain extra deportation powers to deal with. It is clear that in the mid-1860s, when the SCC was established at Shanghai, foreign criminals as a problem population continued to be high on the agenda of British officials. As already described above, the problem of Chinese and foreign criminals, particularly gangs, was an area of great concern to the Shanghai Municipal Council too. It also troubled the local Chinese authorities, who expressed their concerns to the SMC in 1864, and were reported to have urged the need to rid the International Settlement and the Chinese city of both Chinese 'bad characters' and the 'numerous foreign rowdies who infested the port'.[76] Such concerns led the Chinese to agree to the creation of the Shanghai Mixed Court in 1864, described in Chapter 2. In February 1866, British Consul Charles Winchester sought to strengthen co-operation with local Chinese officials, requesting that the SMC supply weekly reports with descriptions of all unemployed foreigners to him in order that he could pass them to the daotai, so that such men could be more easily arrested if they were found in the area surrounding Shanghai. However, it is clear that British consular officials of the time were more enthusiastic about collaboration with the Chinese than were the Council. The SMC expressed the concern that the Chinese might apprehend 'respectable people', either by mistake or 'using the descriptions as a lever against Foreigners', but reluctantly agreed, at the consul's insistence, and passed on details of British subjects only.[77] The problem of foreign 'rowdies' can thus be seen to have been a significant area of concern shared both by consular officials and the SMC, with the former also wishing to engage the Chinese state to a greater degree in resolving it.

This mutual concern led to joint action not long after the SCC opened late in 1865. In December 1866, Judge Hornby requested the assistance of the Shanghai Municipal Police (SMP) in pursuing a gang of four foreigners and four Chinese who it was reported had left Shanghai a few days earlier, 'for the purpose of plunder'.[78] A sergeant and a constable from the SMP were sent with a Chinese gunboat on the mission. It was of course natural for the judge to rely on the SMC and its police force to make arrests, as indeed consuls at Shanghai had already done for some time, but collaboration under Hornby quickly became closer than it had been in the past, as Hornby became a strong advocate for the SMC and for British state support of it. As already noted in Chapter 2, earlier in 1866 Hornby wrote to the FO, at a

76 *Minutes of the SMC*, vol. 2, meeting of 28 September 1864, p. 95.
77 *Minutes of the SMC*, vol. 2, meeting of 18 February 1866, pp. 278–79.
78 *Minutes of the SMC*, vol. 3, meeting of 11 March 1867, p. 53.

time when there were doubts about the future status of the International Settlement, to push for the SMC to be supported. He made his argument on one ground of particular relevance here: that it was important that the SMC should remain a viable local authority so that it could continue to police the International Settlement; the alternatives would be either a 'heavy pecuniary burden' on the British government, or 'fearful loss of life and property' if the Chinese authorities were relied upon to provide security in the Settlement instead, the Chinese being 'utterly unfit' to keep order.[79] The problem of control of criminality at Shanghai was thus used as a justification of the SMC's anomalous position and for deepening engagement between British state structures, especially judicial bodies, and the SMC at Shanghai.

In 1866, Hornby took further steps against the activities of the 'rowdy class'. He wrote to Minister Alcock proposing a new regulation to tackle the problem of foreigners living from crime against Chinese, by attempting to make it impossible for them to engage in 'creek piracy' outside the treaty ports. He explained that it was well known that British subjects frequently left the ports in order to travel into the surrounding country, where 'native boats are constantly pillaged and villages are placed under contribution', rendering 'all foreigners hateful to the masses of the people', but that the court was unable to convict them since evidence was unobtainable. He explained furthermore that it was impossible to deport such men as vagabonds, since 'their crimes enable them to maintain a decent appearance and to live at ease'.[80] Hornby presented a draft to Minister Alcock of a scheme designed, by preventing them leaving the ports for any length of time, to put a stop to their activities. His proposal would give the judge and the consuls the power to require that any 'persons who, it may be reported to them, have no ostensible means of livelihood' produce evidence of their means of subsistence; if they were unable to do so they could be made to report personally to an appointed person at times as instructed by the judge or consul.[81] Those who failed to comply would be imprisoned or deported. Alcock immediately approved the regulations, and sought the FO's retrospective assent to them, which was given.[82] In 1867, Hornby maintained his stance against criminal and destitute Britons, urging consuls in his *Instructions on Consular Jurisdiction*, that it was essential that 'what

79 TNA FO 17/453: Hornby to FO, 8 February 1866.

80 TNA FO 656/23: Hornby to Alcock, 17 December 1866.

81 FO FO 17/474: 'Notification' enclosed in RA to FO 11 March 1867.

82 FO 17/1258 RA to FO, 17 January 1867.

is called in these Countries the "rowdy Class" should be got rid of' by means of consuls' powers of deportation.[83]

It is clear that Hornby's actions against 'the rowdy class' matched both the Legation's and the SMC's priorities in ridding the treaty ports, and especially Shanghai, of violent and criminal gangs comprising British subjects, as well as destitutes with no livelihood other than begging or petty theft. Hornby's actions against Captain Bennet and others who committed acts of violence against Chinese were also clearly well aligned with the policy of Ministers Bruce and Alcock, who spearheaded the 'cooperative policy' in the 1860s. As the attitude of the SMC towards sharing information with the Chinese authorities showed, however, there were differences between the minister and consuls' desire to assist the Chinese to play their part in policing their territory, and the attitude of the SMC, which was generally suspicious of Chinese officials. As already noted, in the longer term, despite his early moves, Hornby showed a marked tendency to favour the stance of the Council, and his influence and the mere fact of the court's location at Shanghai, increased the degree to which the British state became enmeshed, through its project of governance over British subjects in Shanghai, in the work of the SMC over the longer term. This theme is further explored in Chapter 4, relating to the governance of Indian British subjects.

As described in Chapter 2, Hornby grew to be very supportive of the SMC and dismissive of the Chinese government after only a short time at Shanghai.[84] This bias was eventually also apparently expressed in the way that his attitude changed towards British subjects who took the law into their own hands. In 1870, Hornby overturned the decision of the consul at Taiwan in a case where British subjects had been robbed of some camphor, and had subsequently taken direct action in response, with the result that the consul decided to prosecute them. Hornby's action seems to contradict his earlier stance against Captain Bennet and others who used violent actions to punish or exact vengeance on Chinese subjects, rather than rely on Chinese officials to ensure justice. Minister Wade was displeased with Hornby, and the question was referred to the law officers, who described the nub of the issue between the two men thus: 'the Chief Judge apparently thinking that to rely on the Chinese authorities is practically useless in such matters; the Minister thinking that on the

83 Hornby, *Instructions*, p. 19.

84 In his autobiography, he went as far as to call Chinese ministers 'big, obstinate, insincere babies'. Hornby, *Autobiography*, p. 237.

whole and in course of time it is better for our interests to treat them, as really civilized officials.'[85] The law officers declined to intervene and did not criticise Hornby, sending a rather equivocal response in reply to the FO. One side effect of the establishment of a centre of judicial authority in China, was a reduction in the influence of the London-based law officers over legal issues, and Hornby made use of the flexibility given to him to resist moves by British ministers which would lead to greater reliance being placed on Chinese officials. A further example, from the previous year, saw Hornby clashing with Minister Alcock over the latter's attempt to establish a joint tribunal to settle all civil claims between Chinese and foreigners; Hornby strenuously resisted this initiative and it was not implemented.[86] The contrast between Hornby's approach to Chinese officialdom — which stemmed from personal prejudice as well as closeness to Shanghai mercantile interests — and that of Bruce, and other British ministers of the 1860s, could not be greater.

The impact of ideas of racial difference in cases of violence against Chinese

Since the problem of dealing with the most serious crimes, especially those inflicted against Chinese, was said to be the greatest deficiency in the old system which the new SCC was intended to address, it is important to consider how effective this reform was in achieving that aim. Although the evidence discussed above shows that Judge Hornby clearly did use his position as head of this new institution to crack down on British acts of violence, especially those carried out by marauding or destitute British subjects designated 'the rowdy class', there is room for a more detailed examination of the nature and extent of changes to practices under the new court, and a consideration of what the consequences of these practices in cases of serious violence towards Chinese were for victims, witnesses and defendants. The court's approach in such cases had consequences for the development of the treaty ports more generally as sites of colonial practice.

There is one way in which the new institution clearly had an impact on life at the treaty ports: the creation of the court brought the full 'experience' of the British legal system to Chinese soil for the first time, with qualified judges, juries, support staff and the greater use of legal counsel in court

85 TNA FO 83/2253: Law Officers to FO, 11 May 1871.
86 TNA FO 228/484: Hornby to Clarendon, 27 July 1869.

cases.[87] In cases before the court legal conventions were followed more closely than in the earlier consular courts, there was more time spent by counsel making extensive and complex legal arguments, and a number of issues relating to the application of British law in Chinese surroundings were raised for the first time, at least publicly. Cases which dealt with the death of a Chinese at the hands of a foreigner were naturally particularly closely watched and well-publicised. They were widely reported on in both the foreign and Chinese press, and thus highly influential. Moreover, Chinese people — ordinary residents of Shanghai and Chinese officials — played a part in proceedings as either injured parties, witnesses or observers. The role played by this institution in creating Shanghai as a colonial city should therefore be acknowledged and is worthy of further exploration.[88]

There were a number of fairly high-profile cases in the 1860s and 1870s in which Chinese were shot and killed by British subjects. While comparisons of outcomes between court cases are of limited value, since we may question whether the facts of cases are sufficiently similar for us safely to do so, it is possible to tentatively draw the conclusion that, under the new court, more severe sentences were passed against British subjects convicted of manslaughter for such crimes. For example, in 1864 and 1865, there were two cases handled by the local consuls, before the opening of the SCC at Shanghai, where British subjects were found guilty of manslaughter for shooting and killing Chinese and were given very light sentences. The consuls' priorities in both cases seem to have been to have the guilty parties deported. At Hankou a Doctor named Rice fired at a Chinese crowd who were watching a festival near to his house, some of whom were standing on his property. The consul sentenced Rice to a fine and deportation.[89] In the other case, involving a former ship's steward named Dodds who fired what he claimed was a warning shot at a boat near Shanghai, the sentence was slightly heavier — three months' imprisonment plus deportation — and quite possibly reflected the defendant's lower status. The fact that these sentences were very light for the crimes committed, even by the standards of the place and time, is shown by the articles which were published expressing criticism of both sentences in *The North-China Herald*.[90]

87 Although juries were already used in Hong Kong, I stress here the importance of the trial taking place in China, with juries made up of members of the resident British community, witnessed by Chinese officials and residents of Shanghai.

88 John Comaroff has argued persuasively for the way that law was 'constitutive of colonialism': Comaroff, 'Colonialism, Culture, and the Law'.

89 *NCH*, 23 July 1864, p. 118.

90 *NCH*, 4 February 1865, p. 18.

After the opening of the SCC, Judge Edmund Hornby presided over a very similar case to the two above in Shanghai in 1873. A British man, Ford, apparently from a reasonably prosperous background, was found guilty of manslaughter having shot and killed a Chinese 'coolie', who with a group of others, was remonstrating with Ford outside his house over the payment owed for work done by them. Despite expressing considerable sympathy with the defendant in his summing up of the case, Hornby sentenced him to two years' imprisonment, a considerably heavier sentence than the one given to the doctor or the ship's steward by consuls less than ten years earlier.[91]

The *zhixian* (Chinese district magistrate) was reported to have been present in court at the hearing in the Ford case, and it appears that this was not an uncommon practice in cases of serious violent crime against Chinese.[92] The court was therefore an important point of contact between British and Chinese officials, outside their usual interaction through administrative dealings. A case involving British violence leading to the death of a Chinese, which was viewed by Chinese officials as of particular importance, was that of R. v George.[93] This case, from 1869, may appear unusual alongside those already discussed in that a British subject, Robert George, was charged with murder and found guilty by a British treaty port jury. He was executed at Shanghai as a result. However, a closer reading of reports regarding the case reveals that George was described at one point as an 'East-Indian'; given his European name, he was presumably therefore a Eurasian from India. Theories of racial difference were used by the defence to put forward arguments on George's behalf in his trial. The jury were asked to 'think of his excitable temperament, for it is well known how easily people from his country are roused to anger'.[94] His conviction for murder (rather than manslaughter, the more usual charge following the killing of a 'native') and his resulting execution were therefore not so much the anomaly they might at first appear to have been. The use of arguments based on essential racial differences, widely aired in colonial courts elsewhere in the world, show the continuities between the practice of the British court in Shanghai and courts across the British empire.[95] Judge Hornby clearly subscribed to such racial thinking, and made the explicit comment in his autobiography, again akin to common assertions about the weakness of Indian bodies familiar

91 *NCH*, 30 October 1873, pp. 371–80.

92 *NCH*, 30 October 1873, pp. 371–80.

93 Cassel, *Grounds of Judgment*, pp. 73–74. According to Cassel, the case was cited in a Qing handbook for officials.

94 *NCH*, 24 July 1869, p. 384 and p. 389.

95 Kolsky, *Colonial Justice in British India*.

from the Indian legal context, that 'Chinamen have very thin skins, and what an English sailor would hardly feel cuts into their flesh'.[96]

Essentialist assumptions about Chinese characteristics, sometimes implicitly but often overtly racist, were also clearly visible in the detail of some of the cases discussed above. The validity of Chinese oaths was questioned and considered in some depth in both the Ford and George cases. As the nature of Chinese metaphysical beliefs was discussed before them in the court room, the Chinese observers present, including officials, might well have been bemused by the spectacle of British 'experts' on things Chinese (in the Ford case, missionary William Muirhead, who acted as interpreter) putting forth their views on the subject. The truthfulness of Chinese witnesses was questioned too, in ways which must have seemed insulting to those Chinese present. No challenge was made by the judge or prosecution to assertions by the defence in the Ford case regarding 'the mendacity of Chinese witnesses'. Judge Hornby however suggested that the low intelligence of 'Asiatics' meant that they were unlikely to be lying if the story told was long or complex: 'After an experience of nearly 20 years with Asiatic witnesses, I may give you the benefit of my own observation upon the subject. I never knew Asiatic witnesses who were capable of giving anything like cooked answers to a long story.'[97] The crude way in which diverse populations were essentialised and glossed as 'Asiatics' allowed Hornby to lump together the Ottoman subjects he had encountered in his previous post with the Chinese people he now met at Shanghai, and portray them as deficient or questionable participants in legal proceedings. This further highlights the kind of prejudice operating in the minds of British judges such as Hornby.[98]

The need to rely on juries to decide the verdict in serious criminal cases was another way in which Chinese at the treaty ports witnessed the nature of British colonial justice, along with the assumptions and prejudices of British residents of China. British subjects who killed Chinese people were on several occasions acquitted by juries, even of the lesser charge of manslaughter, in the face of strong evidence of guilt. In 1874, one Thomas Fawcett, who had been responsible for overseeing works on a lighthouse being constructed

96 Hornby, *Autobiography*, pp. 252–53. Kolsky has shown how frequently the supposed weakness of Indian bodies was raised in court as a reason why Indians often died at the hands of violent whites in India — Kolsky, *Colonial Justice*.

97 'R. v. Ford', *NCH*, 30 October 1873, p. 379.

98 This kind of thinking has of course been considered in a vast literature, beginning with Edward Said's *Orientalism*. The concept of orientalism has been applied to the study of law, China and the West (with a focus on the United States) by Ruskola in his *Legal Orientalism*.

in Shandong, shot and killed a Chinese man whom he suspected of stealing from the building site. Judge Hornby went on circuit to Yantai to try the case, and very plainly made it clear to the jury that a verdict of manslaughter was appropriate. He was reported to have reminded the jury that — and it is surely telling that he felt the need to do so — 'A Chinaman's life is as precious as that of one of our own countrymen.'[99] The jury, however, acquitted Fawcett, which caused an angry reaction from Chinese observers at the court, as well as Minister Thomas Wade, and also prompted a lengthy discussion in the widely read Chinese newspaper *Shenbao* (申报).[100]

The clearly prejudiced jury at Yantai was not an isolated occurrence, and successive judges expressed concerns about the problem of juries. In 1877, Hornby proposed that special procedures should be adopted to deal with cases where British subjects were accused of crimes against Chinese subjects, including the option for trials to take place without a jury, because it sometimes happened that 'the British community may be known to have ranged themselves on the side of the accused', but the changes he recommended were opposed by Hiram Shaw Wilkinson (then Law Secretary, based at Kanagawa in Japan, later to be judge of the SCC at Shanghai), who was reported to argue that 'if there is a reluctance in British juries to convict where the case rests wholly on native testimony, it is founded on a very justifiable scepticism.'[101] The use of the jury for all serious criminal trials was retained, and concerns about the biased nature of British juries arose again in the twentieth century. Judge de Sausmarez proposed an amendment to the system in 1906, so that the right to a jury trial would not be available in cases where the complainant was Chinese. He stated that juries could not be 'trusted to approach a question from an independent point of view', and went on to explain:

> If a case is of any public interest it has probably been discussed at the various clubs and a jury comes to Court prejudiced. This is particularly so in mixed cases. The different communities do not coalesce and an unreasoning feeling hostile to Chinese or to some foreign nationality is easily roused. I have noticed it in criminal cases where the complainant is a Chinaman.[102]

99 'R v Fawcett', *NCH*, 26 September 1874, p. 321.

100 Hornby, *Autobiography*, p. 243. *Shenbao* — 'Communications to the "Shun-Pao" Regarding the Fawcett Case', *NCH*, 29 October 1874, pp. 428–29. For an examination of *Shenbao* and its significance for Chinese society, see Mittler, *A Newspaper for China*.

101 TNA FO 17/944: 'Sir E. Hornby's draft order in council', report no. 4 by F. Reilly, 28 March 1877.

102 TNA FO 228/1623: De Sausmarez to Satow, 6 April 1906.

One of the major problems of the old system under the Hong Kong Supreme Court was thus clearly not remedied by establishing the SCC at Shanghai.

Injustices to Chinese at the hands of violent Britons entered the public discourse in Shanghai and beyond, especially through press reports in Chinese newspapers such as *Shenbao* (申报), which had a wide circulation throughout China from the 1870s.[103] Both *Shenbao* and its rival *Shanghai Xinbao* (上海新报) took a regular interest in judicial matters, featuring reports of cases heard in the SCC and also the Shanghai Mixed Court. The 1874 correspondence over the Fawcett case referred to above, which was printed in both *Shenbao* and the *NCH*, was dominated by a debate about the jury system. The Chinese correspondents in *Shenbao* demonstrated a fairly detailed understanding of the British system, and made the case against the use of juries in China, arguing that there were so few British subjects from whom to draw juries, that it was often the case that jury members were acquainted with the defendant and could not be impartial. They called for a system of justice which treated Chinese and foreigners equally, a call which had already been made in *Shenbao* in earlier years.[104] Perceived injustices in individual cases, and also dissatisfaction with institutional inequalities, could therefore have effects far beyond those felt by people in the courtroom who witnessed the way that the trials were conducted. Another manslaughter case, dating from 1872, in which a British subject, Ross, was acquitted having shot a Chinese man, was also reported in the *NCH* as well as *Shanghai Xinbao*. In the *NCH*, it was reported that the Chinese City Magistrate had expressed his anger over the case through 'violent expletives' at the inquest held before the trial, which the *NCH* interpreted as an attempt to curry favour with the Chinese 'rabble' in order to extort compensation from the accused.[105] The *NCH*'s interpretation as to the motivation for Chinese actions in the case cannot of course be taken at face value, but the apparent fact of the provocation to anger of the Chinese present at the inquest, demonstrates the power of court cases involving violence against Chinese to attract official and popular attention and to affect the lived experience of Chinese who encountered British law, directly or indirectly.

103 Wagner, 'The Shenbao in Crisis'.

104 'Communications to the "Shun-Pao" Regarding the Fawcett Case', *NCH*, 29 October 1874, pp. 428–29. In 1872, *Shenbao* carrried an article which complained of the lack of reciprocity in judicial arrangements at Shanghai, since British consular officials sat in a judicial capacity in the Shanghai Mixed Court, whereas Chinese officials were not given any such role in the SCC. The earlier *Shenbao* call for equality is referred to in Cassel, *Grounds of Judgment*, pp. 76–77.

105 *NCH*, 21 December 1870, p. 441; *Shanghai Xinbao*, 22 December 1870, p. 2.

The SCC can clearly be seen in this way to have contributed to Shanghai's status as a space where British colonial practice affected the lived experience of residents and visitors. Although the new court may have tended to lead to the issuing of slightly more severe sentences for British subjects in cases of extreme violence towards Chinese, asymmetrical power relations founded on racial difference were clearly still strong factors which determined the way that perpetrators, victims and witnesses were dealt with by the Court, and influenced the way that the court's processes were experienced. Moreover, following the establishment of the SCC the impact of this difference in treatment was all the more immediate, directly witnessed as it was by Chinese and foreigners at court sessions held both in Shanghai and at the other treaty ports.

The sense of crisis in official minds in connection with the subject of British crime, 'rowdy' British subjects and especially violence against Chinese, seems to have subsided somewhat from the end of the 1860s. A number of factors can explain this. First, the end of the rebellions in China returned peace to the hinterlands of the treaty ports and allowed the Qing authorities to regain control over the Chinese population there. The opportunities for Anglo-Chinese criminal gangs to engage in creek piracy and other similar activities were thus reduced. In addition, over time there appear to have been fewer white British seamen at the ports; according to a British official commenting on the reduced need for consular prison accommodation at Shanghai in 1883, this could be attributed to the opening of the Suez canal and the consequent employment of greater numbers of Asian sailors (so-called 'lascars'), who were said to be far less troublesome.[106] Furthermore, as shown above, the effort to improve relations and also to 'set an example' through legal correctness found its high point in the 1860s, and the ministers supportive of the cooperative policy (notably Bruce and Alcock) were followed by officials who took a more aggressive attitude, so that British violence against Chinese, which undoubtedly continued to occur (as the columns of the *NCH* demonstrate), became a lower priority for British diplomats. No major reforms were made to the structures or practices charged with controlling white British crime and criminals after the 1860s. The next serious official panic over control of a population perceived to be violent and deviant, which prompted the mobilisation of British state resources in new ways, would occur early in the twentieth century and

106 TNA FO 656/58: Office of Works to Treasury, 13 February 1883. The Suez Canal opened in 1869. Martin Wiener also suggests that lascar crews were better behaved on board ship than their European counterparts: Wiener, *An Empire on Trial*, p. 23.

would focus on British Indians and the threat they were believed to pose to British and SMC interests. This is addressed in Chapter 4.

White violence in the late 1850s and 1860s prompted a significant institutional response — most importantly the founding of the SCC in 1865 — but it is notable that the heightened concerns were fairly short lived and focussed only on the extreme misbehaviour represented by the 'rowdy class'. A certain degree of violent behaviour on the part of seamen was expected and did not provoke major concern. However, the next chapter will show a high degree of official unease over a comparatively smaller population, 'martial' Indians, who represented a challenge in different ways. There was a reluctance to suspend the rights of white British subjects, and severe sentences, especially capital punishment, were rare. Harald Fischer-Tiné has described similar circumstances in India, and argues that 'white subalterns', although subordinated and marginalised, nevertheless enjoyed a 'racial dividend', in that white criminals received favourable treatment compared to that meted out to Indians.[107] Again, the subsequent chapter will show that in later years, despite the growth of more elaborate and substantial court structures and procedures, judges were more comfortable in altering practices in ways which did not conform to the law in respect of a non-white target population such as Indians.

Conclusion

This chapter has shown that the development of British state structures in China was shaped to a large extent by the presence and activities of British subjects who committed crime in China. In particular, the SCC was established at Shanghai during a period of heightened official alarm over violent crime committed in particular by the problem population referred to as the 'rowdy class'. The new institution was created both as a practical tool to address crime and a means of setting an example to the Chinese government in the context of the new policy of cooperation then being pursued by the British minister and the FO. However, although British officials in China, including Hornby, first judge of the SCC, made strenuous efforts to control British violence and crime, they did so in different ways, with different motivations and with different consequences for the shape of British expansion in China. Mary C. Wright has suggested that Edmund Hornby and the SCC can be viewed as part of the apparatus for British

107 Fischer-Tiné, 'Hierarchies of Punishment in Colonial India'.

cooperation, on the basis of an 1865 judgment in which Hornby allowed the British Crown to prosecute a British subject on behalf of the Chinese government.[108] This chapter, together with Chapter 2, has offered a more detailed and complex view of the court's role, particularly in the key Hornby years, which shows that the long-term impact of the creation of the court was the establishment of a fairly independent institution at Shanghai, frequently in conflict with British officials based at the Legation in Beijing, and able to undermine significant elements of the cooperative policy and promote the colonial expansion being pursued by the SMC which was not based on Britain's rights under the treaties. Again, as already argued in Chapter 2, the establishment of the SCC at Shanghai bolstered the SMC, a body which generally pushed against Chinese government authority and undermined its sovereignty, not least by putting into place a very supportive British official, in particular in the time of Hornby, who was a staunch advocate on its behalf. Thus, a British initiative which was at least in part motivated by an attempt to improve relations with the Chinese (by improving the justice system, and its ability to deal with the 'rowdy class' in particular), and was created by officials who were highly mindful of the treaties between Britain and China, had unforeseen consequences which clearly did not help Britain's relations with the Chinese government or support those whose priority was adherence to the treaties.

Jürgen Osterhammel has summarised the colonial nature of relations at Shanghai:

> The junior British clerk was a sahib, the wealthy, respectable Chinese merchant or comprador was not. Power, status, and colour (the Chinese had not been considered 'yellow' until early in the nineteenth century) correlated in ways characteristic of colonialism all over the world.[109]

Such asymmetrical power relations clearly existed in the courtroom, where even low status white Britons could be assured that British juries would treat them leniently. The analysis in this chapter of the way that British violence against Chinese was handled by the SCC therefore shows one way in which the British state's institutions played a significant role in the making of the treaty ports into colonial spaces. Once the institution of the SCC was established in China, Chinese people were forced into a greater degree of engagement with British law generally and court procedures in particular,

108 The case was R. v. Reynolds and Holtz. Wright, *The Last Stand*, p. 33.
109 Osterhammel, 'Britain and China, 1842–1914', p. 164.

and Chinese officials were allowed only very minimal involvement beyond watching the trials.[110] This all entailed a very different kind of pedagogical project from that which was envisaged by Bruce or Alcock, who as ministers in the 1860s favoured working together with the Chinese, albeit in the hope that they could influence the development of Chinese governance, including law, through what were conceptualised as cooperative actions. In this way they were working within a mode of thought which can be classed as the 'civilising mission', one kind of British approach to colonial relations. Despite the intentions of the superintendent-ministers, however, the SCC at Shanghai offered Chinese — both in person and through reading about cases in the increasingly important Shanghai Chinese press — a sharp lesson in the 'rule of colonial difference', rooted in a view towards China and the Chinese involving much starker inequality.[111]

Bibliography

Bickers, Robert, 'Shanghailanders: The Formation and Identity of the British Settler Community in Shanghai 1843–1937', *Past & Present*, 159, 1 (1998), 161–211.

Bickers, Robert, *Britain in China: Community, Culture and Colonialism, 1900–49* (Manchester: Manchester University Press, 1999).

Bickers, Robert, *Empire Made Me: An Englishman Adrift in Shanghai* (London: Allen Lane, 2003).

Cassel, Pär Kristoffer, *Grounds of Judgment: Extraterritoriality and Imperial Power in Nineteenth-Century China and Japan* (Oxford: Oxford University Press, 2012).

Chatterjee, Partha, *The Nation and Its Fragments: Colonial and Postcolonial Histories* (Princeton, NJ: Princeton University Press, 1993).

Comaroff, John L., 'Colonialism, Culture, and the Law: A Foreword', *Law and Social Inquiry — Journal of the American Bar Foundation*, 26 (2001), 305–14.

Cooper, Frederick and Ann Laura Stoler (eds.), *Tensions of Empire: Colonial Cultures in a Bourgeois World* (Berkeley, CA: University of California Press, 1997).

110 Cassel suggests that Chinese officials may at first have been allowed a meaningful role in trials on the basis that the *zhixian* (district magistrate) was reported to have sat on the bench alongside Hornby in the trial of George discussed above. However, there is no conclusive evidence of any influential role being played in the trial by any Chinese official. It seems very unlikely that Hornby would have been prepared to accept such an intervention, and in any case the verdict was given by a jury, over whom even the British judge had limited influence. Cassel, *Grounds of Judgment*, p. 74.

111 This is of course Partha Chatterjee's well-known phrase. Chatterjee, *The Nation and Its Fragments*, p. 16.

Fairbank, John King, *Trade and Diplomacy on the China Coast: The Opening of the Treaty Ports, 1842–1854* (Stanford, CA: Stanford University Press, 1953).

Fischer-Tiné, Harald, 'Hierarchies of Punishment in Colonial India: European Convicts and the Racial Dividend, c. 1860–1890', in Fischer-Tiné, Harald, and Gehrmann, Susanne (eds.), *Empires and Boundaries: Rethinking Race, Class, and Gender in Colonial Settings* (Abingdon, Oxon: Routledge, 2009), 41–65.

Fischer-Tiné, Harald, *Low and Licentious Europeans: Race, Class, and 'White Subalternity' in Colonial India* (New Delhi: Orient BlackSwan, 2009).

Gerson, Jack J., *Horatio Nelson Lay and Sino-British Relations, 1854–1864*, (Cambridge, MA: Harvard University Press, 1972).

Hevia, James L., *English Lessons: The Pedagogy of Imperialism in Nineteenth-Century China* (Durham, NC: Duke University Press, 2003).

Hornby, Sir Edmund, *Sir Edmund Hornby: An Autobiography* (Boston, MA: Houghton Mifflin, 1928).

Lane-Poole, Stanley, *Sir Harry Parkes in China* (London: Methuen & Co., 1901).

Milne, Graeme J., *People, Place and Power on the Nineteenth-Century Waterfront: Sailortown* (Basingstoke: Palgrave Macmillan, 2016).

Mittler, Barbara, *A Newspaper for China?: Power, Identity, and Change in Shanghai's News Media, 1872–1912* (Cambridge, MA: Harvard University Asia Center, 2004).

Morse, Hosea Ballou, *The International Relations of the Chinese Empire: Vol. 1, The Period of Conflict, 1834–1860* (London: Longmans, Green, 1910).

Munn, Christopher, *Anglo-China: Chinese People and British Rule in Hong Kong, 1841–1880* (Richmond: Curzon, 2001).

Norton-Kyshe, James William, *History of the Laws and Courts of Hongkong*, Vol. 2 (London: T. Fisher Unwin, 1898).

Osterhammel, Jürgen, 'Britain and China, 1842–1914', in Andrew Porter and William Roger Louis (eds.), *The Oxford History of the British Empire: Volume 3, The Nineteenth Century* (Oxford: Oxford University Press, 1999), 146–69.

Ruskola, Teemu, *Legal Orientalism: China, the United States, and Modern Law* (Cambridge, MA: Harvard University Press, 2013).

Said, Edward W., *Orientalism* (London: Routledge & Kegan Paul, 1978).

Scully, Eileen P., *Bargaining with the State from Afar: American Citizenship in Treaty Port China, 1844–1942* (New York: Columbia University Press, 2001).

Symons, Edward William, *The Law Relating to Merchant Seamen: Arranged Chiefly for the Use of Masters and Officers in the Merchant Service* (London: Longman, Brown, Green and Longmans, 1844).

Wagner, Rudolf G., 'The Shenbao in Crisis: The International Environment and the Conflict Between Guo Songtao and the Shenbao', *Late Imperial China*, 20, 1 (1999), 107–43.

Wiener, Martin J., *An Empire on Trial: Race, Murder, and Justice Under British Rule, 1870–1935* (Cambridge: Cambridge University Press, 2009).
Wiswall, F. L., *The Development of Admiralty Jurisdiction and Practice since 1800: An English Study with American Comparisons* (Cambridge: Cambridge University Press, 1970).
Wright, Mary Clabaugh, *The Last Stand of Chinese Conservatism: The T'ung-Chih Restoration, 1862–1874* (Stanford, CA: Stanford University Press, 1957).

4 Indian colonial subjects and British governance in China

Abstract
'Martial' Indians played a key role in British expansion in China; they were both valued as a colonial resource and viewed as a problem population, and their presence prompted a substantial official response. British officials and courts in China dealt with British Indians in particular ways, based on a politics of difference which drove their attitudes and practices. Drawing on individual court cases, the chapter illustrates the ways in which officials discarded judicial norms or exceeded statutory powers when they dealt with Indian British subjects in China. In the process officials worked to support British interests and in particular those of the Shanghai Municipal Council, which relied on the power and resources of the British state.

Keywords: Sikhs, martial race theory, Shanghai Municipal Police, Shanghai gurdwaras, David Petrie, courts

In 1908, at the British Police Court at Shanghai, Jawalla Singh was charged with assault and with being drunk and disorderly in the gurdwara.[1] He was found guilty, and Judge Frederick Bourne sentenced him to a month's imprisonment and threatened him with deportation. The judge was reported making certain comments as he passed sentence:

> It was quite clear to his Worship that prisoner was not a fit man to live in this country. If there were going to be Sikhs here at all they must be good Sikhs.[2]

1 A gurdwara is a Sikh place of worship. There were several at Shanghai (as well as at other treaty ports), and they are discussed in more detail below.
2 'R. (S.M.P.) and Mishra Singh *v.* Jawalla Singh', *The North-China Herald* (*NCH*), 6 March 1908, p. 569. Jawalla Singh was deported after he had served his sentence in prison (*NCH*, 3 April 1908, p. 41).

Thompson, Alex: *British Law and Governance in Treaty Port China 1842-1927. Consuls, Courts and Colonial Subjects.* Taylor & Francis Group, 2024
DOI: 10.5117/9789463720397_CH04

Judge Bourne's comment is notable not only for the patronising manner, commonly adopted by British officials in China towards Indians, in which he addressed Jawalla Singh. It is also noteworthy because he raised a question which was repeatedly asked in relation to Indians of the 'martial races', within which category Jawalla Singh, as a Sikh, was undoubtedly placed: on what terms was the presence of such men in China acceptable or desirable?[3] For although these men were undeniably British subjects, British officials did not view their migration to China, to take advantage of the opportunities created by the foreign presence there, as representing the exercise of their rights as British subjects to benefit from British expansion overseas. British officials were concerned to ensure that British interests were not harmed by the presence and activities in China of British subjects such as Jawalla Singh, and the fitness of Indians to inhabit British colonial spaces in China was constantly under scrutiny. The implications of their presence and actions there were the cause of much official anxiety and activity.

Indians were however distinct from some other marginal British groups in China — such as ethnic Chinese with British nationality, usually derived through a connection with the colonies of Hong Kong or the Straits Settlements — in that official interest in them was not limited to their status as a problem population. 'Good Sikhs' (and 'Sikh' was often used as a shorthand for all 'martial' Indians) were often viewed as a resource which, with careful handling, could give British interests a special advantage and could bolster British prestige in China, especially in Shanghai. Precisely because of their supposed qualities based on racialised thinking, 'martial' Indians could be both a resource and a threat in the eyes of British officials in China, and that is perhaps the reason why they were arguably subjected to more intense measures of control and supervision than any other category of British subjects in China, with important consequences for the treaty ports.

The migration of British Indians to China and elsewhere was facilitated by webs of connections which existed across British imperial spaces, and this migration in turn further expanded and complicated such webs. These facts have been addressed more generally in earlier historical work on India.[4] Historians of China have also given some attention to this process: Robert Bickers argues for the inclusion of Indian influences into any consideration

3 Martial race theory is discussed below. Works on martial race theory include Streets, *Martial Races*; Metcalf, *Ideologies of the Raj*, especially pp. 125–28; Rand, '"Martial Races" and "Imperial Subjects"'.

4 Tony Ballantyne can be credited with contributing the concept of the web to imperial historiography. See his *Orientalism and Race*. See also Metcalf, *Imperial Connections*.

of British expansion in China, and Isabella Jackson's discussion of Indians in the Shanghai Municipal Police (SMP) places British Indians in the framework of 'subempire' developed by Thomas Metcalf in his important work on India as a focal point in an interconnected imperial web.[5] Metcalf's book gives a good account of some aspects of official treatment of Indians, especially those recruited for police forces in China and elsewhere, within the overall framework of Indian 'subempire'. However, the existing literature on India and China includes mostly quite general discussion of connections which existed and offers little detail as to how exactly those connections influenced specific aspects of the British presence in China. Jackson argues for the significance of 'the impact of sub-imperialism on the Shanghai Municipal Police', which seems to hint at the exercise of power from India in some way, but it is not made clear whether Indian Government decisions had much direct impact on Shanghai, or whether this impact was more indirect, the result of the British in Shanghai drawing on Indian colonial knowledge and practices.[6] One role played by this chapter is to define with more precision how India and Indians, in the context of a 'networked' empire, affected the British presence in China through Indian migration and the deployment of Indian manpower there. Specific kinds of colonial authority were constituted in Shanghai to deal with 'martial' Indians, but although there was a clear flow of men and ideas from India, this did not lead to a significant incursion into, or influence over, treaty port China by the Government of India.

British officials adapted law and practice in China to deal with Indians in ways which were deemed appropriate to them. Colonial difference can be seen here operating in an imperial space somewhat different from those settings, such as British India or Dutch Indonesia, in which approaches to colonial subjects have usually been examined.[7] In exploring the way these migrants from India were managed, controlled and disciplined by the British state in China, the transposition of colonial difference from one imperial site (India) to another very different but in some ways fairly closely connected one (treaty port China) can be analysed. In the treaty

5 Bickers, 'Britain and China, and India'; Jackson, 'The Raj on Nanjing Road'. See also Thampi, *Indians in China 1800–1949*; Thampi (ed.), *India and China in the Colonial World*; and for a detailed study focussing on Sikh diaspora and especially revolutionary activities in Shanghai, see Cao, 'Red Turbans on the Bund'.

6 Jackson, 'The Raj on Nanjing Road', p. 1694.

7 There is a huge literature which could be listed under this topic in relation to India. See for example, Chatterjee, *The Black Hole of Empire*; Metcalf, *Ideologies of the Raj*; Kolsky, 'Codification and the Rule of Colonial Difference'. For Indonesia, see Ann Laura Stoler's work, including 'Sexual Affronts and Racial Frontiers'.

ports, British courts regularly dealt with Indians, but the 'rule of colonial difference' was not inscribed in the fundamental structures of the legal system created by the British state in China, in contrast with the situation in India, where the 'European British subject' existed as a legal category with special rights distinct from those accorded to 'natives'.[8] Because the courts in China were not established under circumstances typical of colonial rule, British Indians in China used the same courts and were dealt with under the same laws as other British subjects. The politics of difference was nevertheless clearly evident in the sphere of British law and governance in China and, particularly through reports of court cases, it is possible to see how it operated in the context of the extraterritorial legal system created under the treaties by the British state in China.

Attempts to control Indians led to a further intensification of British state operations in China, and in particular to a closer cooperation with institutions such as the Shanghai Municipal Council (SMC), which was a key employer of Indians and also a body engaged in the policing and defence of Shanghai, aims which local British officials supported in a number of ways.[9] By focussing on the way this relationship worked for the management of 'martial' Indians in China, this chapter will once again demonstrate the connection between British state governance and the SMC, and will show how that relationship remained close at the beginning of the twentieth century. A consideration of the management of Indians in China therefore contributes to our understanding of the nature of the interconnections between the British state and other institutions which engaged in and assisted in the governance of British colonial subjects in China, and thus builds on the discussion of institutions and structures in Chapter 2, further clarifying the nature of colonialism in Shanghai in particular.

'Martial' Indians in China

This chapter is focussed on official attitudes and practices in relation to Indian men who came to China from the north-west of the Indian subcontinent, especially the Punjab, and who often worked as police or watchmen in China. This was a category of Indian British subjects who contemporary British officials tended to group together when addressing issues connected

8 For the situation in India, see Kolsky, *Colonial Justice*, p. 73.

9 For a detailed study of the SMC see Jackson, *Shaping Modern Shanghai*. For policing in Shanghai (although the focus is on the 1920s and '30s), see Bickers, *Empire Made Me*.

with their governance. I refer to this group as 'martial' Indians, since this is a succinct term which reflects contemporary official conceptions of the group's unifying feature, their supposed fighting prowess, without specifying their religious affiliation, which was not always clear.[10] The theory of martial races which informed British imperial military practices in India and elsewhere has been well documented in historical works which examine the theory as an example of race-based, essentialist thinking, which grew in significance in India and Great Britain following the Rebellion of 1857.[11] Martial race theory was widely promoted and justified in contemporary political, military and ethnological works on India.[12] In accordance with this widely espoused theory, British officials in China saw this category of men as having in common a particular essential nature which made them suitable for work related to combat, security and policing.[13]

Men falling into the category of 'martial' Indians, although believed to share important attributes, were not viewed as entirely homogeneous; officials in China often differentiated between subcategories, for example, Sikh, Punjabi Muslim and Pathan. There were thought to be two principal 'types' of Sikh, Majha and Malwa, determined by their place of origin.[14] Sikhs were undoubtedly the largest group of 'martial' Indians in China, and sometimes measures were adopted by officials with Sikhs and Sikh ideas and practices specifically in mind, as will become clear later when I discuss the court and the Shanghai gurdwaras. However, most confusingly, sometimes the label Sikh was used to refer to 'martial' Indians generally, including Muslims from the Punjab or North-west Frontier provinces, a situation which sometimes caused confusion between British officials.[15] The situation is further complicated by the suggestion that some Indians

10 Nor was religion always a very stable category. For a useful discussion of Sikh identity in British India, including a discussion of the British concept of religion as it was applied in India, see Ballantyne, *Between Colonialism and Diaspora*, pp. 41–44.

11 Streets, *Martial Races*.

12 For example: Bonarjee, *A Handbook of the Fighting Races of India*; Barstow, *Handbooks for the Indian Army: Sikhs*; MacMunn, *The Martial Races of India*.

13 The history of 'martial races' played an important part in British evaluations of their suitability for combat-related work. See Rand, '"Martial Races" and "Imperial Subjects"', pp. 11–12.

14 TNA FO 228/2299: table enclosed in HK Governor to Jordan, 22 December 1915. For more on the supposed distinction between the Sikh sub-groups, see Ballantyne, *Between Colonialism and Diaspora*, p. 75.

15 TNA FO 17/1765: HK to CO 9 December 1902 — 'I would first ask whether the term "Sikh" as used by the Foreign Office might possibly be intended in its generic sense as comprising all Indians and not with reference to the special caste known as Sikhs.' Metcalf, *Imperial Connections* (p. 127), states that in Southeast Asia all Indians from the interior of the subcontinent might be called Sikhs.

claimed to be Sikhs in order to enhance their employment prospects, what Ballantyne terms the 'pragmatic embrace of Sikhism'.[16] It seems that British recruitment officers in India also 'created' Sikhs when recruitment from existing followers of Sikhism proved difficult.[17] For the sake of clarity, in this chapter I will only refer to Sikhs when men who were considered to be followers of Sikhism are clearly at issue.

There were also Parsis and Sindhis from India in China, most of whom were merchants or shopkeepers, but there were clear differences in the way these groups were viewed — for one, they were not ascribed martial proclivities — and although Parsis and Sindhis made use of British courts, for example to resolve civil disputes, they had far less interaction with the British authorities.[18] Moreover, they were not on the whole viewed as problem populations, since they generally worked alongside mainstream British trade in ways neither challenging to metropolitan and colonial British interests, nor controversial in terms of relations with the Chinese or other governments. Attitudes towards British Jews, many originally from Baghdad but often British subjects or protégés through a connection with India, can be characterised in much the same way.[19] Finally, aside from 'martial' Indians and merchants, a third group of Indians who were present at the treaty ports, was 'lascars', who were often Bengalis employed as seamen on ships trading to and from India.[20] However, these men rarely seem to have stayed at the ports for extended periods and provoked little or no official response in the form of exceptional measures to address them as a population. Their discipline was to a large extent provided for through ship-based systems of control, and while they appeared quite often in the British courts charged with various crimes, they were usually dealt with swiftly and without controversy.

The growth of 'martial' Indian communities on the China coast appears to have been closely connected to the deployment of Indian soldiers by Britain in China from the First Opium War onwards. Britain made use of Indian forces in China in every significant subsequent British military

16 Ballantyne, *Between Colonialism and Diaspora*, p. 67; reports were also made of this phenomenon occurring in China, for example 'Indians in North China', *The Times of India*, 27 April 1906, p. 4.

17 Streets, *Martial Races*, p. 9.

18 Claude Markovits provides a good overview of the diverse Indian populations in China, see Markovits, 'Indian Communities in China', pp. 55–74. For a more detailed study of Indian Merchants in China (and elsewhere), see Markovits, *The Global World of Indian Merchants*.

19 For Jews, see Betta, 'Marginal Westerners in Shanghai'.

20 For a history of lascars and their role in maritime trade see Jaffer, *Lascars and Indian Ocean Seafaring*.

intervention.[21] Some of these men left the military and found other employment in China. For example, Indian soldiers garrisoned in Hong Kong were recruited for police duties there from the 1840s: probably one of the earliest cases of the use of Indians as police outside India by a British authority.[22] A British regiment of Indian soldiers was based in Shanghai from 1860 to 1864, and although no Indians were recruited for police work in Shanghai or other foreign settlements or concessions in mainland China before the 1880s, British Indians were working as watchmen in Shanghai from at least the late 1860s.[23] It seems likely that these men were ex-soldiers from British regiments in Hong Kong or China. The migration of Indians to China was therefore probably initially triggered by the deployment of Indian troops in Hong Kong and on the mainland, but it is clear that many men found their own way to China, having neither served in the military nor been recruited in India for police or other service in China.

Recruitment of Indians for the Shanghai Municipal Police began in 1884. Six men were recruited locally; it was said that 'no desirable Sikhs can be got from Hongkong [*sic*] at present', but recruiting was soon being done at Hong Kong (later in the same year), and in the Punjab from 1885.[24] Shanghai was always the main centre of Indian settlement on the Chinese mainland, and the SMP the single largest civilian employer. The population of non-military Indians at Shanghai, and presumably therefore also other parts of China, grew only fairly slowly until the turn of the century, when the numbers began to grow more rapidly, rising from 119 in 1895 to 568 in 1905 (see Table 2). It seems likely that the deployment of large numbers of Indian troops in China in response to the Boxer uprising (1900–02) will have played a part in the increase. The unrest caused by the Boxer crisis also probably increased the demand for watchmen, which may have drawn Indians to work in the treaty ports.[25] Another possible influence on migration at this time is famine in India — the Punjab was badly affected by famines in 1896–97 and 1899–1900.[26] In 1906 the SMP resolved to recruit many more Indians

21 Thampi, 'The Indian Community in China and Sino-Indian Relations', p. 73.

22 Ho and Kong, Policing Hong Kong, p. 10; Norton-Kyshe, *History of the Laws and Courts of Hongkong*, Vol. 1.

23 Indian regiment in Shanghai: 'Mr. Holliday on the New Police Scheme', *NCH*, 14 March 1883, p. 303; Indian watchmen: *NCH*, 5 January 1869, p. 9; *NCH*, 22 April 1869, p. 208; *NCH*, 26 June 1869.

24 *NCH*, 12 September 1884, p. 304; *Minutes of SMC*, vol. 8, meeting of 22 September 1884, p. 194; *Minutes of SMC*, vol. 8, meeting of 15 June 1885, p. 267.

25 A similar effect was noted following the upheaval of the 1911 Xinhai Revolution: TNA FO 228/2299: memo by Barrett, 2 December 1912, enclosed in Fraser to Jordan, 27 December 1912.

26 Davis, *Late Victorian Holocausts*. See especially pp. 141–62 and p. 175.

as policemen in response to riots in 1905 which prompted doubts as to the advisability of relying on Chinese for riot control, and extra recruits were obtained from India from 1907 onwards, reinforcing the existing trend for growth in numbers.[27]

Table 2. The Indian population of Shanghai 1880–1925

Year	Number of Indians in Shanghai	Number of Indians employed by SMP
1880	4	nil
1885	58	16*
1890	89	49**
1895	119	69
1900	296	159
1905	568	224***
1910	804	392
1915	1009	564
1920	954	513
1925	1154	772****

Source: SMC, *Annual Reports*, 1895–1930, except:
* Figure is for 1884 from 'Memorandum from the Bubbling Well Road Committee', *The North-China Herald* (*NCH*), 11 February 1885, p. 162.
** Bickers, 'Ordering Shanghai: Policing a Treaty Port, 1854–1900', p. 182.
*** The Ratepayers' Meeting', *NCH*, 16 March 1906, p. 594.
**** 'Municipal Gazette News', *NCH*, 28 November 1925, p. 388.

A typical individual trajectory was described by Amar Singh in 1917, when he was fighting against deportation from China in court proceedings. He left India with the British Army in 1900 and served in Tianjin. He returned to India in 1901 but then travelled to Shanghai in 1903, and found work as a watchman in Shanghai and later with the Shanghai-Nanking [Nanjing] Railway.[28] Indians like Amar Singh were highly mobile, moving both within China between different locations and employers, and also along imperial and other networks connecting India, Singapore, Australia, the United States and many other places. Although recruitment for the SMP and other

27 SMC, Annual Report for 1907, p. 13.
28 TNA FO 228/2705: affidavit of Amar Singh, enclosed in de Sausmarez to Alston, 9 July 1917.

employers sometimes took place in India, in the case of the SMP often with official assistance from the Government of India, Indian migration to China established networks linking British India and China that were not wholly created by British state institutions or by commercial élites. Indeed, it was arguably Indians who played the greatest part in creating these linkages through their choice to seek employment outside India.

The number of Indians in the 'Sikh Branch' of the SMP is shown in Table 2, from which it can be seen that the proportion of the total recorded Indian population of Shanghai employed by the SMP was generally around 40–50%. Indians were employed in smaller numbers in other settlements and concessions: British records from 1915 show that the cities of Hankou, Tianjin and Xiamen, where Indians were also employed in municipal police forces, were the other major centres of population of 'martial' Indians.[29] Indians classified as Sikhs always made up the majority of Indians in China. In Shanghai, all the policemen were said to be Sikhs, but the SMC also employed a number of Muslim Indians, particularly as gaol warders.[30] The total number of Indians known by the British authorities to be resident in China in 1915 was 1,755, but it should be noted that, as British officials were well aware, this was likely to be lower than the true figure.[31] Indians, like other marginal British subjects, often did not register with consuls and may have been overlooked in municipal censuses.

Most 'martial' Indian migrants to China came from villages in rural parts of northern India, where it has been pointed out that there was a long-standing tradition of men from farming families entering military service.[32] Jackson states that Indians in the SMP were 'almost without exception ex-Sepoys from rural families'.[33] While this was undoubtedly the SMC's ideal type of recruit, there is however evidence that a considerable proportion of the men who worked in China had never served in the Indian military, as was also the case in some forces in Malaya, as Metcalf points out.[34] In 1903, the Secretary of the SMC reported that of the 181 Indian police

29 Other treaty ports where Indians were employed as police included Xiamen and Zhenjiang (until the late 1880s). Xiamen — TNA FO 228/3413: Tours to Clive, 12 December 1922; Zhenjiang — *NCH*, 22 February 1889, pp. 205–06.

30 For example, in 1912 there were reported to be 38 Muslim gaol warders — TNA FO 228/2299: memo by E. M. Barrett, 2 December 1912, enclosed in Fraser to Jordan, 27 December 1912.

31 TNA FO 228/2299: enclosure in Hong Kong Governor to Jordan, 22 December 1915 — in which it was also stated that 'probably there is a considerable number of unregistered Indians in China'.

32 Thampi, *Indians in China 1800–1949*, pp. 73–75.

33 Jackson, 'The Raj on Nanjing Road', p. 1680.

34 Metcalf, *Imperial Connections*, p. 112.

currently working in the SMP, ninety-nine had served in the Indian army, meaning that a little over forty-five per cent had not.[35] It seems that the reputation of their 'martial' attributes was enough, if suitable men with actual military experience could not be found.

To understand the marginality of 'martial' Indians, it is important to recognise the linguistic isolation in which most Indians in China lived, including those employed in police forces.[36] It seems that few police or watchmen spoke English or Chinese to any level of fluency, and thus most could only communicate on a deeper level with other Indians. This affected their relations with Chinese, their opportunities in China for work, and it also affected their relationship with the British state and its agents. Relations with the Chinese were notoriously bad. This cannot have been helped by the linguistic divide, which meant that Indian policemen often communicated through actions — sometimes violent — rather than words, with the Chinese, such as rickshaw pullers, who crossed their paths. British officials and employers relied to a large extent on a small number of men with some linguistic abilities to communicate with the majority of Indians. In Hankou in 1914, when opposition to British authority was a particular concern to the British consul there, he informed Minister John Jordan that 'the Municipal Council's two Scotch inspectors have no previous experience of Indians, and, of course, no knowledge of the language, so are entirely dependent on a not very reliable sergeant-major'.[37] European Britons were at once in close and regular contact with Indians but also cut off from them, because communication of a more complex kind was impossible between most Europeans and most Indians. This language gap may have contributed to the chauvinistic tendency to describe Indians as childlike and lacking intelligence. It meant that a great deal of emphasis was placed by the British on obtaining suitable European and Indian staff in leadership roles who could speak both English and Punjabi, but this aim was often unachieved, and the absence of British officers with adequate language skills in the SMP was blamed by Indians themselves for disaffection and insubordination in 1910.[38] The language barrier also had repercussions for the treatment of Indians in legal cases, as will be discussed below.

35 TNA FO17/1765: Memo by J. O. P. Bland dated 31 August 1903 enclosed in Mansfield to Satow, 2 September 1903.

36 A feature of Indian migrant life in many parts of the empire — see Metcalf, *Imperial Connections*, p. 108.

37 TNA FO 228/2299: Fox to Jordan, 20 November 1914.

38 *Minutes of the SMC*, vol. 17, meeting of 17 August 1910, p. 459.

Despite their centrality to British security and prestige in the treaty ports, the lived experience of most 'martial' Indians in China was one of multifaceted and extreme marginality from both other foreigners and Chinese residents. To British élites, the linguistic aspect of this marginality was not always viewed as a disadvantage, because a reason that Indians were valued in policing and as watchmen was the distance it was assumed they would maintain from Chinese residents. In addition, inability to speak English was not seen to be the problem one might think it would be, since there was never any desire to give Indians work which required subtlety or intelligence — they were wanted primarily for their supposed physical abilities and resilience. However, the marginal and isolated nature of Indian communities in China presented difficulties in the exercise of governance. Without channels for obtaining intelligence and communicating effectively, British élites struggled to control 'martial' Indians, and their fears around this issue were frequently expressed in official correspondence. The SMC attempted to resolve part of this problem in the case of Sikhs, the backbone of their security force, through the gurdwaras, which they attempted to maintain influence over as a tool in their repertoire of control. As will be seen later, the British state also co-opted the gurdwaras into official systems of governance over Sikhs, through practices of the courts, which made the gurdwara into an alternative forum for dispute resolution. In addition, the British state adopted specific regulatory measures to enable a closer control over 'martial' Indians in China.

Adapting to new threats: policies and regulations to deal with 'martial' Indians

British officials generally acted specifically to control 'martial' Indians as a group in four sets of circumstances: to restrict the locations such Indians would travel to in China; to control by whom they would be employed; to discipline and control those Indians employed in British or British-dominated concessions or settlements, especially those in police forces; and to counter 'seditious' Indian nationalism and anti-British movements. As they began to do so, they were working through a system of governance created in the 1840s with the purpose of allowing British trade with China to be conducted more freely and conveniently, and which had been revised in the 1860s to deal with the crime and violence of the largely European problem population described in Chapter 3; this was not an apparatus designed to deal with large numbers of colonial subjects moving through the treaty ports and their hinterlands or taking up residence in them. In India, as elsewhere, the British attempted to effect control through a combination of 'native' tradition and colonial law, and in particular from 1860 this was done through the Indian Penal Code, which gave the government wide and draconian powers to discipline its Indian subjects.[39] The movement of 'martial' Indians from India to the treaty ports, under British consular jurisdiction, was seen as problematic by the chief judge in China, Havilland de Sausmarez, in 1910:

> All these men are removed from the restraints which life in their own community imposes on them, and the organization of extraterritorial jurisdiction is ill fitted to deal with so numerous a body of this nature.[40]

British officials addressed this question through alterations to, and adaptation of, the existing institutional apparatus. Various factors and relationships influenced policy and practice in this area, and the changes that were made had significant effects in Shanghai in particular.

Between 1906 and 1917, a series of orders in council and King's regulations were made which were designed specifically to deal with the governance of Indians in China. A large factor in most of these modifications to the British regulatory regime was the influence of issues arising out of the International Settlement of Shanghai and the SMC's use of Indians as a core of its policing and defence force. The first measure to be enacted was the King's regulation entitled 'Peace order and good government of His Majesty's subjects serving the Shanghai Municipal Police' issued in 1906 by Minister John Jordan in response to the refusal of duty of a large proportion of the Indians serving in the 'Sikh Branch' of the SMP.[41] The men had refused duty as the culmination of a set of events over a number of months. The SMC had refused to allow men to resign who it was discovered were moving away, often to America, to seek better pay.

From the late nineteenth century, large numbers of Indians from the Punjab travelled as independent (that is, not indentured) migrants to locations across the British empire and beyond, and to settler colonies and North America in particular. It was such migrants who travelled to and through the Chinese treaty ports in increasing numbers.[42] British and other state

39 Wilson, *India Conquered*. See in particular Chapter 10.

40 *NCH*, 'Municipal Gazette', 1 April 1910, p. 142.

41 SMC, Annual Report for 1907, p. 37.

42 For a summary of Indian migration from the nineteenth century onwards, see Ballantyne, *Between Colonialism and Diaspora*, Chapter 2.

authorities in China and elsewhere reacted in various ways, including in some cases attempting to restrict the flow of migrants. This occurred most famously in 1914 in the case of the *Komagata Maru*, a ship chartered in the face of such restrictions to take Indian migrants to Canada, where it was refused permission to disembark its passengers.[43] The development of Indian revolutionary politics was strongly influenced by the experiences of Indian migrants outside India and by the perceived injustice of this restrictive response to migration. A particular development was the genesis of the secularist pro-independence organisation known as the Ghadar Party.[44] This group was founded in California in 1913 by Indians there whose reactions to the ideas and practices they encountered fed into their activism aimed at ending British rule over India.[45] The considerable mobility of Indians, especially Sikhs from the Punjab, would help to spread Ghadar ideas and organisational structures across the British Empire and also to Indians in China and Japan. When the Government of India suppressed an attempted rebellion by Ghadar supporters centred on Lahore in 1915, it was discovered that several of the alleged participants were former residents of Shanghai, and some were former employees of the SMP.[46]

In 1906, once the SMP refused to accept the resignations of those Indians who wished to move on in search of better opportunities, Indian policemen tried to procure their dismissal in various ways, but instead of dismissing them the SMP disciplined them through fines. The men then asked for an increase in pay and had a petition calling for an increase drawn up by a British lawyer. The SMC refused the request and on 30 September 1906, 103 out of 172 men decided to strike.[47] The strikers' leaders were escorted by a squad of British bluejackets to the British court, where the men were persuaded to return to work by Judge Havilland de Sausmarez.[48] The new King's regulation was issued within weeks of the strike, as an urgent regulation, meaning the Foreign Office (FO) were not consulted before it came into force. Although the regulation applied to any members of the SMP who were British subjects, it was openly declared in the preamble to the Regulation that it was designed to address the problem of Indians refusing duty.[49] The Regulation made it

43 Johnston, *The Voyage of the Komagata Maru*.

44 Ghadar is sometimes spelled 'Ghadr'.

45 Sohi, *Echoes of Mutiny*.

46 SMC, *Annual Report for 1915*, p. 24A; 'Lahore Conspiracy Case, *The Times of India*, 4 November 1915, p. 8.

47 SMC, *Annual Report for 1906*, p. 41; TNA FO 656/106, De Sausmarez to Jordan, 2 October 1906.

48 TNA FO 656/106: de Sausmarez to Jordan, 2 October 1906.

49 TNA FO 656/83: Jordan to de Sausmarez, 12 October 1906.

an offence punishable by the court to disobey superior officers, to desert the service of the SMP, and to persuade or procure another to desert.[50] In December 1906, ten men were deported to India, having been identified as 'ringleaders' of the refusal of duty.[51] The same disciplinary powers over police were extended in 1907 to police forces in British concessions, following a request from the Hankou Municipal Council.[52]

In 1906, at around the same time as the strike occurred, British officials had already been planning various measures to assist the SMP in the disciplinary problems caused by Indians who wished to leave their employment. The acting Crown Advocate had in 1906 drafted a regulation intended to prevent breach of contract by existing members of the force, in response to the events in the months leading up to the strike described above.[53] In addition, in the course of negotiations between the SMC, the Indian government and British officials in China and London over recruitment of 1000 additional men for the SMP from India, the Indian government had raised the question of discipline, fearing repercussions for military discipline in the Indian Army if a suitable regime was not put in place.[54] India favoured military discipline based on the Indian 'Articles of War' for the men under a court martial, but it was feared that this proposal revealed a misunderstanding in India of the nature of the International Settlement at Shanghai — namely that it was not British territory and that its council was constituted as an international body — and while it was accepted by the Minister Jordan and Judge de Sausmarez that greater powers of discipline would be needed given the substantial increase in men contemplated, the minister and judge insisted that discipline would need to be enforced in a way compatible with the existing judicial regime.[55]

Eventually, due to doubts raised by the strike and in particular because of the concerns of Ministers Satow and Jordan (the latter took over as minister in 1906), far fewer than 1000 men were recruited. Satow's view was that 'the Municipal Council are not to be trusted with an army for defence of the

50 'Regulation for the Shanghai Municipal Police', 12 October 1906, *Hertslet's China Treaties* (*HChT*), vol. 2, 1908, pp. 1080–81.

51 SMC, *Report for 1906*, p. 42.

52 TNA FO 656/83: Fraser to Jordan, 21 November 1906, enclosed in Jordan to de Sausmarez, 4 December 1906; 'Regulations respecting maintenance of discipline in the police forces of British concessions', 14 June 1907, in *HChT*, vol. 2, p. 1105.

53 FO 656/106: De Sausmarez to Jordan, 2 October 1906.

54 TNA FO 656/113: Jordan to Shanghai, 19 June 1907.

55 Indian misunderstanding: FO 371/28: Jordan to FO, 17 September 1906; need for disciplinary powers: FO 656/106: De Sausmarez to Jordan, 2 October 1906.

Settlements against attack', and Jordan maintained the same position.[56] The number of Indians nevertheless increased substantially and accordingly, additional disciplinary powers over the force were still sought by the SMC.[57] British officials agreed that they were indeed needed and the basis for these powers was provided in 1909 and 1910 by Orders in Council (OICs), which allowed for a regime closer to military-style discipline by giving the minister the power to confer a warrant on the commander of a foreign concession or settlement police force. This warrant would enable the latter to inflict summary punishment, including imprisonment with hard labour, on members of the force.[58] Despite the earlier doubts about the SMC's recruitment plans, the British state demonstrated its continuing close relationship with the SMC by giving these powers to one of the Council's employees.

King's regulations under the 1909 and 1910 OICs, providing the power of the commander of a police force to inflict summary punishment, were only ever issued in favour of the SMP. Other municipal councils employing Indians, such as Hankou, Tianjin and Xiamen, made do without such powers. Judge de Sausmarez drafted the regulations and warrant, which gave the captain superintendent of the SMP Clarence Bruce the right to fine British members of the force, and to inflict other disciplinary measures, including imprisonment, without needing to apply to the courts. In a letter to the Council accompanying the regulations, which was published in the *Municipal Gazette*, it was made clear that the measures were above all designed to allow the SMP's commander to control Indians in Shanghai, and that the SMC had been fully consulted on its requirements, since 'all the amendments desired by the Council have been inserted.'[59] When de Sausmarez reported to Jordan he explained that he had however been careful to ensure the 'proper subordination' of the captain superintendent to the court.[60]

The outbreak of war in 1914 led to heightened concerns over the loyalty of Indians, and so further regulations were created, again triggered by the situation in Shanghai and also, at least to some extent, the SMC's requirements. These were regulations which would make it illegal to work in enemy employment, and although no mention of it appeared in the text of the regulations which were issued, the regulations were aimed specifically at

56 TNA FO 371/28: Satow to FO to Pelham Warren, 20 April 1906; Jordan to FO, 17 September 1906.

57 *Minutes of the SMC*, vol. 16, 18 December 1907, p. 545.

58 TNA FO 371/28: de Sausmarez to Jordan 28 September 1906; OICs, see Kennett, *British Jurisdiction in China*, pp. 89–90 and 91–92.

59 *Municipal Gazette* (supplement to *The North China Herald*), 31 March 1910, p. 142.

60 FO 656/121: de Sausmarez to Jordan, 5 November 1909.

Indians in Shanghai working for German firms. In August 1915, Fraser wrote to Jordan stating that there were 'a great many Indians still in enemy employ but practically no other British subjects.'[61] Fraser reported that together with SMP Assistant Superintendent Edward I. M. Barrett and leading figures in the gurdwara, he was trying to ensure that the men were registered and were watched.[62] He called for British subjects to be barred by law from employment by the enemy, ending his letter in dramatic fashion (it is clear from Fraser's considerable wartime correspondence that he was excited by the dramas of the war): 'the danger of murderous assault and the like is not imaginary for the enemy are free with money and budmashes are not scrupulous.'[63] In 1916, Fraser wrote to Jordan again following receipt of a letter containing intelligence, collected by Barrett, which contained a list of Indians in German employment, and explaining that the majority were 'known seditionists'. Fraser strengthened his argument by saying that 'Captain Barrett's representation is in my opinion well-founded in that loyal Indians must wonder at our letting disloyal Indians enjoy well-paid employment without interference'.[64] Jordan was persuaded that regulations should be issued, and they were drafted by the Crown Advocate and issued as urgent King's regulations.[65]

Although state officials in general worked closely together and in collaboration with the SMC, there were differences over the best approach. Havilland de Sausmarez was judge of the Supreme Court for China (SCC) at Shanghai from 1905 to 1921, a crucial period for British governance of Indians in China, when major regulatory changes were effected, and also a time when a great deal of activity by Indians provoked British officials into action, particularly during the 1914–18 war. During this time, although he often acted to assist the SMC in exercising control over Indians in Shanghai, de Sausmarez repeatedly asserted the independence of the judiciary in the face of calls for more executive powers to be given to officials to deport Indians under suspicion of anti-British activities or other disruptive behaviour. De

61 TNA FO 228/2299: Fraser to Jordan, 17 August 1915.

62 Edward Ivo Medhurst Barrett was recruited in 1907 to the SMP specifically to lead the Sikh Branch of the force, on the strength of previous experience in the Malay State Guides, a military force which also depended on 'martial' Indians. SMC, *Report for 1907*, p. 229.

63 TNA FO 228/2299: Fraser to Jordan, 17 August 1915; for more on Fraser's wartime role, see Bickers, *Getting Stuck in For Shanghai*; note Fraser's use of the Anglo-Indian term *budmash*, more usually rendered as *badmash*, 'a hooligan, bad character, hoodlum', as defined in Wagenaar et al., *Allied Chambers Transliterated Hindi-Hindi-English Dictionary*, p. 66.

64 TNA FO 228/2702: Fraser to Jordan, 28 March 1916.

65 TNA FO 228/2702: Jordan to Fraser, 8 May 1916; Jordan to FO, 5 June 1916.

Sausmarez took a different approach to Shanghai Consul-General Everard Fraser, who in 1915 called for deportation to be made possible 'in all cases of proved disloyalty in speech, writing or act during the period of the War', and even proposed to take 'executive action' against Tehl Singh, thought to be the Ghadar leader in Shanghai, by effectively kidnapping him with the assistance of the SMP and placing him on a British ship bound for Singapore.[66] Fraser claimed that it would not be possible to deport him through the existing procedure, but de Sausmarez did not agree and nor did Jordan, and indeed Tehl Singh was shortly afterwards deported by de Sausmarez under the existing rules.[67] Referring to Fraser's calls that deportation should be made easier, de Sausmarez expressed his concerns about the new powers being sought, and argued that the proposals were 'opposed to the first principles of English law'. He went on to bring into the open the dilemma of enacting a politics of difference within the constraints of British law in China: 'the very doubtful alternative of the exclusion of Europeans from their action, is an assertion, that an Indian subject of His Majesty is not entitled to the protection granted by Magna Charter [sic] to an Englishman.'[68] British officials in China usually avoided overt expressions of colonial difference in laws or regulations, preferring to resolve the contradiction between the supposed equality of all British subjects, and the everyday fact of the subordination of certain groups, through more informal practices such as are described in connection with the courts in the next section. Despite de Sausmarez's opposition, in the face of mounting pressure to allow more decisive action to be taken against seditious Indians during the war, Jordan was eventually persuaded to support additional deportation powers, but these were framed to apply to all British subjects, and were implemented through the China (War Powers) Order in Council of 1917.[69]

A good deal of the pressure for greater powers came from a new official voice in Shanghai, David Petrie, an officer from the Indian Police (and later Director General of MI5, the British security service) who was sent to Shanghai to coordinate activities against suspected Indian nationalists in East and Southeast Asia in 1916. Before the arrival of Petrie, there is little evidence of the deliberate transfer of personnel, guidance or regulatory models directly from India in connection with the management by the

66 TNA FO 228/2299: telegram from Fraser to Jordan, 29 October 1915.

67 TNA FO 228/2299: telegram from de Sausmarez to Jordan, 4 November 1915; telegram from Fraser to Jordan, 28 December 1915.

68 TNA FO 228/2702: de Sausmarez to Jordan, 23 September 1916.

69 *BaFSP*, vol. 111, 1917–18, pp. 20–21.

British state of Indians in China.[70] The British apparatus of governance in China was not much shaped by direct official Indian involvement, except perhaps in the realm of intelligence, and then only from the arrival of Petrie in Shanghai. In 1894, the India Office showed a reluctance for Indian personnel to become involved in Shanghai affairs when it recommended permission be refused for an Indian Army officer to be allowed to take a position serving the SMC, since it would mean his position, 'outside the control both of the Indian and British Governments, would be altogether anomalous and inconvenient.'[71] It is true that India made a substantial annual contribution to the funding of the British consular service in China, but this payment was paid less than willingly and seems not to have brought with it much power to influence actions in China, if indeed such influence was even sought by the Indian government.[72] On the whole it appears that there was generally no great enthusiasm for involvement in treaty port affairs on the part of the Government of India.

Petrie's appointment in late 1915 came after two events which served to highlight to British officials in China and India the potential threat posed by Indians living and moving through East and Southeast Asia: the trials at Lahore following the Ghadar rebellion in India referred to above, which involved Indians from Shanghai and elsewhere; and a rebellion at Singapore triggered by Ghadarite activists, which resulted in a mutiny by a Singapore-based Indian army regiment in which dozens of Britons were killed.[73] Petrie was tasked with organising intelligence activities throughout all of East and Southeast Asia, not just China, and had originally planned to have his base at Singapore. He chose Shanghai following his initial tour of the region, and with the support of the ministers at Beijing and Tokyo.[74] Petrie was given the title of vice-consul at the Shanghai Consulate-General as a cover. In Shanghai he worked closely with Consul Fraser and SMP Assistant Superintendent Barrett in particular to take action against Indians thought to be associated with the Ghadar Party.[75] This work would continue

70 Cao Yin argues that the SMC modelled its management of Indian police on Hong Kong: Cao Yin, 'The Journey of Isser Singh: A Global Microhistory of a Sikh Policeman', *Journal of Punjab Studies*, 21, 2 (2014), 325–54.

71 IOR: L/PJ/6/377, File 1249, military despatch from the Secretary of State for India, no. 38 of 12 April 1894.

72 TNA FO 228/3050: FO to Palairet, 28 April 1925.

73 For the latter event, see Harper, 'Singapore, 1915, and the Birth of the Asian Underground'.

74 TNA FO 228/2702: Jordan to FO, 11 August 1916.

75 For a detailed description of Petrie's activities within the context of British Indian intelligence efforts against subversion see Popplewell, *Intelligence and Imperial Defence*, especially pp. 258–96.

for a time after the war under Petrie's successor, Godfrey Denham, also an Indian police detective, and Petrie would leave a further legacy when he left in 1919 by recruiting William Beatty from the Indian police to be assistant superintendent in the SMP, who brought with him 50 new recruits for the 'Sikh Branch' from India.[76]

The new powers provided for the minister by the OIC of 1917 were used to deport large numbers of Indians suspected of sedition. The order meant that it was possible for the minister to certify that an individual should be immediately deported, without the chance to give security, if there were 'reasonable grounds for believing that any British subject has acted, is acting, or is about to act in a manner prejudicial to the public safety, or to the defence, peace, or security of His Majesty's Dominions or of any part of them.'[77] It also provided for other lighter punishments, but it seems that it was the more extreme power of deportation which was most used. Petrie drew on information from Barrett of the SMP in particular in compiling lists of men who should be deported, sometimes on very flimsy evidence, which in some cases showed little or no revolutionary activity — the chance to clear out some of Shanghai's Indian 'bad characters' was clearly seized by Barrett. For example, details such as 'very quarrelsome and truculent' were included to try to stiffen the report on Santa Singh, a former member of the SMP and 'station Granthi' (priest) dismissed in 1914.[78] The lists were sent, with details of the reasons for deportation, to the minister, who then issued certificates to the judge, who was not expected to look beyond the certificates and was supposed to merely give effect to the minister's decision. On occasion, the judge did express doubts as to the justice of deportations under the OIC, but Petrie's arguments, which included in one telegram the statement that 'we regard new order as preventive as well as punitive', tended to prevail.[79] British officials in China had in much earlier times, faced with different challenges, sought the power to deport as an executive act. As described in Chapter 3, in 1860, faced with problems arising from the presence of large numbers of Europeans with no ostensible means of livelihood, Minister Bruce had sought similar extended powers to deport British subjects at his own discretion, but had been denied them following

76 For Denham, see Popplewell, *Intelligence and Imperial Defence*, p. 326. Beatty, see FO 671/446: Pearce to Fraser, 14 May 1919.

77 *BaFSP*, vol. 111, 1917–18, pp. 20–21.

78 TNA FO 228/2704: Petrie to Alston, 5 June 1917 and minute of 12 June 1917 thereon (unknown writer).

79 TNA FO 656/142: de Sausmarez to Alston (Chargé d'Affaires), 7 July 1917 and de Sausmarez to Alston, 2 August 1917; TNA FO 228/2704: Petrie (telegram) to Alston, 15 June 1917.

advice from the law officers.[80] After the war, in 1920, the minister's powers were removed, and deportations were once more placed fully in the hands of the courts, but printing and publishing 'seditious matter' was made an offence, punishable by deportation.[81] By contrast, in the same year, the governor of Hong Kong decided he should be able to deport 'undesirable' Indians without reference to the court, a move which drew opposition from the Indian Government, and which demonstrated the unevenness of British approaches to rights and freedoms in different colonial spaces.[82]

No further King's regulations or OICs were issued after 1920 to deal specifically with Indians in China. The SMC and the British state remained bound together in a particularly close relationship through the policing and control of Indians, perhaps more so than in any other area. This was particularly evident in steps taken to deport Indians, which continued after the war. When Mit Singh returned to Shanghai in 1924, having previously been deported, Consul-General Sidney Barton reported that he had 'advised the Municipal Police to prosecute' him, and Singh was duly prosecuted in the Police Court and sentenced to redeportation.[83] One might expect that deportation of British subjects from China, where no new disturbance or crime needed to be dealt with, would be the business of the state, rather than the municipal police, but in practice the line between the state and the SMP was blurred and the latter's interconnections with the British state were very strong. Intelligence activities of the British state continued to work in alignment with the SMP against Indian nationalism in the 1920s, and Indians continued to be deported in large numbers. Fifty-one Indians were deported from China between 1912 and 1924 (in the same period, the total number of other British subjects deported was only six).[84]

The Indian government retreated from an active role for a time and indeed was criticised for not doing enough to prevent Indians returning from deportation after the war. As one Legation official put it, 'This is typical of India who are apt to wash their hands of these Indian undesirables in China, though they can of course be very embarrassing and dangerous

80 TNA FO 83/2251: Law Officers to FO, 8 November 1860.

81 'Order in Council making provision for the deportation of certain offenders', 21 December 1920, in *BaFSP*, vol. 113 (London, 1920), pp. 229–30.

82 FO 228/3413: India Office to CO, 13 November 1922, CO to FO, 5 December 1922.

83 TNA FO 228/3100: Barton to Macleay, 14 August 1924; 'Indian Deportee's Return', *NCH*, 30 August 1924, p. 345.

84 BL IOR/L/PJ/6/1890, file 3823: Legation to India Office, 'List of persons deported from China since 1912', 30 December 1924.

in their activities here.'[85] In 1922 the Government of India turned down a request for Beatty's secondment to the SMC to be extended, despite appeals from the FO, and in 1923 it withdrew its funding for intelligence work in China, so that Denham was not replaced when he left Shanghai that year.[86] Intelligence was left in the hands of London-funded agents until 1927, when an officer from the Punjab Police, Colonel G. H. R. Halland, was sent to be attached to the Shanghai Defence Force as tensions built with the rise of the Guomindang in China and Indians were suspected of linking up with Communist agents.[87] Indian official commitment to British governance in China was intermittent and generally unenthusiastic.

Indians in China and British law in practice

Despite the added regulatory machinery which was introduced to control Indians under the circumstances described above, Indians who were involved in legal proceedings in China were still in principle dealt with under the same laws and regulations which applied to all British subjects, and in the same courts. British courts in China could not apply the Indian Penal Code to Indian British subjects. Another response to the question of how to exercise special control over 'martial' British Indians can be discovered in the everyday practices of the British courts, especially the Police and Supreme Courts at Shanghai. Indians appeared frequently in British courts in China in cases involving a range of criminal and civil matters. A careful reading of the case reports, together with archival records which exist in connection with some more serious cases, reveals certain distinct attitudes and practices in relation to Indians involved in legal proceedings. Indians were treated in particular ways in China, based to a large extent on ideologies and beliefs about the nature of Indians which were widely held by British officials at the time, and the practice of law in particular played a key role in keeping 'martial' Indians in their place within colonial hierarchies in China.

British officials held race-based ideas of group membership which resulted in unevenness in the treatment of British subjects. Judges' attitudes and practices towards 'martial' Indians were undoubtedly influenced by ideas

85 TNA FO 228/3100: minute by W. H. Turner, no date (1924), on Giles to Macleay, 26 June 1924.
86 IOR L/PJ/6/1806: telegram from Viceroy, Simla to India Office, 7 June 1922, and FO to India Office, 8 May 1922; Jeffery, *MI6: The History of the Secret Intelligence Service*, p. 257.
87 TNA FO 228/3589: telegram from Colonial Office to Governors of the Straits Settlements and Hong Kong, 24 February 1927, enclosed in FO to Lampson, 9 March 1927; memo by Halland enclosed in Lampson (telegram) to FO, 19 June 1927.

— in particular based on racial and cultural essences — concerning the supposed nature of Indians. The positive attributes of 'martial' Indians and the ways in which they were thus thought to be useful to British rule have been well documented in the works on martial race theory referred to above, but negative cultural and racial characteristics were also ascribed to this group and were discernible in official discourse on Indians in China. 'Experts' brought in from India from time to time were always ready to share their knowledge with British officials and employers of Indians in China. Major Davidson, of the Indian Army, hired by the SMC in 1910 to enquire into the reasons for disaffection in the Sikh Branch of the SMP, reported that 'The Sikh is a born intriguer; given suitable conditions, and I think he has them here, intrigue will flourish'.[88] Petrie, originally from the Indian police, shared his opinion on the nature of Sikhs in a 1918 despatch to Consul-General Fraser, when he stated 'The ordinary Sikhs employed in the Police are still but little removed from children in their outlook and their mode of thinking'.[89] The perceived capabilities of Sikh policemen were publicly described by the captain superintendent of the SMP in the SMC's *Annual Report for 1906*: 'their lack of intelligence does not permit of their being utilized in the finer spheres of police work.'[90]

Certain aspects of the way that judges dealt with Indians who came before them show that a particular politics of difference, most likely informed in part by the 'experts' referred to above, was clearly at work in the handling of 'martial' Indians in legal cases. Judges frequently adopted a lecturing tone, addressing the perceived deficiencies of Indians, especially Sikhs, in China. The statement quoted at the beginning of this chapter — 'If there were to be Sikhs in China they must be good Sikhs' — suggests that Sikhs were viewed by judges as a group whose presence in China was contingent on the permission of their British rulers. Part of the act of essentialising inherent in the politics of difference was a denial of the individuality of the subject, as judges showed when trying individuals or small numbers of Indians. In such cases, judges often spoke as if Sikhs or Indians were on trial *as a group*, and they frequently addressed the Sikh or Indian community as a whole when castigating behaviour they disapproved of. For example, in 1909, Police Magistrate Gilbert King dealt with a fight between Indians which took place in the very public surroundings of the Shanghai Bund. It was reported in

88 SMA SMP Central Registry Files U102-5-159: 'Report on the condition of the Sikh Police employed by the Shanghai Municipality', Major S. R. Davidson, 28 December 1910.

89 TNA FO 671/446: Petrie to Fraser, 3 December 1918.

90 SMC, *Annual Report for 1906*, p. 13.

the *The North-China Herald* (*NCH*) that he told the interpreter 'to tell all the men in Court — and the room was crowded with Sikhs — that if that sort of thing went on, the Sikhs of Shanghai would have to be confined to a certain part of Shanghai'.[91] Harsh criticism from the bench was common, for example Acting Police Magistrate W. R. Strickland told the Indians in court in a case of assault in 1914, 'It is disgraceful that you people should come here and waste the time of the Court by little lies of your own.'[92] Indians' alleged willingness to lie in court was a frequent complaint made by judges, another supposed trait which was logically easily accommodated alongside the trope of the 'childlike' Indian.

Judges made clear efforts to increase the impact of court proceedings on Indians as a group. In 1906, when dealing with Indian SMP strikers, Judge de Sausmarez reported to Minister Jordan that it was he who personally persuaded the men to return to duty, by assuring them that their grievances would be listened to by the SMC, or by himself or the consul-general, if after one month they had behaved well in their work.[93] After court proceedings dealing with the alleged ringleaders ended, de Sausmarez addressed a group of about 150 strikers from the verandah of the consulate, and according to the press report, lectured them on camaraderie and obedience, before again assuring them that they would be listened to if they worked for one month without any further trouble.[94] In his action, de Sausmarez discharged a function which went far beyond that of a purely judicial figure, showing a preparedness to meet particular circumstances — and the needs of the SMC and International Settlement — by adopting a flexible response.

When in 1909 de Sausmarez presided over the trial of eleven Indian members of the SMP who were suspected of trying to procure their dismissal through various 'insubordinate' acts, a clear attempt was made to create a legal spectacle which would have maximum impact on Indians in the SMP. Attention was paid to the theatre of the courtroom — it was noted that all Indian policemen who could be spared from duty were in the court, providing the audience for the judge to address, and it was also, unusually, noted in the press report that de Sausmarez wore 'the full robes of a judge presiding at a criminal trial', presumably to try to endow him with greater authority. Near the end of the hearing, a lecture was delivered to all Sikhs in court, who were ordered to stand up to hear it. The judge deployed stereotypes of Sikh

91 'Rex (S.M.P.) v. Dewa Singh, Surain Singh and Hazara Singh', *NCH*, 25 September 1909, p. 745.
92 'Mal Sing v. Lachman Singh', *NCH*, 28 March 1914, p. 972.
93 TNA FO 656/106: de Sausmarez to Jordan, 2 October 1906.
94 'The Sikhs in Shanghai', *The Times of India*, 3 November 1906.

characteristics by emphasising honour and pride, saying to them 'you have disgraced your character as Sikhs', and he went on: 'You choose, because you think that there is a little more money to be made, to go off to America and to disregard your honour and your word.'[95] British judges clearly believed that a pedagogical-theatrical approach could have an effect on 'childlike' Indians, and they were ready to adapt their proceedings and their language in this way, to reinforce the colonial hierarchy in Shanghai, and in particular to assist the SMC with discipline over its Indian employees. In 1910, at least eighty men refused to leave when ordered to dismiss following a parade, claiming that they had grievances which they wished to raise with Bruce, the captain superintendent of police, and the British judicial system was once more mobilised to deal with these men. Eighty of the men who were identified as being involved were taken to the British consular gaol and held there until their trial in the Police Court under the King's regulations. In the court they were lectured by both the British magistrate (Gilbert King) and the SMP captain superintendent.[96] Officials of the British state supported the SMC in dealing with this trouble and the SMC's employee, the captain superintendent, was allowed to act in court as an official within the state legal hierarchy; from the perspective of the Indians in court, there can have seemed to have been little difference between their employers (the SMC) and the British state.

A consideration of the exercise in practice of deportation laws gives further evidence of the way in which differentiation between British subjects was effected, within an ostensibly universal legal framework, in ways which highlight the need to view law as a performative resource rather than a collection of rules and principles. As noted above, many more Indians were deported from China than other British subjects. Until the 1916 China (War Powers) Order in Council was passed, the deportation provisions (except in the case of serious offences) provided that a person before the court had the option to provide adequate security to ensure their future good behaviour; only if security was not found would the subject then be deported.[97] It was often the case that Indians thought to be involved in sedition could only be convicted of a minor offence such as a breach of the peace, in which case the court could only deport them on a first offence if they failed to provide

95 'Rex v. Narain Singh, Jhanda Singh, Hazara Singh, Bhan Singh, Puran Singh, Phuman Singh, Jagat Singh, Hazara Singh, Amar Singh, Surain Singh, and Nadan Singh', *NCH*, 23 October 1909, pp. 185–87.

96 'Rex (S.M.P.) *v.* Twenty Indian Police Constables', *NCH*, 29 July 1910, p. 275.

97 See for example Article 83 of the 1904 OIC.

security. When in 1915 the concern was raised that many Indians involved in sedition could get hold of sufficient sums to provide security and thus avoid deportation, de Sausmarez explained that finding security was not easy since it was not merely a question of obtaining enough money but also one of 'finding respectable people approved by court to go bail'.[98] In this way, the court was able to order deportation on the basis of a subjective judgment and thus a flexible criterion of who was sufficiently 'respectable'.

As well as being the most often deported, Indians were without doubt subjected to capital punishment more than any other group of British subjects.[99] Of itself, this fact does not necessarily prove anything about the treatment of Indians by British officials. There is no doubt that over the years a substantial number of Indians killed other people, usually also Indians, in China, often in the course of personal disagreements, what was described as 'factional' infighting, and especially disputes over Indian nationalist causes. But Indians were sometimes found guilty and punished for serious crimes on very thin evidence indeed. In 1905, early on in his role as judge of the SCC, de Sausmarez sat in a case involving the murder of a watchman in which three Indians were jointly accused of the crime. The men were all found guilty by the jury, based on evidence described by the judge as 'almost entirely circumstantial', and all three were sentenced to death.[100] However, as with all capital sentences, under the OIC, the sentence had to be confirmed by the minister before it could be carried out. It was de Sausmarez's duty to write to the minister, giving some advice or comment which might assist in making the decision. This the judge did on 14 July 1905, writing that he could see no reason for mitigation of the sentence of death in the case of any of the men. Later the same day, however, de Sausmarez wrote a second letter to the minister, containing different advice. He explained that both the Crown Advocate and the defending lawyer had written notes to him suggesting that the jury had wrongly convicted one of the men, Verdava Singh. De Sausmarez now declared himself persuaded that the verdict in that case was 'not strictly justified by the evidence', and that the verdict of guilt against Verdava had in fact surprised him. He therefore recommended commuting the sentence in that one case to imprisonment.[101] Minister Satow was initially persuaded to follow de Sausmarez's new advice, but a further intervention was then made

98 TNA FO 228/2299: telegram from de Sausmarez to minister, 4 November 1915.

99 A survey of FO archive files between 1905 and 1915 suggests that in that period, four Indian British subjects were executed. Only one non-Indian British subject was executed.

100 TNA FO 656/106: de Sausmarez to Satow (first letter), 14 July 1905.

101 TNA FO 656/106: de Sausmarez to Satow (second letter), 14 July 1905.

in the case, by Registrar and Acting Judge John Douglas. Douglas, writing with de Sausmarez's permission, explained that he had conducted the case himself (he was magistrate when the case came before the Police Court) and reported that the police Inspector handling the investigation (an SMC employee) had consulted him and kept him informed of developments in the case. Douglas went on to state that the verdict of the jury should not be altered because of the lack of assistance which had been given to the police by Indians who were thought to know the identity of the murderers and because 'the attitude of the Indian community after the trial is a matter of considerable importance'. He enclosed correspondence he had had with de Sausmarez, which revealed that SMP Captain Superintendent Boisragon had impressed on Douglas the importance of going through with the sentence on all three men and that it was believed that the Indian community were 'perfectly satisfied with the correctness of the verdict'. Douglas stated that 'the value of the conviction will be seriously impaired by the one man having his sentence commuted'.[102] The sentences of all three men were confirmed and they were hanged in the Shanghai Gaol.[103] The judges and the minister were prepared to hang a man in the absence of evidence proving his guilt, in order to send out a message to Indians in Shanghai that criminality, and refusal to cooperate with the authorities, would be met with a harsh response. It is difficult to understand their actions except in the light of who that man was — a poor, uneducated, Indian watchman. Only in the case of such a marginal figure would policy objectives outweigh legal norms with such a drastic result. The SMC and British court officials' insistence on the need to discipline Indians in general overrode any individual right to justice in the case of Verdava Singh, even though the penalty he faced was death.

The Courts and the Gurdwara

Court practices in relation to Sikh Indians were significantly different from those applied in cases involving other British subjects, because the gurdwara was frequently given a quasi-official role in British legal proceedings between Sikhs. The first gurdwara in Shanghai was opened in 1903 in the Hongkou district in a temporary building.[104] Subsequently, the SMC contributed land and part of the funding for the building of a new gurdwara which opened in

102 TNA FO 228/1585: Douglas to Satow, 29 July 1905.
103 TNA FO 656/106: Bourne to Satow, 16 August 1905.
104 'The Shanghai Singh-Sabha', *NCH*, 24 November 1905, p. 456.

1908, the opening ceremony being attended by the Chairman of the SMC and the British chief judge, Havilland de Sausmarez.[105] A gurdwara for the use of policemen was opened by the SMC at Gordon Road Police Station in 1916, in order to try to eliminate conflict between police and watchmen over the running of the older gurdwara.[106] British officials and senior representatives of the SMC took a close interest in gurdwara affairs, and at times promoted, supported and collaborated with the committees and priests (*granthis*) of gurdwaras with a view to bolstering the loyalty and discipline of Sikh adherents. The granthi for the gurdwara which opened in 1908 was on the payroll of the SMC, and later that year it was reported that 'his influence for good is already making itself felt'.[107] However, the following year, the SMC's Watch Committee reported that 'the controlling effect of the gurdwara is not as great as was anticipated'.[108] When the Gordon Road gurdwara was opened in 1916 a further granthi was employed by the SMC.[109] In this way, the SMC and British officials were following the same practices undertaken in the Indian Army, where it has been well documented that Sikhism was made use of through its institutions as a force for promoting habits and behaviour desirable to the British among Sikh soldiers.[110] There are numerous examples from court reports in China of judges turning cases over to the gurdwara personnel to resolve. There was no provision in the OICs or any regulation for the involvement of the gurdwara in deciding legal hearings, so it seems that the judges adjusted their practice of the law on their own initiative. In 1908, Assistant Judge Frederick Bourne heard a debt case involving Man Singh and Bela Singh, in which each party claimed that the other owed him money.[111] Bourne 'ordered the parties to refer the matter to the Granthi' and adjourned the case for one week. When the case was resumed, the granthi was called for, and following a lecture by the judge about the readiness of Sikhs to commit perjury despite having sworn on their 'sacred books', the granthi was asked to arbitrate in the dispute.[112]

105 'The Sikh Gurdwara', *NCH*, 16 August 1907, p. 386.

106 SMC *Annual Report*, 1915, p. 24A.

107 'Municipal Budget, 1908', p. 11, Appendix to SMC *Annual Report*, 1907. It should be noted that there were gurdwara officials at the Hongkou Gurdwara who did not collaborate with British officials, and some took part in anti-British activities. See 'A Stormy Petrel of Shanghai', *NCH*, 31 July 1926, p. 269.

108 *Minutes of the SMC*, vol. 17, 6 October 1909, p. 123.

109 SMC *Annual Report*, 1916, p. 90C.

110 Ballantyne, *Between Colonialism and Diaspora*, p. 66.

111 'Man Singh *v.* Bela Singh', *NCH*, 3 January 1908, p. 28. Cases involving debts owed to Indian moneylenders (usually, but not always, by other Indians) were very common.

112 'Man Singh *v.* Bela Singh', *NCH*, 10 January 1908, pp. 84–85.

A further debt case was referred to the gurdwara by Bourne in 1912, but this time the judge was not satisfied with the standard of justice which was on offer. He explained why he had asked the gurdwara to intervene:

> When I heard this case, and after hearing the evidence, I made up my mind that I ought to give judgement for the defendant, but it seemed to me that I might not understand Indian custom sufficiently to do justice between the parties as efficiently as would be done by the gurdwara, where I understand that matters in litigation are tried by juries of the men's own country, who understand the customs better than I.[113]

In this case, the parties were said to have agreed to the gurdwara being asked to settle the matter, but the judge explained why this solution was in the end not satisfactory to him: 'Some time passed and I inquired from the Captain Superintendent what conclusion the gurdwara had come to, and it appears that all they did was to draw lots as to which of the parties was in the right.'[114] It might be expected that such a revelation would put a stop to farming out part of the administration of justice to the gurdwara, but it seems that it did not, and the gurdwara continued to be deployed as one of a number of tools available to British officials, affording them some flexibility when choosing how best to exercise control.

Most of the cases which the gurdwara officials were invited to preside over or participate in were civil cases. However, in 1908 Judge Bourne, sitting in the Police Court, heard a case in which Jawalla Singh alleged that four Sikh men had assaulted him and adjourned it in order that the granthi could 'look into the matter'. Having done so, the granthi told the judge that the complainant was lying and asked the judge to punish Jawalla for taking a false oath. Jawalla's response was to try to assert his rights to British justice as a British subject, as the *NCH* reported: 'Complainant stated that the Granthi had nothing to do with the consulate and it would be better for his Worship to decide the case.' It was reported that the judge responded that 'he did not want complainant to tell him how to do his duty'. The judge found against Jawalla, and said he would refer the case to the Crown Advocate for a possible perjury prosecution. Among his final comments was reportedly the statement that 'The Sikh community had decided the matter and he was quite sure that justice was being done, and that complainant should be

113 'Mehar Singh *v.* Paratab Singh', *NCH*, 4 May 1912, p. 348.
114 'Mehar Singh *v.* Paratab Singh', *NCH*, 4 May 1912, p. 348.

severely punished.'[115] Jawalla was thus denied his rights as a British subject and subservience to the gurdwara was enforced by an official of the British state in China.

Bourne was not the only judge to use the gurdwara as a forum for the settlement of legal disputes between Sikhs. In 1909 Motal Singh accused Isser Singh of stealing some silver items from him. Judge Gilbert King found that he could not be sure of Isser Singh's guilt, so discharged him, but then reported the case to Captain Barrett of the SMP 'so that it might be inquired into at the gurdwara', thereby effectively handing the case to the gurdwara as an alternative legal forum.[116] That this course of action involved the SMP officer responsible for the Sikh Branch is also significant, showing how the court worked closely with the SMP. In 1926, King officiated in a debt case between two Sikhs, in which the 'Sikh community' had already given its judgment. It was reported that the judge upheld the decision exactly as it had been made by the two parties' 'fellow-countrymen' at the gurdwara.[117] It is not certain why some cases and not others were referred to the gurdwara. It does seem that frequently this course of action was taken in cases where the evidence of the parties was conflicting and it appeared that one was committing perjury. Passing the case to the gurdwara must have been an appealing course of action in such circumstances, where the frustration of judges was sometimes evident. The fact that nearly all cases involving Indians would have required interpreters must also have made the cases more tiresome. The involvement of the gurdwara may also have been connected with a wish to remain aloof from Indians and their disputes, a phenomenon which Jonathan Saha has described among British officials in Burma.[118] The way the gurdwara was resorted to by British judges is clear evidence that judges based their approach to Sikhs in their courts on general understandings of the proper means to govern non-European colonial subjects elsewhere in the world, incorporating the widespread view that British law could not be universally applied in view of the importance of maintaining the customs and traditions of the colonised. Their approach was no doubt also heavily influenced by the understanding that SMC control over Sikhs in Shanghai was, in line with practices in the Indian Army, in part effected through the gurdwara and its officials.

115 'Jawalla Singh *v.* Hernam Singh, Mall Singh, Norain Singh and Goordat Singh', *NCH*, 6 March 1908, p. 568.
116 'Motal Singh v. Isser Singh', *NCH*, 26 June 1909, pp. 747–48.
117 'Missing Promissory Note', *NCH*, 20 February 1926.
118 Saha, 'A Mockery of Justice?', p. 211.

Metcalf and others have described how the British in India grappled with universalising ideals of rule of law at the same time as they were convinced that local people required custom and tradition to structure their societies and ensure stability.[119] Judge de Sausmarez was clearly very attached to certain fundamental British legal principles, illustrated by his efforts to defend the separation of powers and maintain a judiciary independent of the executive against calls for greater deportation powers. But, judging from his handling of the murder case referred to above, and the practices of his junior colleagues while he was chief judge, these British officials in China were not attached to universal principles which would give Indians as individual British subjects the same treatment as European Britons. When the judges intervened in the governance of 'martial' Indians in China, it is difficult to ascertain the extent to which they were deliberately importing their understanding of specifically Indian legal procedures into their courtrooms, but it seems likely that, although none had professional experience of law in India, at least vague notions of the Indian legal system would have been known to them. At times, judges attempted to follow procedures and courtroom etiquette as they were understood to be practised in India. In a murder case in 1907, Judge de Sausmarez ordered that Indians watching the trial should not bring sticks into the courtroom, since this 'was looked upon in India as a mark of disrespect and should not be allowed here'.[120] It was clear from the case decided by Bourne in 1912 referred to above that 'custom' played an important role in his thinking.

The judges' use of the gurdwara was, it seems, an improvised response based less on a particular model of legal practice from India or elsewhere, and more on general ideas about governing colonial subjects and in particular the importance of religion in structuring the lives of Sikhs, and especially 'good Sikhs'. Religious observance was thought to be an essential component of the ideal Sikh, so it is not surprising that officials should support the gurdwaras and acknowledge and underpin their authority. As stated earlier, the SMC supported gurdwaras in Shanghai and incorporated these bodies into their structures in order to use them in the control and discipline of the Sikh policemen they employed. British

119 Metcalf, *Imperial Connections*, p. 17; Cohn, *Colonialism and Its Forms of Knowledge*.

120 'Rex *v.* Varyam Singh alias Surjen Singh', *NCH*, 15 November 1907, p. 416. De Sausmarez had family connections with India, including through his uncle George de Sausmarez who was a general in the Indian Army. These connections may perhaps have informed his view of Indian cultural practices.

judges' attitudes and practices in relation to the gurdwara dovetailed with the SMC's approach, by giving the gurdwara additional power and authority over Sikhs in Shanghai. The court was also ready to play a role in a performance of state power targeting 'martial' Indians, by adapting practices and indeed selectively applying British law and procedures to their cases. All of these practices assisted the SMC in its management of its employees and in policing the Shanghai International Settlement, and this was therefore another key way in which British officials in China facilitated and bolstered the governance of this particular, and peculiar, imperial formation.

Conclusion

The migration of Indians, and the state's response thereto, influenced British expansion and the development of the treaty ports through a variety of processes and with a number of important effects. It is clear that there were two main consequences for the British state's presence in China. First, the main institutions involved in the state's project of governance over British subjects in China, the minister, consuls and courts, worked together to supplement their regulatory repertoire in order to meet the challenges they believed Indians created for British governance. Second, they did this in a way which was most often designed to support the Shanghai Municipal Council, the main non-military employer of Indian manpower in China. This was perhaps the area of work, out of all their activities in China, where British officials and SMC employees collaborated most closely of all. The SMC needed Indians, or at least thought it needed them, because of its peculiar status as the British-dominated governing authority of a large and commercially important city, inhabited by several thousand foreigners and hundreds of thousands of Chinese by the early twentieth century. The SMC's decision to employ large numbers of Indians clearly led to an increased level of activity and deployment of resources on the part of the British state in China, and thus influenced the development of British governance in China.

The presence of Indians in large numbers in the SMP, and the way they were jointly managed by the SMC and British state institutions, clearly influenced the implementation of policing at the International Settlement at Shanghai. This had implications both for the institutions built at that place and also the lived experience of Shanghai residents who encountered Indian police in their everyday lives, much as British colonial subjects in

Britain's colonies at Hong Kong and elsewhere in Southeast Asia did. The actions of the British state therefore contributed in a significant way to the creation of Shanghai and, to a lesser extent, other British concessions where Indian police were deployed, as sites where colonial relations were enacted and experienced.

The migration of Indians to China led also to increased, but surprisingly limited, activity in, and direction of resources to, China on the part of the government of India. The latter rarely tried to assert influence over British governance in China. When India sent Petrie and then Denham to Shanghai between 1916 and 1923 this was done following repeated requests from consuls and diplomats in East Asia for assistance and only because the Government of India was concerned about the ultimate effects in India of rebellious activities taking place in China and elsewhere. Rather than being a projection of power outwards from India, their presence was very much the continuation of the pattern in other areas, whereby demands for resources were made on India, to pay, to provide guidance, to provide personnel. Given this picture, if we are to use China as an example of Indian 'subempire', we cannot understand the latter term as suggesting an expansionist impulse emanating from the Government of India.

We can however see that when Indians migrated to China, and as a result sometimes appeared in British courts in China, certain ideas and practices accompanied them. Indians in China were not freed from the effects of colonial difference which was a feature of Indian everyday experience in India. They found themselves in a milieu in which the essentialist views described in this chapter, in particular in connection with Sikhs, determined the way those in authority treated them. It would be more precise to say that the ideas and practices travelled to China separately from Indians themselves of course — they came with British officials in their thoughts and convictions, whether those officials came direct from Great Britain, or after colonial experience elsewhere — but these ideas and practices were clearly activated when, for example, an Indian stood before a British judge in the dock at the Shanghai British court, and was sentenced to death based on circumstantial evidence. Contrary to the rhetoric of officials and despite the constraints of its basis in domestic rather than Indian colonial law, British law as practised in Shanghai was constitutive of a hybrid colonial state, with its own set of governmental priorities, in which 'martial' Indians were highly marginalised and subjected to heavy and harsh discipline rooted in race-based thinking.

Bibliography

Ballantyne, Tony, *Orientalism and Race: Aryanism in the British Empire* (New York: Palgrave Macmillan, 2002).

Ballantyne, Tony, *Between Colonialism and Diaspora: Sikh Cultural Formations in an Imperial World* (Durham, NC: Duke University Press, 2006).

Barstow, A. E., *Handbooks for the Indian Army: Sikhs* (Calcutta: Government of India, 1928).

Betta, Chiara, 'Marginal Westerners in Shanghai: The Baghdadi Jewish Community, 1845–1932', in Robert Bickers, and Christian Henriot (eds.), *New Frontiers: Imperialism's New Communities in East Asia, 1842–1953* (Manchester: Manchester University Press, 2000), 38–54.

Bickers, Robert, *Empire Made Me: An Englishman Adrift in Shanghai* (London: Allen Lane, 2003).

Bickers, Robert, Getting *Stuck in For Shanghai: Putting the Kibosh on the Kaiser from the Bund: The British at Shanghai and the Great War* (London: Penguin, 2014).

Bickers, Robert, 'Britain and China, and India, 1830s–1947', in Robert Bickers and Jonathan J. Howlett, (eds.), *Britain and China, 1840–1970: Empire, Finance and War* (Abingdon: Routledge, 2016), 58–83.

Bonarjee, P. D., *A Handbook of the Fighting Races of India* (Calcutta: Thacker, Spink & Co., 1899).

Cao, Yin, 'The Journey of Isser Singh: A Global Microhistory of a Sikh Policeman', *Journal of Punjab Studies*, 21, 2 (2014), 325–54.

Cao, Yin, 'Red Turbans on the Bund: Sikh Migrants, Policemen, and Revolutionaries in Shanghai, 1885–1945', National University of Singapore, PhD thesis, (2016).

Chatterjee, Partha, *The Black Hole of Empire: History of a Global Practice of Power* (Princeton, NJ: Princeton University Press, 2012).

Cohn, Bernard S., *Colonialism and Its Forms of Knowledge: The British in India* (Princeton, NJ: Princeton University Press, 1996).

Colley, Linda, 'Britishness and Otherness: An Argument', *Journal of British Studies*, 31, 4 (1992), 309–29.

Davis, Mike, *Late Victorian Holocausts: El Niño Famines and the Making of the Third World* (London: Verso, 2001).

Harper, Tim, 'Singapore, 1915, and the Birth of the Asian Underground', *Modern Asian Studies*, 47, 6 (2013), 1782–811.

Ho, Lawrence K. K. and Chu Yiu Kong, *Policing Hong Kong, 1842–1969 — Insiders' Stories* (Hong Kong: City University of Hong Kong Press, 2012).

Jackson, Isabella, 'The Raj on Nanjing Road: Sikh Policemen in Treaty-Port Shanghai', *Modern Asian Studies*, 46, 6 (2012), 1672–704.

Jackson, Isabella, *Shaping Modern Shanghai: Colonialism in China's Global City* (Cambridge: Cambridge University Press, 2017).

Jaffer, Aaron, *Lascars and Indian Ocean Seafaring, 1780–1860: Shipboard Life, Unrest and Mutiny* (Woodbridge: Boydell Press, 2015).

Jeffery, Keith, *MI6: The History of the Secret Intelligence Service, 1909–1949* (London: Bloomsbury, 2010).

Johnston, Hugh J. M., *The Voyage of the Komagata Maru: The Sikh Challenge to Canada's Colour Bar* (Vancouver: UBC Press, 2014).

Kennett, W. B., *British Jurisdiction in China. Orders in Council, 1904–1915, with Amended and Repealed Articles Noted, and an Index* (Shanghai: North-China Daily News & Herald, 1916).

Kolsky, Elizabeth, 'Codification and the Rule of Colonial Difference: Criminal Procedure in British India', *Law and History Review*, 23, 3 (2005), 631–83.

MacMunn, George Fletcher, *The Martial Races of India* (London, 1933).

Markovits, Claude, *The Global World of Indian Merchants, 1750–1947: Traders of Sind from Bukhara to Panama* (Cambridge: Cambridge University Press, 2000).

Markovits, Claude, 'Indian Communities in China, c. 1842–1949', in Robert Bickers and Christian Henriot (eds.), *New Frontiers: Imperialism's New Communities in East Asia, 1842–1953* (Manchester: Manchester University Press, 2000), 55–74.

Metcalf, Thomas R., *Ideologies of the Raj* (Cambridge: Cambridge University Press, 1995).

Metcalf, Thomas R., *Imperial Connections: India in the Indian Ocean Arena, 1860–1920* (Berkeley, CA: University of California Press, 2008).

Norton-Kyshe, James William, *History of the Laws and Courts of Hongkong* (London: T. Fisher Unwin, 1898)

Popplewell, Richard James, *Intelligence and Imperial Defence: British Intelligence and the Defence of the Indian Empire, 1904–1924* (London: Frank Cass, 1995).

Rand, Gavin, '"Martial Races" and "Imperial Subjects": Violence and Governance in Colonial India, 1857–1914', *European Review of History: Revue Européenne D'histoire*, 13, 1 (2006), 1–20.

Saha, Jonathan, 'A Mockery of Justice? Colonial Law, the Everyday State and Village Politics in the Burma Delta, c. 1890–1910', *Past & Present*, 217, 1 (2012), 187–212.

Sohi, Seema, *Echoes of Mutiny: Race, Surveillance, and Indian Anticolonialism in North America* (Oxford: Oxford University Press, 2014).

Stoler, Ann Laura, 'Sexual Affronts and Racial Frontiers: European Identities and the Cultural Politics of Exclusion in Colonial Southeast Asia', in Frederick Cooper and Ann Laura Stoler (eds.), *Tensions of Empire: Colonial Cultures in a Bourgeois World* (Berkeley, CA: University of California Press, 1997), 198–237.

Streets, Heather, *Martial Races: The Military, Race and Masculinity in British Imperial Culture, 1857–1914* (Manchester: Manchester University Press, 2004).

Thampi, Madhavi (ed.), *India and China in the Colonial World* (New Delhi: Social Science Press, 2005).

Thampi, Madhavi, 'The Indian Community in China and Sino-Indian Relations', in Thampi, Madhavi (ed.), *India and China in the Colonial World* (New Delhi: Social Science Press, 2005), 66–82.

Thampi, Madhavi, *Indians in China 1800–1949* (New Delhi: Manohar Publishers & Distributors, 2005).

Wagenaar, H. W., S. S. Parikh, D. F. Plukker and R. V. van Zanten, *Allied Chambers Transliterated Hindi-Hindi-English Dictionary* (New Delhi: Allied Chambers, 1993).

Wilson, Jon E., *India Conquered: Britain's Raj and the Chaos of Empire* (London: Simon & Schuster, 2016).

5 The colonial state and governance beyond sovereignty

Abstract
The need to govern British subjects prompted important actions by the British state, which in turn influenced colonialism as it was experienced in China. British settlers in the treaty ports, and especially at Shanghai, were provided with the law courts which allowed settlers to live, do business in and (collaboratively) control these colonial spaces. These courts underpinned areas of foreign life as well as having powerful effects on the lives of Chinese who lived at the treaty ports. The Shanghai International Settlement was effectively governed through a hybrid colonial state, one of the principal constituents of which was the British state.

Keywords: British state, Shanghai Municipal Council, informal empire, imperial networks, marginal Britons

At the most fundamental level, the preceding pages represent an exercise in writing institutions, processes and practices of the British state into the internationalised history of China. The British state created substantial structures and engaged in a range of practices to implement consular jurisdiction in China following the opening of the treaty ports in 1842, and these actions continued to develop and have profound effects, at least until British government policy changed in the 1920s to become one of retrenchment and withdrawal.

The actions in terms of the structures and practices which were created and implemented by the state in this period amounted to a project of governance which had significant consequences for the development of the treaty ports and for China-Britain relations. These findings challenge the findings of some writers who have perhaps relied too much on the analytical framework based on the categories of formal and informal empire, which is frequently deployed by scholars interested in British expansion in China.

Thompson, Alex: *British Law and Governance in Treaty Port China 1842-1927. Consuls, Courts and Colonial Subjects.* Taylor & Francis Group, 2024
DOI: 10.5117/9789463720397_CH05

Descriptions of empire or colonialism at the treaty ports as 'nearly invisible' or 'restricted', apparently based on a binary understanding which contrasts areas classed as 'formal' and 'informal' empire, reflect assumptions about the nature of the treaty ports which do not accord with the evidence of the actual institutions, processes and practices which developed in those places.[1]

In putting extraterritoriality into practice in the treaty ports, the British state did not simply withdraw rights from the Chinese state; it inhabited the space made by extraterritoriality by engaging in a range of practices and connections, which had consequences for the development of the treaty ports, especially Shanghai. How, in practice, did the state extend its governance in China? Overall, taking the findings presented in the preceding pages together, we can conclude that the state project of governance unfolded in response to the challenge of managing the diverse British population in a blended fashion: there was a whole range from planned, intentional expansion of structures at one end of the spectrum (often initiated by the Foreign Office and the minister) to incipient, and sometimes haphazard, 'mission creep' at the other. The history of the Supreme Court for China, which was an institution central to the project of governance described in this book, can provide examples of both kinds of processes. It was founded in the 1860s through a mostly London-led procedure, described in Chapter 2, in which the law officers were consulted, and experience in the Ottoman Empire was heavily drawn upon. But it developed in response to situations unfolding at the treaty ports, especially Shanghai, often in ways which were led by figures at Shanghai, where it was based. For example, as shown in Chapter 3, the chief judge, Edmund Hornby, soon embedded himself within the Shanghai mercantile community, and worked to support the aims of the Shanghai Municipal Council (SMC) in ways which did not align with the policy of the then minister, Rutherford Alcock. In Chapter 4 we saw how, in the early twentieth century, after the SMC had recruited 'martial' Indians to form a key part of its security apparatus, the British court responded to deal with these new circumstances. Some of the means by which the court moved to meet the specific local conditions were informal adaptations of procedures and interventions which had no basis whatsoever in law.

A key means by which the state's role has been illuminated in these pages is through a focus on the governance of marginal British subjects in China. This has shown that the development of the British state's structures and practices in China was influenced to a considerable extent by the

1 Darwin, *Unfinished Empire*, pp. 391–92; Goodman and Goodman, *Twentieth Century Colonialism and China*, p. 2.

perceived need to respond to the presence and activities of marginal groups. In Chapter 3 we saw that the need to discipline and control British seafarers was recognised from the opening of the first five ports in the 1840s, but further challenges presented by groups such as 'the rowdy class' played a key role in the decision to create the most important institution for governance, the Supreme Court for China at Shanghai. Later, the perceived need to discipline 'martial' Indians in China led to significant additions and reforms to the British machinery of governance, described in Chapter 4, as well as the deployment of methods not provided for under legal statutes or established principles. The focus on marginal subjects at the treaty ports has allowed for a sustained analysis of the everyday practices of the state, in particular the role of the courts. This has shown how colonial relations, in the production of which the British state was an important force, shaped the Chinese treaty ports, both as part of the British imperial settler world, and also as colonised zones inhabited by Chinese and others.

The British state therefore played a role in China-Britain relations as they unfolded on the ground, in the everyday colonial life of the major treaty ports. It did so in conjunction with certain other formations, some of which have been more thoroughly researched, for example the SMC and the customs. The findings in this book complement work by others who have examined the history of foreign involvement in nineteenth- and early twentieth-century China within a wider colonial context, including the extensive work of Robert Bickers on the treaty ports, James Hevia's *English Lessons*, Isabella Jackson's work on the SMC, Catherine Ladds' research on the customs, and Pär Cassel's writing on extraterritoriality.[2] This growing body of work which has explored Sino-foreign interactions in the treaty century has often described foreign and Chinese everyday lived experiences at the treaty ports but before now there has generally been little attention given to the British state's practices of governance in China.

Among the most significant of the findings presented here is that British state expansion led to the intertwining of the British state and the SMC, leading in turn to a deep interconnectedness at an institutional level which has not been sufficiently recognised or described. In this way we know much more about the development and operation of governance at Shanghai, commercially and culturally arguably China's most important city from the mid-nineteenth century. Isabella Jackson, in the most comprehensive

2 See Bickers, *Britain in China and Empire Made Me* as well other books and articles; Hevia, *English Lessons*; Jackson, *Shaping Modern Shanghai*; Ladds, *Empire Careers*; Cassel, *Grounds of Judgment*.

survey written of the SMC, states that 'from the days of the Taiping Rebellion (1850–1864), the Council's driving concern was the protection of life and property'.[3] As this book has shown, it was in those two key areas that British officials and institutions, especially the courts and court officials, were crucial to the functioning of the International Settlement. The SMC relied on the British state to the extent that, in effect, it was a hybrid colonial state which governed the Shanghai International Settlement; an assemblage in which SMC personnel and British state agents and institutions were the primary actors.[4] Although there was no name for this assemblage, so that its outlines are difficult to trace and its influence is not always in plain view, its agency cannot be doubted. The SMC could not govern Shanghai's International Settlement alone and any attempt to account fully for the governance of the Settlement must incorporate a role for the British state.

British state institutions based in Shanghai supported the work of the Council from the very first years of the existence of the International Settlement, often in ways which did not ultimately align well with the official British policy being promoted by the British ministers at Beijing in the 1860s. The supportive role in relation to the SMC continued over time and became embedded in a kind of taken-for-granted set of practices and relationships, focussed in particular around the key areas of policing and law. As demonstrated in Chapter 4, by the time the SMC was grappling with the problem of disciplining its Indian workforce, the British judge of the Supreme Court for China automatically mobilised his resources — not least his position in a hierarchy of British authority — to assist the SMC. The way that the court adapted clearly represented a response to the requirements of the SMC, with the British court personnel and officers of the council working together as though they were part of a single authority. The degree of autonomy enjoyed by the British court facilitated its assistance of the SMC and allowed the Council to develop its own apparently autonomous status. However, while the SMC was autonomous to a degree, it was not independent: it relied on the British state, especially the latter's local institutions, as well as military back-up, in key ways related to its essential functions in connection with the management of law, land and power.[5] If, as John Comaroff has argued, 'cultures of legality were constitutive of colonialism, tout court', then the

3 Jackson, *Shaping Modern Shanghai*, pp. 28–29.

4 The term assemblage used to describe the modern state is borrowed from Joyce and Mukerji, 'The State of Things'.

5 These were the key underpinnings of the treaty ports, according to Bickers and Jackson: *Treaty Ports in Modern China*, p. 9.

British state in partnership with the SMC was instrumental in bringing Shanghai as a colonial city into being.[6]

The British state's role in China is best considered alongside existing work on imperial networks and the circulation of ideas and practices, and throughout this book I have brought to attention the existence and nature of connections along such networks which have not generally been visible in previous work. Chapters two, three and four all clarified the way in which imperial networks connected the treaty ports with Hong Kong, India and the Ottoman Empire. Such connections developed through various transfers of people, ideas and practices, sometimes in unexpected ways, and with effects on China-Britain relations and the development of the treaty ports. Connections were made and unmade in the course of the development of the British project of governance. The colony of Hong Kong was initially envisaged as a territorial foothold which would service the needs of British interests in the newly opened ports, and for that reason shared a government and legal system with the treaty ports. However, there were disputes and conflicts of interest between British colonial officials in Hong Kong and British officials based in Beijing and at the treaty ports and this shared arrangement was found to be inadequate to the task of delivering British aims for consular jurisdiction. Chapters two and three showed how, because of these problems, connections between British governance at the treaty ports and Hong Kong colonial governance were largely severed in the legal and administrative domains.

Imperial connections with British India have previously been described by other scholars, and connections of certain kinds are indeed confirmed in the research presented here, in particular in Chapter 4 on 'martial' Indians.[7] However, the case of British governance in China — in particular its application to the control of Indian colonial subjects — shows with greater clarity the nuances of those connections, which were strong in some areas but surprisingly weak in others. For example, in the area of institutional ties, neither the Government of India nor its court system were closely linked to their British counterparts in China. By contrast with the considerable political interference by the Government of India in polities situated to the west of India, in Persia and the Gulf, there was only very weak interest in active involvement in the treaty ports, despite the commercial importance of the opium trade.[8] Although British expansion relied on Indian manpower, the British Indian

6 Comaroff, 'Colonialism, Culture, and the Law', p. 309.
7 Metcalf, *Imperial Connections*; Jackson, 'The Raj on Nanjing Road'.
8 Onley, 'The Raj Reconsidered'.

state projected itself very little into the treaty ports and had limited influence there. There was a transfer of ideas about Indians and of certain practices towards them from India to the treaty ports, but this was largely done outside formal structures — the Indian legal system was not drawn on to create the formal structures of British systems of governance in China, but instead more general ideas and practices were adopted. We may call this Indian influence subimperial, as some historians have done, but we should clarify what we mean by that term — specifically whether influence was 'pushed' outwards from an Indian centre, whether it was extracted by actors based in the treaty ports seeking to take advantage of what they saw as India's useful resources, both physical and intellectual or cultural, or whether indeed ideas and practices were borrowed unreflectively or subconsciously. Although determining the answer to this question has not been a central aim of this book, my findings suggest the latter two types of processes were more important.[9]

Although primarily focussed here on the British state's relationships to its own marginal subjects, the analysis made of British governance, especially in Chapter 3, has also demonstrated that the way that consular jurisdiction was implemented by Britain in China affected the lived experiences of Chinese people at the treaty ports. The institution of the British court at Shanghai was a setting in which Chinese participants and witnesses in trials, and also readers of the Chinese press, could clearly experience the asymmetrical relations characteristic of colonialism, and cases which were controversial could have a significant impact, even beyond Shanghai. The use of Indians in municipal police forces has also been pointed to by earlier writers as evidence of the colonial trappings of everyday treaty port life, a state of affairs deliberately promoted by the SMC and clearly affecting the experience of residents of the treaty ports, foreign and Chinese.[10] Chinese at the treaty ports frequently experienced harsh treatment at the hands of Indian policemen and watchmen, who were chosen by imperial élites specifically for their suitability in meting out such treatment to the Chinese population. The British state played an important role in facilitating this state of affairs, and the effects it produced, especially in the way that the disciplining of Indians working in security roles was enabled through the specific policies and practices which were adopted to deal with them.

With the occasional exception, mostly in relation to marginal Europeans, the existing literature on foreign settlers and sojourners in China has done

9 Metcalf and Jackson have both described the relationship as subimperial. Metcalf, *Imperial Connections*, p. 29; Jackson, 'The Raj on Nanjing Road', p. 1694.

10 Jackson, 'The Raj on Nanjing Road', pp. 1688–89.

little more than refer to the existence of marginal colonisers in passing, to highlight the stratified nature of settler communities at the treaty ports and their similarity to other colonial sites across the British empire. The focus in the later chapters of this book on marginal groups, especially Chapter 4 on 'martial' Indians, has demonstrated that cultural factors, together with challenges inherent in the context of the treaty ports and British colonies, fed into the politics of difference which determined how these groups were handled by state actors. The state did a good deal of the work of managing difference which was an essential part of the maintenance of colonial space. That these processes, involving attempts at boundary maintenance, were important in Shanghai and the other treaty ports comes out in earlier work, but the role of the state in this process has not been analysed in any great detail.[11] This work also has broader implications for debates over the importance of the management of difference in empires more generally. It shows that the management of difference affected official practices in important ways, influenced by the specific circumstances of the treaty ports and their place within imperial networks, to produce the British official stance in relation to different British marginal groups covered in this research. In short, Indians in particular were managed in specific ways tied to cultural understandings of their identities and it is impossible to understand the British approach to governing them without an appreciation of the politics of difference.

The findings presented here suggest that we might more broadly incorporate the state into our considerations of the British presence in China. Other aspects of the British state's actions in China could fruitfully be investigated. For example, state policies and practices through the consulates and courts in supporting and facilitating the expansion of British commercial activities in China might provide further evidence for the importance of the state in the development of the treaty ports, which were all of course primarily intended as centres of trade. State interaction with commercial interests at the level of the Foreign Office and Legation, for example in relation to railway loans, has been explored.[12] However, there is room for more work on everyday, lower-level commercial activities and interactions through Britain's institutions and officials at the treaty ports. Such an analysis would most likely uncover another set of connections and networks linking the ports to other parts of the world, and other individuals, organisations and groups.

11 See for example Bickers, *Britain in China*, especially Chapter 3.

12 Edwards, *British Diplomacy and Finance in China*; Hillier, *Mediating Empire*, especially pp. 154–57.

This book has highlighted that extraterritoriality was about more than a loss of Chinese sovereignty: as it was implemented through consular jurisdiction it resulted in a serious endeavour by the British state to control British subjects in China. As a consequence of this process, the British state played an important role in the development of colonialism in China, in ways which have hitherto been overlooked or underemphasised. Throughout its chapters, this book has examined the British state's project of governance in China and connected it with the institutions, practices and culture which grew up in the Chinese treaty ports, a colonial world dominated by Britain. And it has given due weight, for the first time, to the roles played by British officials, through regulations, institutions and everyday practices, in creating, shaping and perpetuating this world.

Bibliography

Bickers, Robert, *Britain in China: Community, Culture and Colonialism, 1900–49* (Manchester: Manchester University Press, 1999).

Bickers, Robert, *Empire Made Me: An Englishman Adrift in Shanghai* (London: Allen Lane, 2003).

Bickers, Robert and Isabella Jackson (eds.), *Treaty Ports in Modern China: Law, Land and Power* (Abingdon: Routledge, 2016).

Cassel, Pär Kristoffer, *Grounds of Judgment: Extraterritoriality and Imperial Power in Nineteenth-Century China and Japan* (Oxford: Oxford University Press, 2012).

Comaroff, John L., 'Colonialism, Culture, and the Law: A Foreword', *Law and Social Inquiry-Journal of the American Bar Foundation*, 26 (2001), 305–14.

Darwin, John, *Unfinished Empire: The Global Expansion of Britain* (London: Allen Lane, 2012).

Edwards, E. W., *British Diplomacy and Finance in China, 1895–1914* (Oxford: Clarendon Press, 1987).

Goodman, Bryna, and David S. G. Goodman, *Twentieth Century Colonialism and China: Localities, the Everyday, and the World* (Abingdon: Routledge, 2012).

Hevia, James L., *English Lessons: The Pedagogy of Imperialism in Nineteenth-Century China* (Durham, NC: Duke University Press, 2003).

Hillier, Andrew, *Mediating Empire: An English Family in China, 1817–1927* (Netherlands: Amsterdam University Press, 2020).

Jackson, Isabella, 'The Raj on Nanjing Road: Sikh Policemen in Treaty-Port Shanghai', *Modern Asian Studies*, 46, 6 (2012), 1672–704.

Jackson, Isabella, *Shaping Modern Shanghai: Colonialism in China's Global City* (Cambridge: Cambridge University Press, 2017).

Joyce, Patrick, and Chandra Mukerji, 'The State of Things: State History and Theory Reconfigured', *Theory and Society*, 46, 1 (2017), 1–19.
Ladds, Catherine, *Empire Careers: Working for the Chinese Customs Service, 1854–1949* (Manchester: Manchester University Press, 2013).
Metcalf, Thomas R., *Imperial Connections: India in the Indian Ocean Arena, 1860–1920* (Berkeley, CA: University of California Press, 2008).
Onley, James, *The Arabian Frontier of the British Raj: Merchants, Rulers, and the British in the Nineteenth-Century Gulf*, (Oxford: Oxford University Press, 2007).

Bibliography

Archives

British Library, London
India Office records

- L: India Office Departmental Records
  - L/MIL: India Office: Military Department Records
  - L/P&J: India Office: Public and Judicial Department Records
  - L/P&S: India Office: Political and Secret Department Records
- R: Records received in London and incorporated in India Office Records:
  - R/2: India: Crown Representative: Indian States Residencies Records

Kings College London, Foyle Special Collections,
The Foreign and Commonwealth Office Historical Collection

- KNN11 GRE: King's regulations, etc., 1905–14
- KNN11.1915 GRE: King's regulations, etc., 1915
- KNN11.1916 GRE: King's regulations, etc., 1916

Shanghai Municipal Archives (SMA): SMP Central Registry Files U102–5–159

The National Archives, Kew
Colonial Office records

- CO 129 — Hong Kong, original correspondence
- CO 273 — Straits Settlements, original correspondence

Foreign Office records

- FO 17 — Political and other departments: general correspondence before 1906, China
- FO 83 — Law officers' reports
- FO 96 — Political and Other Departments: Miscellanea, Series II
- FO 97 — Political and Other Departments: Supplements to General Correspondence before 1906
- FO 228 — Consulates and legation, China: general correspondence, series I
- FO 233 — Northern department and Foreign Office: consulates and legation, China: miscellaneous papers and reports
- FO 369 — Consular department: general correspondence from 1906
- FO 371 — Political and other departments: general correspondence from 1906–66
- FO 405 — China and Taiwan confidential print

- FO 656 — Supreme Court, Shanghai, China: general correspondence
- FO 663 — Consulate, Amoy, China: general correspondence and registers
- FO 665 — Consulate, Foochow, China: general correspondence and registers
- FO 671 — Consulate, Shanghai, China: general correspondence and registers
- FO 678 — Foreign Office: Various Consulates, China: Deeds
- FO 763 — Consulate, Tamsui, Japan: General Correspondence and Registers of Correspondence
- FO 1092 — Supreme Court, Shanghai, China: judges' and magistrates' notebooks

US National Archives and Records Administration (US NARA): RG 8274, Archives of the SMP Special Branch

Published sources

Barstow, A. E., *Handbooks for the Indian Army: Sikhs* (Calcutta: Government of India, 1928).

Blackstone, William, and Coleridge, John Taylor, *Commentaries on the Law of England: Book the Third* (London: Cadell, 1825).

Bonarjee, P. D., *A Handbook of the Fighting Races of India* (Calcutta: Thacker, Spink & Co., 1899).

British Parliamentary Papers, House of Commons, *Papers relative to the Establishment of a Court of Judicature in China, for the Purpose of Enabling the British Superintendents of Trade to Exercise Control over the Proceedings of British Subjects, in their Intercourse with each other and with the Chinese*, vol. 41, [c.128], (1838).

British Parliamentary Papers, House of Commons, *China No. 3 (1864) Papers relating to the Affairs of China*, vol. 63, [c.3295], (1864).

British Parliamentary Papers, House of Commons, *Report of the Royal Commissioners for inquiring into the laws of naturalisation and allegiance: together with an appendix containing an account of British and foreign laws, and of the diplomatic correspondence which has passed on the subject, reports from foreign states, and other papers*, vol. 25, [c.4109], (1869).

British Parliamentary Papers, House of Commons, *Reports on Consular Establishments in China, 1869*, vol. 69, [c.44], (1870).

Bruce, John, *Annals of the Honorable East-India Company*, Vol. 3 (London: Cox, Son and Baylis, 1810).

Giles, Herbert Allen, *A Glossary of Reference on Subjects Connected with the Far East* (Shanghai: Kelly & Walsh, 1900).

Great Britain, Foreign Office, *British and Foreign State Papers*, 170 vols. (London, 1812–1968).

Hall, William Edward, *A Treatise on the Foreign Powers and Jurisdiction of the British Crown* (Oxford: Clarendon Press, 1894).

Hertslet, Godfrey E. P. (ed.), *Hertslet's China Treaties: Treaties, &c., between Great Britain and China; and between China and foreign powers; and orders in council, rules, regulations, acts of Parliament, decrees, &c., affecting British interests in China in force on the 1st January 1908*, 2 vols. (London: HMSO, 1908).

Hertslet, Godfrey E. P., (ed.), *Hertslet's Commercial Treaties*, 31 vols. (London: multiple publishers, 1840–1925)

Hornby, Sir Edmund, *Instructions to Her Majesty's Consular Officers in China and Japan, on the Mode of Conducting Judicial Business, with Comments on the China and Japan Order in Council, 1865, and the Rules of Procedure Framed under It* (Shanghai: A. H. de Carvalho, 1867).

Hornby, Sir Edmund and Rennie, Sir Richard, *Instructions to Her Majesty's Consular Officers in China and Japan, on the Mode of Conducting Judicial Business, with Comments on the China and Japan Order in Council, 1865, and the Rules of Procedure Framed under It* (Shanghai: Kelly & Walsh, 1885).

Hornby, Sir Edmund, *Sir Edmund Hornby: An Autobiography* (Boston, MA: Houghton Mifflin, 1928).

Jenkyns, Sir Henry, *British Rule and Jurisdiction beyond the Seas* (Oxford: Clarendon Press, 1902).

Kennett, W. B., *British Jurisdiction in China. Orders in Council, 1904–1915, with Amended and Repealed Articles Noted, and an Index* (Shanghai: North-China Daily News & Herald, 1916).

Koo, V. K. Wellington, *The Status of Aliens in China*, (New York: Columbia University Press, 1912).

Kotenev, Anatol M., *Shanghai: Its Mixed Court and Council* (Shanghai: North China Daily News & Herald Limited, 1925).

Lane-Poole, Stanley, *The Life of Sir Harry Parkes, K.C.B., G.C.M.G., Sometime Her Majesty's Minister to China and Japan.*, Vol. 1 (London: Macmillan and Co., 1894).

Lane-Poole, Stanley, *Sir Harry Parkes in China* (London: Methuen & Co., 1901).

The London Gazette, 1842–1927.

MacMunn, George Fletcher, *The Martial Races of India* (London, 1933).

Major, A. G., *A Compendium of Instructions to H.M. Consular Officers in China* (Beijing: British Embassy, 1927).

Major, A. G., *A Compendium of Instructions to H.M. Consular Officers in China*, 2 vols., (Beijing: British Embassy, 1935).

Morse, Hosea Ballou, *The International Relations of the Chinese Empire: Vol. 1, The Period of Conflict, 1834–1860* (London: Longmans, Green, 1910).

Morse, Hosea Ballou, *The International Relations of the Chinese Empire: Vol. 2, The Period of Submission, 1861–1893* (London: Longmans, Green, 1918).
Morse, Hosea Ballou, *The International Relations of the Chinese Empire: Vol. 3, The Period of Subjection, 1894–1911* (London: Longmans, Green, 1918).
Morse, Hosea Ballou, *The Chronicles of the East India Company, Trading to China 1635–1834* (Boston: Harvard University Press, 1926).
North-China Daily News, 1865–1951.
The North-China Herald, 1850–1941.
Norton-Kyshe, James William, *History of the Laws and Courts of Hongkong* (London: T. Fisher Unwin, 1898).
Shanghai Municipal Council, *Annual Reports* (Shanghai: Kelly & Walsh, 1900–27).
Shanghai Times, 1914–21.
Shanghai Xinbao 上海新报, 1861–72.
Symons, Edward William, *The Law Relating to Merchant Seamen: Arranged Chiefly for the Use of Masters and Officers in the Merchant Service* (London: Longman, Brown, Green and Longmans, 1844).
Teichman, Eric, *The Consular Officer's Vade-Mecum* (Tientsin Press, 1920).
The Times of India, 1842–1927.
Tuson, E. W. A., *The British Consul's Manual: Being a Practical Guide for Consuls, as Well as for the Merchant, Shipowner, and Master Mariner, in All Their Consular Transactions* (London: Longman and Co., 1856).
Ward, A. W. and G. P. Gooch (eds.), *The Cambridge History of British Foreign Policy, 1783–1919: Volume III: 1866–1919* (Cambridge: Cambridge University Press, 1923).
Wright, Arnold and H. A. Cartwright (eds.), *Twentieth Century Impressions of Hong-Kong, Shanghai, and Other Treaty Ports of China: Their History, People, Commerce, Industries, and Resources* (London: Lloyd's Greater Britain Publishing Co., 1908).
Zhang Qian (ed.), *The Minutes of Shanghai Municipal Council* (Shanghai: Shanghai guji chubanshe, 2002).

Secondary works

Anderson, Clare, *Legible Bodies: Race, Criminality and Colonialism in South Asia* (Oxford: Berg, 2004).
Anderson, David M. and David Killingray (eds.), *Policing the Empire: Government, Authority, and Control, 1830–1940* (Manchester: Manchester University Press, 1991).
Atwell, Pamela, *British Mandarins and Chinese Reformers: The British Administration of Weihaiwei (1898–1930) and the Territory's Return to Chinese Rule* (Oxford: Oxford University Press, 1985).

Ballantyne, Tony, *Orientalism and Race: Aryanism in the British Empire* (New York: Palgrave Macmillan, 2002).

Ballantyne, Tony, *Between Colonialism and Diaspora: Sikh Cultural Formations in an Imperial World* (Durham, NC: Duke University Press, 2006).

Ballantyne, Tony, and Antoinette M. Burton, *Moving Subjects: Gender, Mobility, and Intimacy in an Age of Global Empire* (Urbana: University of Illinois Press, 2009).

Berridge, G. R., *British Diplomacy in Turkey: 1583 to the Present; a Study in the Evolution of the Resident Embassy* (Leiden: Martinus Nijhoff Publishers, 2009).

Betta, Chiara, 'Marginal Westerners in Shanghai: The Baghdadi Jewish Community, 1845–1932', in Robert Bickers, and Christian Henriot (eds.), *New Frontiers: Imperialism's New Communities in East Asia, 1842–1953* (Manchester: Manchester University Press, 2000), 38–54.

Bethencourt, Francisco, *Racisms: From the Crusades to the Twentieth Century* (Princeton, NJ: Princeton University Press, 2014).

Bickers, Robert, 'Shanghailanders: The Formation and Identity of the British Settler Community in Shanghai 1843–1937', *Past & Present*, 159, 1 (1998), 161–211.

Bickers, Robert, *Britain in China: Community, Culture and Colonialism, 1900–49* (Manchester: Manchester University Press, 1999).

Bickers, Robert, *Empire Made Me: An Englishman Adrift in Shanghai* (London: Allen Lane, 2003).

Bickers, Robert, 'Ordering Shanghai: Policing a Treaty Port, 1854–1900', in David Killingray, Margarette Lincoln and Nigel Rigby, (eds.), *Maritime Empires: British Imperial Maritime Trade in the Nineteenth Century* (Woodbridge: Boydell Press, 2004), 173–94.

Bickers, Robert, 'Purloined Letters: History and the Chinese Maritime Customs Service', *Modern Asian Studies*, 40, 3 (2006), 691–723.

Bickers, Robert, (ed.), *Settlers and Expatriates: Britons Over the Seas* (Oxford: Oxford University Press, 2010).

Bickers, Robert, *The Scramble for China: Foreign Devils in the Qing Empire, 1832–1914* (London: Allen Lane, 2011).

Bickers, Robert, 'Incubator City: Shanghai and the Crises of Empires', *Journal of Urban History*, 38, 5 (2012), 862–78.

Bickers, Robert, 'British Concessions and Chinese Cities, 1910s–1930s', in Billy K. L. So, and Madeline Zelin (eds.), *New Narratives of Urban Space in Republican Chinese Cities* (Leiden: Brill, 2013), 296.

Bickers, Robert, Getting *Stuck in For Shanghai: Putting the Kibosh on the Kaiser from the Bund: The British at Shanghai and the Great War* (London: Penguin, 2014).

Bickers, Robert, 'Britain and China, and India, 1830s–1947', in Robert Bickers and Jonathan J. Howlett, (eds.), *Britain and China, 1840–1970: Empire, Finance and War* (Abingdon: Routledge, 2016), 58–83.

Bickers, Robert, *Out of China: How the Chinese Ended the Era of Western Domination* (London: Penguin, 2017).

Bickers, Robert and Christian Henriot (eds.), *New Frontiers: Imperialism's New Communities in East Asia, 1842–1953* (Manchester: Manchester University Press, 2000).

Bickers, Robert and Isabella Jackson (eds.), *Treaty Ports in Modern China: Law, Land and Power* (Abingdon: Routledge, 2016).

Boorman, Howard Lyon, Richard C. Howard and Joseph Kai Huan Cheng, *Biographical Dictionary of Republican China* (New York: Columbia University Press, 1971).

Brooks, Barbara, 'The Japanese Consul in China, 1895–1937', *Sino-Japanese Studies*, 10, 1 (1997), 8–32.

Brooks, Barbara, 'Japanese Colonial Citizenship in Treaty Port China: The Location of Koreans and Taiwanese in the Imperial Order', in Robert Bickers and Christian Henriot (eds.), *New Frontiers: Imperialism's New Communities in East Asia, 1842–1953* (Manchester: Manchester University Press, 2000).

Brooks, Barbara, *Japan's Imperial Diplomacy: Consuls, Treaty Ports, and War in China, 1895–1938* (Honolulu: University of Hawai'i Press, 2000).

Brown, Nathan J., 'The Precarious Life and Slow Death of the Mixed Courts of Egypt', *International Journal of Middle East Studies*, 25, 1 (1993), 33–52.

Burbank, Jane and Frederick Cooper, *Empires in World History: Power and the Politics of Difference* (Princeton, NJ: Princeton University Press, 2010).

Cao, Yin, 'The Journey of Isser Singh: A Global Microhistory of a Sikh Policeman', *Journal of Punjab Studies*, 21, 2 (2014), 325–54.

Cao, Yin, 'Red Turbans on the Bund: Sikh Migrants, Policemen, and Revolutionaries in Shanghai, 1885–1945', National University of Singapore, PhD thesis, (2016).

Carroll, John M., 'Colonial Hong Kong as a Cultural-Historical Place', *Modern Asian Studies*, 40, 2 (2006), 517–43.

Cartier, Carolyn L., *Globalizing South China* (Oxford: Blackwell, 2001).

Cassel, Pär Kristoffer, *Grounds of Judgment: Extraterritoriality and Imperial Power in Nineteenth-Century China and Japan* (Oxford: Oxford University Press, 2012).

Cassel, Pär Kristoffer, 'Extraterritoriality in China: What We Know and What We Don't Know', in Robert Bickers and Isabella Jackson (eds.), *Treaty Ports in Modern China: Law, Land and Power* (Abingdon: Routledge, 2016), 23–42.

Chappell, Jonathan, 'Maritime Raiding, International Law and the Suppression of Piracy on the South China Coast, 1842–1869', *The International History Review*, 40, 3 (2018), 473–92.

Chatterjee, Partha, *The Nation and Its Fragments: Colonial and Postcolonial Histories* (Princeton, NJ: Princeton University Press, 1993).

Chatterjee, Partha, *The Black Hole of Empire: History of a Global Practice of Power* (Princeton, NJ: Princeton University Press, 2012).

Chen, Li, 'Law, Empire, and Historiography of Modern Sino-Western Relations: A Case Study of the "Lady Hughes" Controversy in 1784', *Law and History Review*, 27, 1 (2009), 1–53.

Chow, Phoebe, *Britain's Imperial Retreat from China, 1900–1931* (London: Routledge, 2017).

Coates, P. D., *The China Consuls: British Consular Officers, 1843–1943* (Hong Kong: Oxford University Press, 1988).

Cohen, Jerome Alan, Fu-mei Chang, and R. Randle Edwards (eds.), *Essays on China's Legal Tradition* (Princeton, NJ: Princeton University Press, 1980)

Cohn, Bernard S., *Colonialism and Its Forms of Knowledge: The British in India* (Princeton, NJ: Princeton University Press, 1996).

Colley, Linda, 'Britishness and Otherness: An Argument', *Journal of British Studies*, 31, 4 (1992), 309–29.

Colley, Linda, Britons*: Forging the Nation, 1707–1837* (London: Vintage, 1996).

Collingham, E. M., *Imperial Bodies: The Physical Experience of the Raj, c.1800–1947* (Hoboken, NJ: Wiley, 2001).

Comaroff, John L., 'Reflections on the Colonial State, in South Africa and Elsewhere: Factions, Fragments, Facts and Fictions', *Social Identities*, 4, 3 (1998), 321–61.

Comaroff, John L., 'Colonialism, Culture, and the Law: A Foreword', *Law and Social Inquiry-Journal of the American Bar Foundation*, 26 (2001), 305–14.

Cooper, Frederick and Ann Laura Stoler (eds.), *Tensions of Empire: Colonial Cultures in a Bourgeois World* (Berkeley, CA: University of California Press, 1997).

Darwin, John, *Unfinished Empire: The Global Expansion of Britain* (London: Allen Lane, 2012).

Davis, Mike, *Late Victorian Holocausts: El Niño Famines and the Making of the Third World* (London: Verso, 2001).

Day, Jenny Huangfu, *Qing Travelers to the Far West: Diplomacy and the Information Order in Late Imperial China* (Cambridge: Cambridge University Press, 2018).

Dikötter, Frank, *Crime, Punishment and the Prison in Modern China* (C. Hurst & Co., 2002).

Dirks, Nicholas B., *Colonialism and Culture* (Ann Arbor: University of Michigan Press, 1992).

Edwards, E. W., *British Diplomacy and Finance in China, 1895–1914* (Oxford: Clarendon Press, 1987).

Edwards, R. Randle, 'Ch'ing Legal Jurisdiction Over Foreigners', in Jerome Alan Cohen, Fu-mei Chang, and R. Randle Edwards (eds.), *Essays on China's Legal Tradition* (Princeton, NJ: Princeton University Press, 1980), 222–69.

England, Vaudine, *Fortune's Bazaar: The Making of Hong Kong* (London: Corsair, 2023).

Esselstrom, Erik, *Crossing Empire's Edge: Foreign Ministry Police and Japanese Expansionism in Northeast Asia* (Honolulu: University of Hawai'i Press, 2009).

Fairbank, John King, *Trade and Diplomacy on the China Coast: The Opening of the Treaty Ports, 1842–1854* (Stanford, CA: Stanford University Press, 1953).

Fairbank, John King and Denis Crispin Twitchett (eds.), *The Cambridge History of China: Republican China, 1912–1949*, Pt. 1 (Cambridge: Cambridge University Press, 1978).

Feuerwerker, Albert, *The Foreign Establishment in China in the Early Twentieth Century* (Ann Arbor: Center for Chinese Studies, University of Michigan, 1976).

Fischer-Tiné, Harald, 'Hierarchies of Punishment in Colonial India: European Convicts and the Racial Dividend, c. 1860–1890', in Fischer-Tiné, Harald, and Gehrmann, Susanne (eds.), *Empires and Boundaries: Rethinking Race, Class, and Gender in Colonial Settings* (Abingdon, Oxon: Routledge, 2009), 41–65.

Fischer-Tiné, Harald, *Low and Licentious Europeans: Race, Class, and 'White Subalternity' in Colonial India* (New Delhi: Orient BlackSwan, 2009).

Fischer-Tiné, Harald and Michael Mann (eds.), *Colonialism as Civilizing Mission: Cultural Ideology in British India* (London: Anthem Press, 2004).

Fischer-Tiné, Harald and Susanne Gehrmann (eds.), *Empires and Boundaries: Rethinking Race, Class, and Gender in Colonial Settings* (Abingdon, Oxon: Routledge, 2009).

Fitzgerald, John, 'Equality and the "Unequal Treaties": Chinese Émigrés and British Colonial Routes to Modernity', in Bryna Goodman and David S. G. Goodman, (eds.), *Twentieth Century Colonialism and China: Localities, the Everyday, and the World* (Abingdon: Routledge, 2012), 180–96.

Gallagher, John and Ronald Robinson, 'The Imperialism of Free Trade', *The Economic History Review*, New Series, 6, 1 (1953), 1–15.

Gerson, Jack J., *Horatio Nelson Lay and Sino-British Relations, 1854–1864*, (Cambridge, MA: Harvard University Press, 1972).

Goodman, Bryna, and David S. G. Goodman, *Twentieth Century Colonialism and China: Localities, the Everyday, and the World* (Abingdon: Routledge, 2012).

Gorman, Daniel, 'Wider and Wider Still?: Racial Politics, Intra-Imperial Immigration and the Absence of an Imperial Citizenship in the British Empire', *Journal of Colonialism and Colonial History*, 3, 3 (2002).

Grant, Kevin, Philippa Levine, and Frank Trentmann (eds.), *Beyond Sovereignty: Britain, Empire, and Transnationalism, c. 1880–1950* (Basingstoke: Palgrave Macmillan, 2007).

Greenberg, Michael, *British Trade and the Opening of China 1800–1842* (Cambridge: Cambridge University Press, 1969).

Harper, Marjory, and Stephen Constantine, *Migration and Empire* (Oxford: Oxford University Press, 2010).

Harper, Tim, 'Singapore, 1915, and the Birth of the Asian Underground', *Modern Asian Studies*, 47, 6 (2013), 1782–811.

Harrison, Henrietta, *The Making of the Republican Citizen: Political Ceremonies and Symbols in China 1911–1929* (Oxford: Oxford University Press, 2000).

Hevia, James L., *English Lessons: The Pedagogy of Imperialism in Nineteenth-Century China* (Durham, NC: Duke University Press, 2003).

Hillier, Andrew, *Mediating Empire: An English Family in China, 1817–1927* (Netherlands: Amsterdam University Press, 2020).

Ho, Lawrence K. K. and Chu Yiu Kong, *Policing Hong Kong, 1842–1969 — Insiders' Stories* (Hong Kong: City University of Hong Kong Press, 2012).

Hunt, Alan, *Governance of the Consuming Passions: A History of Sumptuary Law* (London: Macmillan, 1996).

Hutcheon, Jane, *From Rice to Riches* (Sydney: Pan Macmillan Australia, 2003).

Jackson, Isabella, 'The Raj on Nanjing Road: Sikh Policemen in Treaty-Port Shanghai', *Modern Asian Studies*, 46, 6 (2012), 1672–704.

Jackson, Isabella, *Shaping Modern Shanghai: Colonialism in China's Global City* (Cambridge: Cambridge University Press, 2017).

Jackson, Will, *Madness and Marginality: The Lives of Kenya's White Insane* (Manchester: Manchester University Press, 2013).

Jaffer, Aaron, *Lascars and Indian Ocean Seafaring, 1780–1860: Shipboard Life, Unrest and Mutiny* (Woodbridge: Boydell Press, 2015).

Jeffery, Keith, *MI6: The History of the Secret Intelligence Service, 1909–1949* (London: Bloomsbury, 2010).

Johnston, Hugh J. M., *The Voyage of the Komagata Maru: The Sikh Challenge to Canada's Colour Bar* (Vancouver: UBC Press, 2014).

Joyce, Patrick, *The State of Freedom: A Social History of the British State Since 1800* (Cambridge: Cambridge University Press, 2013).

Joyce, Patrick, and Chandra Mukerji, 'The State of Things: State History and Theory Reconfigured', *Theory and Society*, 46, 1 (2017), 1–19.

Karatani, Rieko, *Defining British Citizenship: Empire, Commonwealth and Modern Britain* (London: Frank Cass, 2003).

Kayaoglu, Turan, *Legal Imperialism: Sovereignty and Extraterritoriality in Japan, the Ottoman Empire, and China* (Cambridge: Cambridge University Press, 2010).

Keeton, George Williams, *The Development of Extraterritoriality in China*, Vol. 1 (London: Longmans, Green & Co., 1928).

Keeton, George Williams, *The Development of Extraterritoriality in China*, Vol. 2 (London: Longmans, Green & Co., 1928).

Killingray, David, Margarette Lincoln and Nigel Rigby (eds.), *Maritime Empires: British Imperial Maritime Trade in the Nineteenth Century*, (Woodbridge: Boydell Press, 2004).

Kolsky, Elizabeth, 'Codification and the Rule of Colonial Difference: Criminal Procedure in British India', *Law and History Review*, 23, 3 (2005), 631–83.
Kolsky, Elizabeth, *Colonial Justice in British India* (Cambridge: Cambridge University Press, 2010).
Kuehn, Thomas, *Empire, Islam, and Politics of Difference: Ottoman Rule in Yemen, 1849–1919* (Leiden: Brill, 2011).
Ladds, Catherine, *Empire Careers: Working for the Chinese Customs Service, 1854–1949* (Manchester: Manchester University Press, 2013).
Lambert, David and Alan Lester (eds.), *Colonial Lives across the British Empire: Imperial Careering in the Long Nineteenth Century* (Cambridge: Cambridge University Press, 2006).
Lees, Lynn Hollen, 'Being British in Malaya, 1890–1940', *The Journal of British Studies*, 48, 1 (2012), 76–101.
Lester, Alan, *Imperial Networks: Creating Identities in Nineteenth-Century South Africa and Britain* (Abingdon: Routledge, 2005).
Lester, Alan, 'Imperial Circuits and Networks: Geographies of the British Empire', *History Compass*, 4, 1 (2006), 124–41.
Leung, Yuen-sang, *The Shanghai Taotai: Linkage Man in a Changing Society, 1843–90* (Honolulu: University of Hawai'i Press, 1990).
Lovell, Julia, *The Opium War: Drugs, Dreams and the Making of China* (Basingstoke: Macmillan, 2011).
Magubane, Zine, 'The Boundaries of Blackness: African-American Culture and the Making of a Black Public Sphere in Colonial South Africa', in Harald Fischer-Tiné and Susanne Gehrmann (eds.), *Empires and Boundaries: Rethinking Race, Class, and Gender in Colonial Settings* (Abingdon: Routledge, 2009), 212–32.
Markovits, Claude, *The Global World of Indian Merchants, 1750–1947: Traders of Sind from Bukhara to Panama* (Cambridge: Cambridge University Press, 2000).
Markovits, Claude, 'Indian Communities in China, c. 1842–1949', in Robert Bickers and Christian Henriot (eds.), *New Frontiers: Imperialism's New Communities in East Asia, 1842–1953* (Manchester: Manchester University Press, 2000), 55–74.
Merry, Sally Engle, 'Law and Colonialism', *Law & Society Review*, 25, 4 (1991), 889–922.
Metcalf, Thomas R., *Ideologies of the Raj* (Cambridge: Cambridge University Press, 1995).
Metcalf, Thomas R., *Imperial Connections: India in the Indian Ocean Arena, 1860–1920* (Berkeley, CA: University of California Press, 2008).
Meyer, Maisie J., *From the Rivers of Babylon to the Whangpoo: A Century of Sephardi Jewish Life in Shanghai* (Lanham, MD: University Press of America, 2003).
Milne, Graeme J., *People, Place and Power on the Nineteenth-Century Waterfront: Sailortown* (Basingstoke: Palgrave Macmillan, 2016).
Mittler, Barbara, *A Newspaper for China?: Power, Identity, and Change in Shanghai's News Media, 1872–1912* (Cambridge, MA: Harvard University Asia Center, 2004).

Mizutani, Satoshi, *The Meaning of White: Race, Class, and the 'Domiciled Community' in British India 1858–1930* (Oxford: Oxford University Press, 2011).

Mommsen, Wolfgang J., and Jürgen Osterhammel, *Imperialism and After: Continuities and Discontinuities* (London: Allen & Unwin, 1985).

Moore, Alasdair, *La Mortola: In the Footsteps of Thomas Hanbury* (London: Cadogan Guides, 2004).

Munn, Christopher, *Anglo-China: Chinese People and British Rule in Hong Kong, 1841–1880* (Richmond: Curzon, 2001).

Oldham, James, 'Special Juries in England: Nineteenth Century Usage and Reform', *The Journal of Legal History*, 8, 2 (1987), 148–66.

Onley, James, *The Arabian Frontier of the British Raj: Merchants, Rulers, and the British in the Nineteenth-Century Gulf,* (Oxford: Oxford University Press, 2007).

Osterhammel, Jürgen, 'Semi-Colonialism and Informal Empire in China: Towards a Framework of Analysis', in W. Mommsen and J. Osterhammel (eds.), *Imperialism and After: Continuities and Discontinuities* (London: German Historical Institute, 1986), 290–314.

Osterhammel, Jürgen, 'British Business in China, 1860s–1950s', in Davenport-Hines, R. P. T. and Geoffrey Jones, eds., *British Business in Asia since 1860.* (Cambridge: Cambridge University Press, 1989), 189–216.

Osterhammel, Jürgen, 'Britain and China, 1842–1914', in Andrew Porter and William Roger Louis (eds.), *The Oxford History of the British Empire: Volume 3, The Nineteenth Century* (Oxford: Oxford University Press, 1999), 146–69.

Parry, Clive (ed.), *Law Officers' Opinions to the Foreign Office, 1793–1860: A Reproduction of the Manuscript Series with Index and Commentaries*, Vol. 19 (Farnborough: Gregg International Publishers, 1970).

Pennell, C. R., 'The Origins of the Foreign Jurisdiction Act and the Extension of British Sovereignty', *Historical Research*, 83, 221 (2009), 465–85.

Popplewell, Richard James, *Intelligence and Imperial Defence: British Intelligence and the Defence of the Indian Empire, 1904–1924* (London: Frank Cass, 1995).

Potter, Simon J., and Jonathan Saha, 'Global History, Imperial History and Connected Histories of Empire', *Journal of Colonialism and Colonial History*, 16, 1 (2015).

Rand, Gavin, '"Martial Races" and "Imperial Subjects": Violence and Governance in Colonial India, 1857–1914', *European Review of History: Revue Européenne D'histoire*, 13, 1 (2006), 1–20.

Rhodes, Edward, *Presence, Prevention, and Persuasion: A Historical Analysis of Military Force and Political Influence* (Oxford: Lexington, 2004).

Rhoads, Edward J. M., *Manchus and Han: Ethnic Relations and Political Power in Late Qing and Early Republican China, 1861–1928* (Seattle: University of Washington Press, 2011).

Rich, Paul B., *Race and Empire in British Politics* (Cambridge: Cambridge University Press, 1990).

Ristaino, Marcia R., *Port of Last Resort: The Diaspora Communities of Shanghai* (Stanford, CA: Stanford University Press, 2001).

Roberts, Christopher, *The British Courts and Extra-Territoriality in Japan, 1859–1899* (Leiden: Global Oriental, 2013).

Ruskola, Teemu, *Legal Orientalism: China, the United States, and Modern Law* (Cambridge, MA: Harvard University Press, 2013).

Ruxton, Ian C. (ed.), *The Diaries of Sir Ernest Satow, British Envoy in Peking (1900–06)*, 2 volumes (Morrisville, NC: Lulu Press, 2006).

Ruxton, Ian C. (ed.), *The Diaries of Sir Ernest Mason Satow, 1883–1888: A Diplomat in Siam, Japan, Britain and Elsewhere* (Morrisville, NC: Lulu Press, 2016).

Saha, Jonathan, 'A Mockery of Justice? Colonial Law, the Everyday State and Village Politics in the Burma Delta, c. 1890–1910', *Past & Present*, 217, 1 (2012), 187–212.

Said, Edward W., *Orientalism* (London: Routledge & Kegan Paul, 1978).

Scully, Eileen P., 'Prostitution as Privilege: the "American Girl" of Treaty-Port Shanghai, 1860–1937', *The International History Review*, 20, 4 (1998), 855–83.

Scully, Eileen P., *Bargaining with the State from Afar: American Citizenship in Treaty Port China, 1844–1942* (New York: Columbia University Press, 2001).

Sharafi, Mitra, *Law and Identity in Colonial South Asia: Parsi Legal Culture, 1772–1947* (Cambridge: Cambridge University Press, 2014).

Shea, Victor, and William Whitla (eds.), *Essays and Reviews: The 1860 Text and Its Reading* (Charlottesville: University Press of Virginia, 2000).

Sohi, Seema, *Echoes of Mutiny: Race, Surveillance, and Indian Anticolonialism in North America* (Oxford: Oxford University Press, 2014).

Steinmetz, George, 'Return to Empire: The New U.S. Imperialism in Comparative Historical Perspective', *Sociological Theory*, 23, 4 (2005), 339–67.

Steinmetz, George, 'The Colonial State as a Social Field: Ethnographic Capital and Native Policy in the German Overseas Empire before 1914', *American Sociological Review*, 73, 4 (2008), 589–612.

Stephens, Thomas B., *Order and Discipline in China: The Shanghai Mixed Court, 1911–27* (Seattle: University of Washington Press, 1992).

Stoler, Ann Laura, 'Rethinking Colonial Categories: European Communities and the Boundaries of Rule', in Nicholas B. Dirks, *Colonialism and Culture* (Ann Arbor: University of Michigan Press, 1992).

Stoler, Ann Laura, *Race and the Education of Desire: Foucault's History of Sexuality and the Colonial Order of Things* (Durham, NC: Duke University Press, 1995).

Stoler, Ann Laura, 'Sexual Affronts and Racial Frontiers: European Identities and the Cultural Politics of Exclusion in Colonial Southeast Asia', in Frederick

Cooper and Ann Laura Stoler (eds.), *Tensions of Empire: Colonial Cultures in a Bourgeois World* (Berkeley, CA: University of California Press, 1997), 198–237.

Stoler, Ann Laura, 'On Degrees of Imperial Sovereignty', *Public Culture*, 18, 1 (2006), 125–46.

Stoler, Ann Laura, *Along the Archival Grain: Epistemic Anxieties and Colonial Common Sense* (Princeton, NJ: Princeton University Press, 2010).

Stoler, Ann Laura, and Carole McGranahan, 'Refiguring Imperial Terrains', *Ab Imperio*, 2 (2006), 17–58.

Streets, Heather, *Martial Races: The Military, Race and Masculinity in British Imperial Culture, 1857–1914* (Manchester: Manchester University Press, 2004).

Tan, Carol G. S., *British Rule in China: Law and Justice in Weihaiwei 1898–1930* (London: Wildy, Simmonds and Hill, 2008).

Thampi, Madhavi (ed.), *India and China in the Colonial World* (New Delhi: Social Science Press, 2005).

Thampi, Madhavi, 'The Indian Community in China and Sino-Indian Relations', in Thampi, Madhavi (ed.), *India and China in the Colonial World* (New Delhi: Social Science Press, 2005), 66–82.

Thampi, Madhavi, *Indians in China 1800–1949* (New Delhi: Manohar Publishers & Distributors, 2005).

Thomas, Nicholas, *Colonialism's Culture: Anthropology, Travel and Government* (Cambridge: Polity Press, 1994).

Van de Ven, Hans J., *Breaking with the Past: The Maritime Customs Service and the Global Origins of Modernity in China* (New York: Columbia University Press, 2014).

Wagenaar, H. W., S. S. Parikh, D. F. Plukker and R. V. van Zanten, *Allied Chambers Transliterated Hindi-Hindi-English Dictionary* (New Delhi: Allied Chambers, 1993).

Wagner, Rudolf G., 'The Shenbao in Crisis: The International Environment and the Conflict Between Guo Songtao and the Shenbao', *Late Imperial China*, 20, 1 (1999), 107–43.

Wakeman, Frederic E., *Policing Shanghai, 1927–1937* (Berkeley, CA: University of California Press, 1996).

Wang, Gungwu, *Anglo-Chinese Encounters since 1800: War, Trade, Science, and Governance* (Cambridge: Cambridge University Press, 2003).

Ward, Kerry, *Networks of Empire: Forced Migration in the Dutch East India Company* (Cambridge: Cambridge University Press, 2008).

Whewell, Emily, 'British Extraterritoriality in China: The Legal System, Functions of Criminal Jurisdiction, and its Challenges, 1833–1943', University of Leicester PhD thesis (2015).

Wiener, Martin J., *An Empire on Trial: Race, Murder, and Justice Under British Rule, 1870–1935* (Cambridge: Cambridge University Press, 2009).

Wilson, Jon E., *India Conquered: Britain's Raj and the Chaos of Empire* (London: Simon & Schuster, 2016).

Wiswall, F. L., *The Development of Admiralty Jurisdiction and Practice since 1800: An English Study with American Comparisons* (Cambridge: Cambridge University Press, 1970).

Wright, Ashley, 'Maintaining the Bar: Regulating European Barmaids in Colonial Calcutta and Rangoon', *The Journal of Imperial and Commonwealth History*, 45, 1 (2017), 22–45.

Wright, Mary Clabaugh, *The Last Stand of Chinese Conservatism: The T'ung-Chih Restoration, 1862–1874* (Stanford, CA: Stanford University Press, 1957).

Yeh, Wen-hsin, *Shanghai Splendor: Economic Sentiments and the Making of Modern China, 1843–1949* (Berkeley, CA: University of California Press, 2007).

Young, Crawford, *The African Colonial State in Comparative Perspective* (New Haven: Yale University Press, 1994).

Index

For Product Safety Concerns and Information please contact our EU
representative GPSR@taylorandfrancis.com
Taylor & Francis Verlag GmbH, Kaufingerstraße 24, 80331 München, Germany

www.ingramcontent.com/pod-product-compliance
Ingram Content Group UK Ltd.
Pitfield, Milton Keynes, MK11 3LW, UK
UKHW022124190926
475702UK00013B/1627
* 9 7 8 1 0 4 1 1 7 6 4 4 2 *